Re-conceiving Property Rights in the New Millennium

This book constitutes Volume II of a set of two Volumes. Volume II considers the possibility of a new, sustainable land relations policy for Southern African Development Community (SADC) States that are currently mired up in land disputes that have become the subject of domestic, regional and international tribunals, including the SADC Tribunal and the Washington-based International Centre for the Settlement of Investment Disputes (ICSID). It shows that land relations in the SADC have always been, and will perhaps remain, a matter for constitutional regulation. Because constitutional laws defer to no other laws, except by legislative design, legal contests appear to be the least likely means by which these disputes will eventually be settled in the sub-region. Only human rights-inspired policies that respond to the call for social justice by acknowledging both the current and the underlying contexts to the disputes, and also to the developmental aspirations of these States hold the most potential to resolve these disputes. This book recommends efficient pedagogical counter-apartheid-rule psychological distortions of the significance of human dignity (PECAPDISHD) as a pre-requisite and corollary to the dismantling of the salient physical legacy of apartheid-rule in affected SADC States. This book shows that PECAPDISHD's potential and benefits would be enormous.

Ben Chigara is Professor of International Laws at Brunel University, UK.

Re-conceiving Property Rights in the New Millennium

Towards a New Sustainable Land Relations Policy

Edited by
Ben Chigara

Routledge
Taylor & Francis Group
LONDON AND NEW YORK

First published 2012
by Routledge
2 Park Square, Milton Park, Abingdon, Oxon OX14 4RN

Simultaneously published in the USA and Canada
by Routledge
711 Third Avenue, New York, NY 10017

Routledge is an imprint of the Taylor & Francis Group, an informa business

First issued in paperback 2013

British Library Cataloguing in Publication Data
A catalogue record for this book is available from the British Library

Library of Congress Cataloging in Publication Data
Re-conceiving property rights in the new millennium: towards a new sustainable land relations policy / edited by Ben Chigara.
p. cm.
ISBN 978-0-415-67870-4 (hbk) – ISBN 978-0-203-80656-2 (ebk) 1. Southern African Development Community. 2. Land reform – Law and legislation – Africa, Southern. 3. Land tenure – Law and legislation – Africa, Southern. I. Chigara, Ben.
KQC672.R4 2011
346.6804'32 – dc22
2011005402

ISBN: 978-0-415-67870-4 (hbk)
ISBN: 978-0-203-80656-2 (ebk)
ISBN: 978-0-415-85974-5 (pbk)

Typeset in Baskerville
by Taylor & Francis Books

We shall all become, when our capacities to choose to recognize, promote and protect the inherent dignity of all individuals regardless shall have become second nature in all our dealings with others.

***

(Ben Chigara, PhD Professor of International Laws, Brunel University, UK)

Contents

Table of cases

List of abbreviations

ACHPR	African Charter on Human and Peoples' Rights
ADMADE	Administrative Design for Game Management Areas
AIDS	Acquired Immune Deficiency Syndrome
ANC	African National Congress Angola
APRM	African Peer Review Mechanism
AU	African Union
BEE	Black Economic Empowerment
BIT	Bilateral Investment Treaty
CAADP	Comprehensive Africa Agriculture Development Programme
CAMPFIRE	Communal Areas Management Programme for Indigenous Resources
CBD	Convention on Biological Diversity
CBNRM	Community-Based Natural Resource Management
CBNRMP	Community-Based Natural Resource Management Programme
CEDAW	Convention on the Elimination of all forms of Discrimination against Women
CESCR	UN Committee on Economic, Social and Cultural Rights
CIL	Customary International Law
CITES	Convention on International Trade of Endangered Species
CKGR	Central Kgalagadi Game Reserve
CLARA	Communal Land Rights Act No 11 of 2004
COMPASS	Community Partnerships for Sustainable Resource Management
CPA	Communal Property Association
DME	Department of Minerals and Energy
DRC	Democratic Republic of Congo
DUAT	*a direito de use e aproveitamento de terra* ('right of use and benefit')
ESAP	Economic Structural Adjustment Programme
ESC	Economic, Social and Cultural
EU	European Union
FANR	Food, Agriculture and Natural Resources
FAO	Food and Agriculture Organization of the United Nations
FDI	Foreign Direct Investment
FRELIMO	Frente de Libertação de Moçambique

GDP	Gross Domestic Product
GRAIN	Genetic Resources Action International
HRBA	Human Rights-Based Approach to Development
HRC	Human Rights Committee
ICCPR	International Covenant on Civil and Political Rights
ICERD	International Convention on the Elimination of All Forms of Racial Discrimination
ICESCR	International Covenant on Economic, Social and Cultural Rights
ICSID	International Centre for the Settlement of Investment Disputes
IFAD	International Fund for Agricultural Development
IFLOMA	Manica Forestry Industries
IFPRI	International Food Policy Research Institute
ILO	International Labour Organization
Inter-Am Ct HR	Inter-American Court of Human Rights
IWGIA	International Work Group for Indigenous Affairs
LCC	Land Claims Court
LRP	Land Relations Policy
MCP	Malawi Congress Party
MDG	Millennium Development Goals
MPLA	Movimento Popular da Libertação de Angola (Angola)
NEPAD	New Partnership for Africa's Development
NGO	Non-Governmental Organization
NRM	Natural Resource Management
OAU	Organisation of African Unity
PECAPDISHD	pedagogical counter-apartheid-rule psychological distortions of the significance of human dignity
SADC	Southern African Development Community
SADCC	Southern African Development Co-ordination Conference
SAPs	Structural Adjustment Programmes
SLRSF	Southern African Development Community Land Reform Support Facility
SMIF	Sustainable Management of Indigenous Forests
SWAPO	South West Africa People's Organization (Namibia)
UDHR	Universal Declaration of Human Rights
UN	United Nations
UNCCD	United Nations Convention to Combat Desertification
UNESCO	United Nations Educational, Scientific and Cultural Organization
UPA (FNLA)	Union of Peoples of Angola (Frente Nacional de Libertaço de Angola)
ZANLA	Zimbabwe African National Liberation Army (Zimbabwe)
ZANU	Zimbabwe African National Union (Zimbabwe)
ZAPU	Zimbabwe African Peoples Union (Zimbabwe)
ZIPRA	Zimbabwe People's Revolutionary Army (Zimbabwe)

List of contributors

Sibo Banda is a lecturer in the Law Department at National University of Ireland Maynooth. He holds an LLB (Hons) degree from the University of Malawi, an LLM degree in Law in Development, from the University of Warwick, UK. He completed his PhD degree at University College Cork in Ireland. Dr Banda's research interests are focused on investigating the public and private divide in the practice of law and in legal theory. His research covers the use of fundamental rights in private law; legal pluralism in the Malawi legal system and the competing conceptions of property in the age of fundamental rights. Dr Banda's recent publications include 'Taking Indirect Horizontality Seriously in Ireland: A Time to Magnify the Nuance', (2009) *Dublin University Law Journal*, 31: 263–97 and 'Constitutional Mimicry and Common Law Reform in a Rights-Based Post-Colonial Setting: The Case of South Africa and Malawi', (2009) *Journal of African Law*, 53(1): 142–70.

Ben Chigara, PhD, Nottingham University; LLM with Distinction and Josephine Ono Prize, Hull University; BA (Hons), Keele University; CE, University of Zimbabwe. Ben joined Brunel University from Warwick in 2003. He is the founding Director of the Centre for International and Public Law (CIPL) that was inaugurated by Lord Bill Brett on 11 May 2004. He is the founding Director of Brunel University's flagship Master of Law programmes in International Economic Law, International Intellectual Property and European and International Commercial Law. He is the founding Deputy Head (Operations) of the Brunel Law School which was unhinged from the School of Social Sciences and Law in 2005. Ben has also held lectureships at Warwick University, Leeds University and Oxford Brookes University; and various teaching positions at Nottingham University, Denmark, Louisville and Zimbabwe. He is the author of several books, book chapters and journal articles. He is a current and serving consultant to the European Scientific Foundation, the European Commission, the International Labour Organization (ILO) and the Organization for Security and Cooperation in Europe's (OSCE) Office for Democratic Institutions and Human Rights (ODIHR). He is the Professor of International Laws at Brunel University, London.

Edward Lahiff received his PhD in Development Studies from the School of Oriental and African Studies at the University of London in 1997. He spent ten years in southern Africa working with rural non-governmental organisations and as Senior Lecturer in Land and Agrarian Studies at the University of the Western Cape. From February 2009 he served as Doctoral Programme Officer with the Trinity International Development Initiative (TID) and Coordinator of the International Doctoral School in Global Health at the Centre for Global Health, Trinity College Dublin. In October 2010, he took up the position of Lecturer in International Development at University College Cork. Dr Lahiff has published widely on land reform, rural livelihoods and natural resources in southern Africa.

Sibongile Manzana is currently serving as a diplomat in Malawi. Prior to her current posting, she served both on the multilateral and bilateral desks, where she worked on issues pertaining to human rights, specifically civil and political rights and the enhancement of relations between South Africa and other countries. She has received training in multilateral negotiations, defending the country's position at international forums such as the United Nations Human Rights Council. She also observed and reported on elections in the Democratic Republic of Congo in 2006. She holds a Master of Philosophy (MPhil) in Environmental Management, Honours in Forced Migration studies and BA International Relations degrees. Her MPhil research focused on Environmental Rights. Sibongile's professional interests integrate diplomacy, research, sustainable development and environmental issues.

Rachel Murray is Professor of International Human Rights Law at the University of Bristol. Her specialist areas are human rights in Africa, particularly the African Charter and its Commission on Human and Peoples' Rights and the Organization of African Unity/African Union. She has written widely in this area, including books with Hart Publishing and Cambridge University Press (*Human Rights in Africa, from Organization of African Unity to African Union*, Cambridge: Cambridge University Press, 2004; *The African Charter on Human and Peoples' Rights. The System at Work*, with Malcolm Evans, Cambridge: Cambridge University Press, 2008; *The African Commission on Human and Peoples' Rights and International Law*, Oxford: Hart Publishing, 2000), and articles in leading legal human rights journals. She also advises organisations and individuals on how to use the African human rights system, including drafting cases and participating in its meetings. She is on the editorial board of a number of journals including the *Journal of African Law* and the *African Journal of International and Comparative Law*. Her other area of interest is national human rights institutions (*The Role of National Human Rights Institutions at the International and Regional Levels*, Oxford: Hart Publishing, 2007). She holds and directs two major grants with the AHRC. The first was to evaluate the role of national preventive mechanisms under the Optional Protocol to the UN Convention against Torture. The second examines the implementation of human rights standards and the role of soft law. She is a member of the Board of the human rights organisation,

Interights, a Fellow of the Human Rights Centre at the University of Essex and a member of the AHRC's Peer Review College. She currently directs the Centre for Human Rights Implementation at the University of Bristol.

Clement Ng'ong'ola is an Associate Professor in the Department of Law at the University of Botswana. He has been a member of the Department since 1986. He is from Malawi. He studied law at the Universities of Malawi, Exeter and London, obtaining a PhD from the School of Oriental and African Studies, University of London, in 1983, for a thesis on 'Law and Agrarian Change in Malawi'. He has conducted research and published extensively on law and land tenure issues in Southern Africa, and is now a noted authority on law and land issues in Botswana. Several High Court and Court of Appeal decisions refer to his writings and in this way acknowledge his scholarship on these issues.

Lyn Ossome is doctoral candidate in the Department of Political Studies, University of the Witwatersrand. She is a feminist researcher and activist, with a long-term interest in human rights work. Her published works have focused on the functionality of structured violence in democracies, land and agrarian reform, migration, sexuality and aid effectiveness.

Annika Rudman is a Senior Lecturer at the Department of Public Law, University of Stellenbosch. She holds an LLB and an LLM in International Human Rights Law, University of Lund and a second LLM in Public International Law, University of Utrecht as well as a PhD in Peace and Development Research, University of Gothenburg. Dr Rudman specialises in Public International Law and International Human Rights Law and has carried out extensive research in the areas of gender, land reform and customary law in Southern Africa, formalisation of property rights and sustainable development in Sub-Saharan Africa and feminist legal theory. She has been affiliated with the Universities of Lund and Malmo in Sweden as well as the University of Dar Es Salaam in Tanzania. Dr Rudman has published and contributed in a number of publications: *Land reform, development and social justice – A gender perspective on communal land tenure* (South Africa: Juta, forthcoming 2011), *Equality Before Custom? – A study of property rights of previously disadvantaged women under land reform and communal tenure in post-apartheid South Africa* (University of Gothenburg, School of Global Studies, 2009) and 'Human Rights in Africa', in Spang, M. (ed) *Mänskliga rättighteter – ett ofullbordat uppdrag* (The Hague: Liber Publications, 2009) to mention a recent few.

Munyaradzi Saruchera is a researcher and development consultant with Labyrinth Environment and Development Consulting, South Africa (and Malawi). He has more than 15 years' work experience in development research with national, regional and international non-governmental organisations in Zimbabwe, Botswana, South Africa and Malawi. Munyaradzi's work experience spans different sectors that include community development and social change, learning, monitoring and evaluation, rural development and agrarian reform, biodiversity conservation, natural resources management, smallholder farmers and seed security. Currently studying for a PhD (Sociology) with Stellenbosch University, his research examines the role of social capital and social networks in smallholder farmers' response to climate and environmental changes in Malawi. Munyaradzi has studied political science and regional and policy studies for his Honours and Masters degrees, respectively. His work interests are in community development and social change, the sociology of development and the quality of relationships as both an indicator of success and a function of successful and viable enterprises in the development discourse. Munyaradzi is an Ashoka Fellow, a member of the International Peace Research Association (IPRA), Promoting Local Innovations (PROLINNOVA) Network, the International Association for the Study of Common Property (IASCP) and the Mankind Project in South Africa.

Manisuli Ssenyonjo PhD (University of Nottingham) is a Senior Lecturer in Law at Brunel University, London and an Advocate of Uganda's Courts of Judicature. He has published extensively on human rights issues in Africa. He is the author of *Economic, Social and Cultural Rights in International Law* (Oxford: Hart Publishing, 2009), co-editor of *International Human Rights Law: Six Decades after the UDHR and Beyond* (Aldershot: Ashgate, 2010) and editor of *Economic, Social and Cultural Rights* (Aldershot: Ashgate, 2011).

Acknowledgements

Many, many hours of thought, reflection and professionalism of many, many experts in many places, including Australia, the United States, Europe, Canada and Africa have resulted in this piece of work. These colleagues comprise the invisible majority that needs must remain anonymous in consequence of convention's requirement of non-disclosure of independent expert advisers to projects of this nature. Nonetheless, their visibility is apparent in every chapter of the book as the reader will easily tell. To them all – thank you.

Foreword

The law defines land as 'real property' in nearly all jurisdictions. This distinguishes land from all other forms of property and tells us unequivocally that in any community, land is the most prized possession. In the *Island of Palmas* case (1928), Judge Huber observed that land was the critical signifier of Statehood. No State could exist without ownership over a portion of the globe to the exclusion of all other States.[1]

There is only so much land for any nation, in fact, so finite an amount that competition for the best land – whatever the critical purpose in each community – is an inescapable fact of life. Every form of civilization has been characterised by allocation of land rights. In southern Africa, land relations policies of pre-colonial, colonial and even post-colonial administrations have tended to exclude women from the land game. Colonial administrations had extended this disenfranchisement of women to 'natives' in general, and then actively campaigned through a series of legal measures to convert them from land owners and farmers in their own right to farm tenants, wage earners and mine labourers that depended on European enterprises for their existence. Settler Europeans became the new land owners and farmers *par-excellence* from the land thefts of Latin Americans, to the 'denationalisation' of American Indians, then in Australia and New Zealand and the infamous Land Act of 1912 and 1936 in South Africa.

Colonial-rule land games were guided by constitutional pieces of legislation that completely disregarded indigenous peoples' own interests in land as farmers in their own right. Consequently, the legacy of foreign rule in southern Africa is typified by unequal land distribution between the native blacks and settler white Europeans. This fact had galvanised the struggle for political independence from foreign rule that had gripped the African sub-region until the collapse of apartheid-rule in South Africa in 1994 when the first majority rule government led by President Mandela took office.

I had the privilege of serving in that government as Minister of Water Affairs and Forestry, from 1994 to 1999, and then as Minister of Education between 1999 and 2004. Immediately after President Mandela's government had taken office, it had categorized land reform in the same basket of acute concerns as national security and development. Water rights or many would prefer to call it theft, followed the apartheid policy of land expropriation. My task was to prepare and promulgate a Water Act for a post-colonial and a post-apartheid society. This was done in 1998 with the National Water Act which is now used as a paradigm in other post-colonial countries.

The government wasted little time in legislating to begin to correct the distortions of apartheid-rule regarding land rights in South Africa. In the same year of taking office, the first non-racial government had passed the Restitution of Land Rights Act of 1994. This was followed by the Land Reform (Labour Tenants) Act of 1996; and the Extension of Security of Tenure Act of 1997. A Land Claims Court empowered to hold hearings in any part of the country was established. The Court was also empowered to conduct its proceedings in an informal way where appropriate.

The challenge to reform land distribution in the Southern African Development Community (SADC) today requires a cultural paradigmatic shift of near seismic proportions. The passing of legislation for judicial enforcement alone is not sufficient to muster the change required. The people demand and deserve more. It is a reform that touches all with need for land and all with land in excess of their need. It is a challenge that only those with hearts that are strong enough to concede the right of others to be as valid as their own will find manageable. Change with efficiency; reform with a heart and commitment. A recognition that much has still to be done is necessary.

Professor Ben Chigara's two-volume set on this vital matter is a thorough and rigorous effort to date, in my view, to both flag the enormity of the challenge of undoing the distortions in land allocation on racial lines and to end the failed land games of yester-year in a humane manner.

Its combination of pedagogy of the oppressed, rational choice theory, and *humwefficiency* to arrive at a formulation of a strategy for the realisation of the transformation required to achieve the required culture change among all stakeholders in the SADC land issues is commendable.

The contributors have responded so well to the challenge set by him.

Professor Chigara's initiative is to be highly commended.

Professor Kader Asmal
Minister of Water Affairs and Forestry 1994–99
Minister of Education 1999–2004
South Africa

Note

1 *Netherlands v US* (1928) 2 RIAA 829.

Part 1

Socio-economic and cultural issues around land

1 Land ownership and economic, social and cultural rights in the Southern African Development Community

*Manisuli Ssenyonjo**

1.1 Introduction

Several human rights (such as adequate housing, adequate food, work, water and sanitation) are affected by access to land. Inequitable land ownership patterns and landlessness give rise to a host of interrelated human rights violations including hunger and inadequate food, inadequate housing, poor health, and extreme poverty. While there is a clear relationship between access to land and the enjoyment of economic, social and cultural (ESC) rights, there is no explicit right to land protected in international human rights instruments. However, human rights related to the access, control and ownership of land have been established in the international legal instruments for particular vulnerable groups such as indigenous peoples[1] and women.[2]

Despite the fact that 'land constitutes the main asset from which the rural poor are able to derive a livelihood … [m]illions of families, though they toil on the land, do not enjoy ownership rights over it and are considered landless'.[3] The focus of this chapter is on selected issues on land ownership and ESC rights in the Southern African Development Community (SADC). All SADC Member States are States parties to at least one international human rights treaty protecting ESC rights such as the African Charter on Human and Peoples' Rights (African Charter)[4] and the International Covenant on Economic, Social and Cultural Rights (ICESCR).[5]

By way of context, this chapter begins by examining the legal framework for the protection of ESC rights in the SADC in section 2. It then considers the protection of the human right to property and its implication for land ownership in the SADC in section 3. The chapter also examines the application of the principle of non-discrimination to land ownership in the SADC in section 4, and further considers 'property status' as a prohibited ground of discrimination in section 5. Section 6 illustrates briefly the relationship between land ownership and ESC rights using the example of the rights to adequate food and adequate housing. Section 7 offers some concluding observations.

1.2 The protection of ESC rights in the SADC: a general overview

The founding Treaty of the Southern African Development Community 1992/1993, (SADC Treaty)[6] does not entrench individual and group human rights. Thus, it does not explicitly protect ESC rights including the right to property. Instead, it binds Member States to act in accordance with, among other standards, the principles of 'human rights, democracy and the rule of law'.[7] Such principles include equality, non-discrimination, participation, accountability, the rights of access to the courts, the right to a fair hearing and respect for international treaty and customary international law.[8]

Creatively, the SADC Tribunal has interpreted the principles of 'human rights, democracy and the rule of law' to mean that it is seized with the jurisdiction to entertain 'any dispute concerning human rights, democracy and the rule of law'.[9] This reveals the possibility for utilizing the SADC Tribunal for future cases of human rights violations including ESC rights. Furthermore, Article 5 of the SADC Treaty, which spells out the objectives of SADC, arguably entails the obligation to respect, protect and fulfil all human rights including ESC rights. More specifically by Article 5(1)(a) of the SADC Treaty States parties undertake, *inter alia*, to:

> promote sustainable and equitable economic growth and socio-economic development that will ensure poverty alleviation with the ultimate objective of its eradication, enhance the standard and quality of life of the people of southern Africa and support the socially disadvantaged through regional integration.

In relation to land ownership, this can be understood as entailing protection from arbitrary deprivation of land, as well as equitable and non-discriminatory access of land. While these and other objectives do not necessarily create directly enforceable human rights obligations on Member States, they entrench the aspirational ideals that should inspire the law, policy and practice of all SADC Member States.

Indeed SADC Member States have a positive obligation under the SADC Treaty to promote the achievement of the objectives of SADC, and also the negative obligation to refrain from taking any measure likely to undermine the achievement of these objectives and the sustenance of the principles of human rights, democracy and the rule of law. This can be discerned from Article 6(1) of the SADC Treaty which provides:

> Member States undertake to adopt adequate measures to promote the achievement of the objectives of SADC, and shall refrain from taking any measure likely to jeopardize the sustenance of its principles, the achievement of its objectives and the implementation of the provisions of this Treaty.

Given that one of the objectives of SADC, as noted above, is to 'promote sustainable and equitable economic growth and socio-economic development that will ensure poverty alleviation', it is essential that Member States implement measures to ensure protection from arbitrary deprivation of land, while at the same time protecting equitable and non-discriminatory access, acquisition, ownership, inheritance and control of land especially by vulnerable groups including women. This can be achieved by implementing SADC Member States' human rights obligations recognized under the SADC Charter on Fundamental Social Rights (SADC Social Charter).[10] Under this Charter, SADC Member States recognize the:

> universality and indivisibility of basic human rights proclaimed in instruments *such as* the United Nations Universal Declaration of Human Rights, the African Charter on Human and Peoples' Rights, ... and other relevant international instruments.[11]

Thus, all the human rights stated in these instruments are directly legally binding to the SADC Member States through the above provision. Furthermore, the inclusion of the words 'such as' and 'other relevant international instruments' in Article 3(1) above indicate that the list of international instruments referred to above is by no means intended to be exhaustive but merely illustrative. It follows that other human rights instruments may be incorporated in this category. As a result, the rights protected in other relevant regional human rights instruments (e.g. the Protocol to the African Charter on Human and Peoples' Rights on the Rights of Women in Africa[12]) and international human rights instruments (e.g. the ICESCR and the International Covenant on Civil and Political Rights (ICCPR)[13]) are included implicitly in Article 3(1) of the SADC Social Charter. Among the rights protected in some of the applicable human rights instruments relevant to land ownership is the right to property which has significant implications for land ownership and the enjoyment of ESC rights in the SADC.

1.3 The protection of the human right to property: implications for land ownership

Although both the ICESCR and the ICCPR do not protect the right to property, this right was declared in Article 17 of the Universal Declaration of Human Rights (UDHR),[14] which provides that 'Everyone has the right to own property alone as well as in association with others' and that 'No one shall be arbitrarily deprived of his property'. The significance of this provision in Africa is reflected in the protection accorded to the right to property in Article 14 of the African Charter which provides:

> The right to property shall be guaranteed. It may only be encroached upon in the interest of public need or in the general interest of the community and in accordance with the provisions of appropriate laws.

While Article 17 of the UDHR declares the right of 'everyone' to own property, Article 14 of the African Charter avoids to explicitly protect the right of 'everyone' to own property. Instead, it simply provides that the right to property shall be guaranteed leaving States with a margin of discretion in determining the scope of the right to property. In relation to land ownership, Article 14 of the African Charter raises two main issues. First, Article 14 does not define the content of the right to property and its beneficiaries. Does Article 14 guarantee the right to private and communal land ownership? Second, what constitutes 'public need' or the 'general interest of the community' to justify permissible encroachment on the right to property? Since these are broadly framed, the implication is that States have a potentially wide margin of discretion to define 'public need' and 'general interest' of the community in a particular national context. This is particularly the case given that there is no explicit mention of 'prompt, effective and adequate compensation' prior to the compulsory deprivation of property.

Although Article 14 of the African Charter does not explicitly mention land ownership, the right to property protected in this Article extends to land and housing given the broad definition of property:

> "Property" can be defined as those material things which can be possessed, as well as any right which may be part of a person's patrimony; that concept includes all movables and immovables, corporeal and incorporeal elements and any other intangible object capable of having value.[15]

In interpreting Article 14, the African Commission on Human and Peoples' Rights (African Commission) stated that the 'right to property necessarily includes a right to have access to property of one's own and the right not for one's property to be removed',[16] invaded or encroached upon.[17] Understood in this context, Article 14 entails among other things the following:

- protection from arbitrary deprivation of property;
- equitable and non-discriminatory access, acquisition, ownership, inheritance and control of land and housing, especially by women;
- adequate compensation for public acquisition, nationalization or expropriation;
- equitable and non-discriminatory access to affordable loans for the acquisition of property;
- equitable redistribution of land through due process of law to redress historical and gender injustices;
- recognition and protection of lands belonging to indigenous communities;
- peaceful enjoyment of property and protection from arbitrary eviction;
- equal access to housing and to acceptable living conditions in a healthy environment.[18]

The African Commission has interpreted the scope of the right to property in the African Charter by stating that it encompasses two main principles.[19] The first principle, which is of a general nature, provides for the principle of ownership and peaceful enjoyment of property.[20] The role of the State is to respect and protect this right against any form of encroachment, and to regulate the exercise of this right in order for it to be accessible to everyone (including particularly vulnerable groups of people such as indigenous peoples), taking public interest into due consideration.[21]

In the *Centre for Minority Rights Development (Kenya) and Minority Rights Group International on behalf of Endorois Welfare Council v Kenya*,[22] it was alleged that the Government of Kenya in violation of Article 14 of the African Charter forcibly removed the Endorois community[23] from their ancestral lands in Kenya, without proper prior consultations, adequate and effective compensation. The African Commission found, among others, a violation of Article 14 noting, *inter alia*, that the State had not only denied the Endorois community all legal rights in their ancestral land, rendering their property rights essentially illusory, but in the name of creating a Game Reserve and the subsequent eviction of the Endorois community from their own land, the State had violated the very essence of the right itself, and cannot justify such an interference with reference to 'the general interest of the community' or a 'public need'.[24]

The decision is noteworthy because the Commission emphasized the African Charter's protection for collective claims to land rights as property by indigenous communities. It marked the first time the African Commission has recognized indigenous peoples' rights over traditionally owned land under the African Charter. In the SADC context, respecting the right to property entails, among others, an obligation on Member States to refrain from forced evictions of indigenous peoples from their ancestral land. An important first step is to recognize the existence of indigenous peoples in States where they exist rather than failing to recognize their existence in the territories of some SADC Member States.[25]

The second principle provides for the possibility, and conditions of deprivation of the right to property.[26] Article 14 of the African Charter recognizes that States are in certain circumstances entitled, among other things, to control the use of property in accordance with the 'public or general interest', by enforcing such laws as they deem necessary for the purpose.[27] The confiscation of private property without the legitimate interest of public need or in the general interest of the community (such as those pursued in measures of economic reform or measures designed to enhance greater social justice within the community) would be arbitrary and in violation of Article 14. In the SADC context, the SADC Tribunal has confirmed that those compulsorily deprived of land have the right under international law to be paid, and the correlative duty of the expropriating State to pay fair compensation in respect of expropriated lands.[28] This applies to nationals and non-nationals, a standard which appears to move beyond general international law which protects *alien* property against expropriation without compensation.[29] In general, compensation should reasonably reflect the existing market value of the acquired property.

The State obligation to ensure equitable and non-discriminatory access to affordable loans for the acquisition of property is essential, given that Article 10(2) of the SADC Social Charter protects the individual right to 'receive sufficient resources'. This Article provides that persons who have been unable to either enter or re-enter the labour market and have no means of subsistence 'shall be entitled to receive sufficient resources and social assistance'. While at the time of writing the SADC Tribunal had not yet interpreted the scope of the individual entitlement to 'receive sufficient resources' and the corresponding State obligation to provide such resources, a wider reading of this provision would entail access to land resources. In this respect, States and other actors would be obliged to provide equitable and non-discriminatory access to affordable loans to enable disadvantaged individuals to acquire land.

1.4 Non-discrimination and land ownership in the SADC

Article 6(2) of the SADC Treaty specifically prohibits discrimination by providing that:

> SADC and Member States shall not discriminate against any person on grounds of gender, religion, political views, race, ethnic origin, culture, ill health, disability, or such other ground as may be determined by the Summit.

It is useful to note that the grounds of prohibited discrimination in the SADC Treaty are limited. For example, there is no specific mention of grounds such as nationality, age, sexual orientation, marital and family status, place of residence, economic and social situation. Before any such grounds can be added to the list of prohibited grounds of discrimination in the SADC Treaty, there is a requirement for such determination to be made by the SADC Summit.

It follows, therefore, that the obligation of SADC Member States to respect, protect and fulfil the principle of non-discrimination, direct and indirect, in all fields including land ownership under the SADC Treaty is limited only to the specific prohibited grounds listed in Article 6(2) of the SADC Treaty. However, since the SADC Treaty cannot be interpreted and applied contrary to other applicable international instruments binding on the SADC Member States,[30] other prohibited ground of discrimination can be read into the SADC Treaty. In particular, given that all the SADC Member States are parties to the African Charter, they have a general obligation to eliminate discrimination in land ownership, formally (in law) and substantively (in practice). This is because non-discrimination is a 'fundamental principle' in the African Charter essential to the exercise and enjoyment of all human rights including the right to property.[31] In this regard, Article 2 of the African Charter emphatically stipulates that:

> Every individual shall be entitled to the enjoyment of the rights and freedoms recognized and guaranteed in the present Charter without distinction of any kind such as race, ethnic group, colour, sex, language, religion, political or any other opinion, national and social origin, fortune, birth or other status.

Relying on comparative human rights law, the African Commission has stated that a violation of the principle of non-discrimination arises if:

> a) equal cases are treated in a different manner; b) a difference in treatment does not have an objective and reasonable justification; and c) if there is no proportionality between the aim sought and the means employed.[32]

The African Commission has further stated that to determine whether one has been the victim of discrimination or not, the allegation has to be weighed against the three tests set above:

> Was there equal treatment? If not, was the differential treatment justifiable? Was the aim of the difference in treatment proportionate to the aim sought and means employed? These three benchmarks are cumulative requirements and hence the non-compliance with any of the three requirements makes a treatment discriminatory.[33]

It can be discerned from the African Commission's jurisprudence that States parties to the African Charter, including the SADC Member States, have a general obligation not only to refrain from discrimination on the prohibited grounds[34] but also to take temporary special measures in favour of marginalized groups, which suffer historical or persistent prejudice in order to attenuate or suppress conditions that perpetuate discrimination.[35] As the Commission has clearly stated, 'in certain cases, positive discrimination or affirmative action helps to redress imbalance'.[36] For example, in order to ensure that women have equal access to land as men, States have to 'take corrective and positive action' to eliminate discrimination against women in law and in fact.[37]

It is to be noted that discrimination constitutes any distinction, exclusion, restriction or preference or other differential treatment that is directly or indirectly based on the prohibited grounds of discrimination and which has the intention or effect of nullifying or impairing the recognition, enjoyment or exercise by everyone, on an equal footing, of all the rights and freedoms protected in the African Charter.[38]

Direct discrimination in land ownership occurs when an individual is treated less favourably in land ownership than another person in a similar situation for a reason related to a prohibited ground, which can not be justified objectively. For example, laws denying women a right to inherent land on an equal footing with men directly discriminate against women. Under Article 83 of Law No. 68–012 of 4 July 1968 on succession, women in Madagascar are discriminated against regarding inheritance of immovable property within their families. In some States customary land is traditionally inherited by the man's family in accordance with rules of male primogeniture, to the detriment of widows and, especially, female children.[39]

On the other hand, indirect discrimination in land ownership occurs when a law, policy or land programme which appear neutral at face value, has a disproportionate impact on the ownership of land as distinguished by prohibited grounds of discrimination. Among others, the principle of non-discrimination when applied to land requires States to prohibit any distinction, exclusion, restriction or preference (in laws, policies and practices) which is based on any prohibited ground.

Significantly, prohibited grounds of discrimination are not limited to the specific grounds listed above in Article 2 of the African Charter but also include another general ground – 'other status' – given that the 'nature of discrimination varies according to context and evolves over time'.[40] Thus, the African Commission has accepted that 'other status' includes 'disability, age or sexual orientation',[41] grounds of discrimination not explicitly mentioned in Article 2 of the African Charter. There seems to be no good reason why 'other status' should also not include other grounds such as marital and family status, gender identity, health status, place of residence, economic and social situation.

To comply with their obligations under the African Charter, the SADC Member States should protect the right to property without discrimination on all grounds explicitly prohibited in the African Charter and other ground implied in the Charter under 'other status'. This means, for example, that although nationality is not an explicitly prohibited ground of discrimination in Article 6(2) of the SADC Treaty, SADC Member States should not discriminate on the basis of nationality since this is prohibited under other human rights treaties ratified by the SADC Member States including the African Charter. It follows that the arbitrary expulsion/deportation of non-nationals depriving them of land is an encroachment on the right to property in violation of Article 14 of the African Charter.[42]

Surprisingly, rather than adopting anti-discrimination laws and ensuring that effective and enforceable remedies are available to individuals in case of discrimination,[43] some SADC Member States have adopted laws with discriminatory effect in land ownership. For example, the Government of Zimbabwe embarked on a programme of land reform in the year 2000. The programme was constitutionally recognized in section 16A of the Constitution, which was introduced by the Constitution of Zimbabwe Amendment (No. 16) Act 2000. Subsequently, the programme was further entrenched when the Legislature enacted section 16B through the Constitution of Zimbabwe Amendment (No. 17) Act 2005 (Amendment 17). The legal effect of section 16B(2)(a) was to compulsorily acquire all agricultural land that was identified in the notices of acquisition. Consequently, full title in such land vested in the State with effect from 14 September 2005. Moreover, by virtue of section 16B(2)(b), no compensation is payable for this land except for any improvements effected thereon before it was acquired. The Amendment 17 also ousted the jurisdiction of the courts to entertain any challenge concerning such compulsory land acquisitions by providing that a person having any right or interest in the land compulsorily acquired 'shall not apply to a court to challenge the acquisition of the land by the State, and no court shall entertain any such challenge'.[44]

The validity of Amendment 17 was challenged before the SADC Tribunal in the case of *Mike Campbell (Pvt) Limited and Others v The Republic of Zimbabwe*.[45] In this case, 79 applicants, all white farmers in Zimbabwe, were deprived of their agricultural lands under Zimbabwe's Constitutional Amendment 17 without having had the right of access to the courts and the right to a fair hearing. The applicants alleged before the SADC Tribunal that their land was compulsorily acquired and effectively ownership vested to the State without compensation and access to the courts. The applicants claimed, *inter alia*, that this compulsory acquisition was discriminatory in effect on the basis of race because the targeted agricultural lands were all owned by white Zimbabwean farmers only. The State argued that its compulsory land acquisition policy was for the benefit of people who were disadvantaged under colonialism and thus it was a means of correcting colonially inherited land ownership inequities. After noting that there was no explicit mention of race, ethnicity or people of a particular origin in Amendment 17 as to make it racially discriminatory, the Tribunal held:

> Since the effects of the implementation of Amendment 17 will be felt by the Zimbabwean white farmers only, we consider it, although Amendment 17 does not explicitly refer to white farmers, as we have indicated above, its implementation affects white farmers only and consequently constitutes indirect discrimination or de facto or substantive inequality.

The Tribunal concluded that in implementing Amendment 17, Zimbabwe discriminated against the applicants on the basis of race and thereby violated its obligation under Article 6(2) of the Treaty. The Tribunal also found that the criteria adopted by Zimbabwe in relation to its land reform programme was not based on reasonable and objective criteria but arbitrary and based primarily on considerations of race. The State was directed to pay fair compensation to the applicants.

The decision of the Tribunal is significant partly because while its order to pay compensation, strictly regarded, is confined to the 79 applicants in this case, its ramifications extend to the former owners of all the agricultural land that has been acquired without compensation by the Government of Zimbabwe since 2000 in terms of section 16B of the Constitution.[46] In effect, enforcement of the decision *vis-à-vis* the 79 applicants in particular and compliance with it generally would ultimately necessitate the Government having to reverse all the land acquisitions without compensation that have taken place since 2000.[47]

It is important to note that the Tribunal found discrimination on the basis of race in the implementation of Zimbabwe's land reform programme under Amendment 17 because of the lack of objective criteria. What happened in practice was that land from white farmers was compulsorily acquired without fair compensation and yet such land ended up being primarily awarded to ruling party adherents.[48] Thus, the Tribunal observed that if:

> (a) the criteria adopted by the Respondent [Zimbabwe] in relation to the land reform programme had not been arbitrary but reasonable and objective; (b) fair compensation was paid in respect of the expropriated lands, and (c) the lands expropriated were indeed distributed to poor, landless and other disadvantaged and marginalized individuals or groups, rendering the purpose of the programme legitimate, the differential treatment afforded to the Applicants would not constitute racial discrimination.

In sum, in order to comply with the obligations of the SADC Member States under the SADC Treaty and applicable human rights instruments with respect to non-discrimination, laws, policies and practices relating to land ownership should be regularly reviewed. Where necessary, relevant laws should be amended in order to ensure that they do not discriminate or lead to discrimination, whether formally or substantively, in relation to the exercise and enjoyment of the right to property. As confirmed by the SADC Tribunal, in the event of compulsory acquisition of land, the expropriating State must pay fair compensation and expropriation must serve a legitimate aim. Unfortunately, there is less political will to implement the decisions of the SADC Tribunal.

Despite the jurisprudential value of the above case, it has not been enforced in Zimbabwe. Thus its practical significance has been minimal. In a later case brought in the Zimbabwean High Court for enforcement of the SADC Tribunal judgment, the High Court declined to enforce it by ruling that such decisions are not binding on Zimbabwe![49] The High Court stated that enforcing the judgment 'would be to challenge the decision of the Supreme Court within its jurisdictional domain and thereby undermine the authority of that Court in Zimbabwe'.[50] It also observed that to enforce the judgment 'the Government would be required to contravene and disregard what Parliament has specifically enacted in section 16B of the Constitution' yet the Constitution is the Supreme law of Zimbabwe.[51] Any such result, according to the High Court, this would be contrary to domestic law and public policy.[52] In effect domestic law was invoked to justify non-compliance with Zimbabwe's international legal obligations as a State party to the SADC Treaty and its Protocol. Yet as a matter of international law 'A party may not invoke the provisions of its internal law as justification for its failure to perform a treaty'.[53] Indeed, the SADC Tribunal's decisions are legally binding and enforceable within the territories of the State concerned.[54] However, Zimbabwe has continued to challenge the jurisdiction of the Tribunal stating that 'any decisions that the Tribunal may have made or may make in the future against the Republic of Zimbabwe are null and void'.[55] In these circumstances, on 17 August 2010 the Summit of the SADC Heads of State and Government decided 'that a review of the role functions and terms [sic] of reference of the SADC Tribunal should be undertaken and concluded within 6 months'.[56] Whether this really represents a move to undermine the role of the Tribunal in handing down decisions involving human rights issues remains to be seen.

1.5 Property status as a prohibited ground of discrimination

Property status is a prohibited ground of discrimination in international human rights law. For example, Article 2(2) of the ICESCR lists the prohibited grounds of discrimination in the exercise of ESC rights as 'race, colour, sex, language, religion, political or other opinion, national or social origin, *property*, birth or other status'. A similar list is provided in Article 2 of the UDHR and Article 2(1) of the ICCPR. Thus, the principle of non-discrimination on the basis of property status is clearly well established in international human rights law. As the UN Committee on Economic, Social and Cultural Rights (CESCR) has noted:

> Property status, as a prohibited ground of discrimination, is a broad concept and includes real property (e.g. land ownership or tenure) and personal

property (e.g. intellectual property, goods and chattels, and income), or the lack of it. The Committee has previously commented that Covenant rights, such as access to water services and protection from forced eviction, should not be made conditional on a person's land tenure status, such as living in an informal settlement.[57]

It is often the case that the individuals and groups living in poverty often face discrimination because they lack property. Poverty is 'a human condition characterized by sustained or chronic deprivation of the resources, capabilities, choices, security and power necessary for the enjoyment of an adequate standard of living and other civil, cultural, economic, political and social rights'.[58] Economic growth in several SADC Member States has not, in itself, led to sustainable development, and individuals and groups of individuals continue to face socio-economic inequality, often because of entrenched historical and contemporary forms of discrimination. Women and girls bear a disproportionate burden of poverty, and children growing up in poverty are often permanently disadvantaged.

In some SADC Member States such as Madagascar almost 69 per cent of the population continues to live in poverty, especially women, young people and persons living in rural and remote areas.[59] In 2009 in the Democratic Republic of Congo (DRC), 75 per cent of the population lived in extreme poverty, 83 per cent of the population had no access to safe drinking water, while 70 per cent had no access to hygienic sanitation facilities and only 1 per cent of the population had access to electricity.[60] While life expectancy at birth in the year 2010 in some non-African States (such as Norway, Australia, Canada, Sweden, Japan, Switzerland, France, Iceland and Spain) was over 80 years, in several SADC States (such as Angola, DRC, Lesotho and Zimbabwe) it was below 50 years,[61] 30 years lower.

Some of the forms of discrimination perpetuating poverty are based on property status. For example, the restriction of access to credit and mortgages to persons with land titles excludes a significant proportion of the population without land titles to accessing credit and mortgages. This disproportionately affects women in the SADC rural areas because historically women in this sub-region were discriminated against in land inheritance and thus owing to their lack of collateral they have limited access to credit. In order to realize the SADC objective relating to the promotion of sustainable development, discrimination on the basis of property status must be addressed in accordance with international, regional and sub-regional human rights standards.

In short, SADC Member States must 'take all appropriate measures to eliminate discrimination against women by any person, organization or enterprise'[62] with respect to ownership and inheritance of land. This includes discrimination emanating from both State and non-State actors. For example, laws and policies discriminating against women in the inheritance of land must be eliminated immediately, and replaced by laws protecting non-discriminatory inheritance. In this respect Article 21 of the Protocol on the Rights of Women in Africa provides:

1. A widow shall have the right to an equitable share in the inheritance of the property of her husband. A widow shall have the right to continue to live in the matrimonial house. In case of remarriage, she shall retain this right if the house belongs to her or she has inherited it.
2. Women and men shall have the right to inherit, in equitable shares, their parents' properties.

The elimination of discrimination against women is in accordance with Article 18 of the SADC Protocol on Gender and Development[63] which protects non-discriminatory 'access to property and resources' in the following terms.

> States Parties shall, by 2015, review all policies and laws that determine access to, control of, and benefit from, productive resources by women in order to:
>
> (a) end all discrimination against women and girls with regard to water rights and property such as land and tenure thereof;
> (b) ensure that women have equal access and rights to credit, capital, mortgages, security and training as men; and
> (c) ensure that women and men have access to modern, appropriate and affordable technology and support services.

In addition to reviewing discriminatory laws and policies against women in land ownership, States must provide for appropriate remedies to any person (including any woman) whose rights or freedoms have been violated.[64] Such remedies should include prompt and adequate compensation, reparation, restitution, rehabilitation, guarantees of non-repetition and public apologies. Further, SADC Member States should ensure that such remedies (as determined by competent judicial, national human rights institutions and/or ombudspersons, administrative or legislative authorities/institutions, or by any other competent authority provided for by law) are effectively implemented in practice.[65] Such institutions should effectively address the individual and structural nature of the harm caused by discrimination in the field of land ownership. These institutions should adjudicate or investigate land-related complaints promptly, impartially and independently, and address alleged violations relating to land ownership, including actions or omissions by private actors.

It should be noted that widespread poverty among women and poor socio-economic conditions are among the causes of discrimination against women and violation of women's human rights in SADC.[66] This has disproportionately affected rural women and women head of households, particularly in view of their precarious living conditions and lack of access to ownership of land, inheritance, education, credit facilities and community services.[67] In order to address such critical issues affecting women, SADC Member States have to make the promotion of gender equality an explicit component of relevant national development plans and policies, in particular those aimed at poverty alleviation and sustainable development.[68] In this regard it is essential that special attention is paid to the rights of rural women and women heads of households, ensuring that they participate in decision-making processes and have full access to credit facilities. Where necessary, States should adopt and enforce land laws to protect rural women such as the Village Lands Act No. 5 of 1999 in Tanzania, which protects the right of women to acquire, own and use land equally with men. This should be accompanied by educational programmes to enhance women's, especially rural women's, awareness of their land and property rights through legal literacy programmes and extension services, as well as the expansion of legal assistance to rural women wishing to file claims of discrimination.

1.6 Land ownership and ESC rights

Land ownership laws and policies adopted by SADC Member States have an impact, positive or negative, on the progressive enjoyment of ESC rights. This section uses the example of the right of everyone to an adequate standard of living and two of its components, namely, the rights to adequate food and housing,[69] to demonstrate the relationship between land ownership laws in some SADC Member States and the right to an adequate standard of living. A particular challenge is to ensure the right to an adequate standard of living to individuals and groups of people who have special needs or are particularly more vulnerable.

1.6.1 Adequate food

The right to adequate food is at the core of the right to an adequate standard of living as there is no life without food or life is shorter and more prone to mental or physical ill-health with hunger, malnutrition, or under-nutrition. Thus the right to adequate food is indivisibly linked to the inherent dignity of the human person. This right is realized when 'every man, woman and child, alone or in community with others, has physical and economic access at all times to adequate food or means for its procurement'.[70] The core content of the right to adequate food implies:

> The availability of food in a quantity and quality sufficient to satisfy the dietary needs of individuals, free from adverse substances, and acceptable within a given culture;
> The accessibility of such food in ways that are sustainable and that do not interfere with the enjoyment of other human rights.[71]

Availability refers to the possibilities either for feeding oneself directly from productive land or other natural resources, or for well functioning distribution, processing and market systems that can move food from the site of production to where it is needed in accordance with demand.[72] It follows that laws relating to land ownership can impact negatively on the availability of food especially where such laws deprive peasants and people living in rural areas of cultivable land. For example, Madagascar's Law No. 2007–36 of 14 January 2008, relating to investment law allows land acquisition by foreign investors, including land for agricultural purposes. This has an adverse impact on the access of peasants and people living in rural areas to cultivable lands, which leads to a negative impact on the realization by the Malagasy population of the right to food.[73] In order to facilitate the acquisition of land by peasants and persons living in rural areas (and the availability of adequate food), Madagascar should revise Law No. 2007–36.

However, the domestic enforcement of many ESC rights in several SADC Member States remains problematic because these rights are essentially not enshrined in the Constitution or other domestic legislation of a number of SADC Member States (e.g. Mauritius), although some individual rights proclaimed in national constitutions are relevant to these ESC rights. Where some ESC rights have been protected, in several States this has not been done on an equal footing with other rights. The effect is that most ESC rights have not been explicitly incorporated in the domestic law and cannot be directly invoked by individuals before national courts. This situation has a restrictive impact on the scope of the competencies of the institutional guarantees of human rights to enforce ESC rights, including courts, the National Human Rights Commissions, and the Offices of the Ombudsmen.

1.6.2 Adequate housing

An adequate standard of living requires that everyone has a place to have adequate housing so as to live in security, peace, and dignity. There are several requirements for adequate housing including legal security of tenure.[74] As explained by the CESCR:

> Tenure takes a variety of forms, including rental (public and private) accommodation, cooperative housing, lease, owner-occupation, emergency housing and informal settlements, including occupation of land or property. Notwithstanding the type of tenure, *all persons should possess a degree of security of tenure which guarantees legal protection against forced eviction*, harassment and other threats. States parties should consequently take immediate measures aimed at conferring legal security of tenure upon those persons and households currently lacking such protection, in genuine consultation with affected persons and groups.[75]

Freedom from forced evictions – the permanent or temporary removal against their will of individuals, families and/or communities from the homes and/or land which they occupy, without the provision of, and access to, appropriate forms of legal or other protection[76] – is thus at the core of the right to adequate housing. The African Commission confirmed that the right to adequate housing is implicitly protected in the African Charter,[77] which as noted above, is legally binding on all SADC Member States. It is helpful to recall that the right to adequate housing, like other human rights, imposes three types or levels of obligations on SADC Member States: (a) the obligation to respect; (b) the obligation to protect; and (c) the obligation to fulfil.[78]

The first obligation to *respect* requires States to refrain from interfering, directly or indirectly, with the enjoyment of the right to adequate housing by for example abstaining from forced evictions. The second obligation to *protect* requires States to take steps to prevent third parties (who instruct or carry out forced evictions) from interfering in the right to adequate housing by protecting the tenure of existing housing against interference or forced evictions by third parties and to enforce such measures. Lastly, the obligation to *fulfil* requires States to take appropriate legislative, administrative, judicial, budgetary, promotional and other measures aimed at the full realization of the right to adequate housing by facilitating the opportunity of everyone to find affordable housing and to provide necessary housing to particularly vulnerable individuals and groups.

In order to comply with the above obligations, SADC Member States should protect ESC rights including the right to adequate housing in national law (the constitution or other legislation) as this can enhance the judicial protection of these rights. For example Article 26 of the Constitution of South Africa (1996) provides:

1. Everyone has the right to have access to adequate housing.
2. The state must take reasonable legislative and other measures, within its available resources, to achieve the progressive realisation of this right.
3. No one may be evicted from their home, or have their home demolished, without an order of court made after considering all the relevant circumstances. No legislation may permit arbitrary evictions.

On the basis of the above Constitutional protection of access to adequate housing, the Constitutional Court of South Africa in the *Government of the Republic of South Africa and Others v Grootboom and Others*[79] held that section 26(2) of the Constitution requires the State to devise and implement within its available resources a comprehensive and coordinated programme progressively to realize the right of access to adequate housing. The programme must include 'reasonable measures' such as to provide relief for people who have no access to land, no roof over their heads, and who are living in intolerable conditions or crisis situations. The Court observed that a 'programme that excludes a significant segment of society cannot be said to be reasonable'.[80] Furthermore, the Court stated that 'Those whose needs are the most urgent and whose ability to enjoy all rights therefore is most in peril, must not be ignored by the measures aimed at achieving realization of the right'.[81] On the facts, the Court found that the state of the housing programme in the area of the Cape Metropolitan Council fell short of compliance with the above constitutional requirements in that it failed to make reasonable provision within its available resources for people in the Cape Metropolitan area with no access to land, no roof over their heads, and who were living in intolerable conditions or crisis situation.

In addition, SADC Member States should ensure, prior to carrying out any evictions (e.g. in connection with conflict over land rights, development and infrastructure projects, with land acquisition measures, associated land redistribution programmes, sale and transfer of mortgaged property, etc) and particularly those involving large groups, that all feasible alternatives are explored in consultation with the affected persons, with a view to avoiding, or at least minimizing, the need to use force.[82] Legal remedies or procedures should be provided to those who are affected by eviction orders in particular all the individuals concerned should have a right to adequate compensation for any property, both personal and real, which is affected.[83]

However, several SADC Member States have failed to refrain from forced evictions. For example, in 2008–09 the CESCR found that many families in Luanda (Angola), Madagascar and the DRC were forcibly evicted from their homes/land without being provided with adequate compensation or offered alternative accommodation.[84] As a result the Committee urged States to:

> take all appropriate measures to ensure that forced evictions take place as a last resort and that persons forcibly evicted from their homes are provided with adequate compensation or offered alternative accommodation, in line with the guidelines adopted by the Committee in its general comment No. 7 (1997) on the right to adequate housing (art. 11 (1) of the Covenant): Forced evictions.[85]

In cases where eviction is considered to be justified, it should be carried out in strict compliance with the relevant procedural protections of international human rights law and in accordance with general principles of reasonableness and proportionality. Procedural protections which should be applied in relation to forced evictions include:

> (a) an opportunity for genuine consultation with those affected; (b) adequate and reasonable notice for all affected persons prior to the scheduled date of eviction; (c) information on the proposed evictions, and, where applicable, on the alternative purpose for which the land or housing is to be used, to be made available in reasonable time to all those affected; (d) especially where groups of people are involved, government officials or their representatives to be present during an eviction; (e) all persons carrying out the eviction to be properly identified; (f) evictions not to take place in particularly bad weather or at night unless the affected persons consent otherwise; (g) provision of legal remedies; and (h) provision, where possible, of legal aid to persons who are in need of it to seek redress from the courts.[86]

All SADC Member States must therefore protect individuals against forced evictions without access to courts of law even in cases where State or non-State actors conclude 'agreements' with individuals to forfeit the right of access to the courts. This issue was considered by the SADC Tribunal in *Tembani v Republic of*

Zimbabwe.[87] In this case, the applicant was a registered owner of a farm of 1265 hectares in Zimbabwe that he had voluntarily offered as security to a parastatal bank called the Agricultural Bank of Zimbabwe (ABZ). This was offered on the security of the farm to acquire a loan in an agreement in which the applicant agreed to forfeit his right of access to a court of law. When he defaulted repaying the loan, his farm was seized and sold without giving him recourse to any court of law. Under Zimbabwe's relevant domestic law,[88] the domestic courts' competence to entertain matters arising out sale in execution of a debt had been ousted. In a number of cases the Supreme Court of Zimbabwe had confirmed that lenders can take possession of the property offered as security without recourse to courts of law in case the parties entered into an agreement which gave powers to the lender to take possession of the defaulting debtor without recourse to any court of law.[89]

The SADC Tribunal considered whether the applicant had been denied access to the courts and deprived of a fair hearing, in breach of Articles 4(c)[90] and 6(1)[91] of the SADC Treaty when his immovable property, a farm, which he had mortgaged to ABZ as security for his loans, pursuant to various loan agreements, had been seized and sold by ABZ after he had defaulted on his debts. The SADC Tribunal relying on its previous decision[92] and comparative judicial decisions by the Constitutional Court of South Africa,[93] stated that:

> It is settled law that the concept of the rule of law embraces at least two fundamental rights, namely, the right of access to the courts and the right to a fair hearing before an individual is deprived of a right, interest or legitimate expectation.

On this basis it was held that the relevant domestic law,[94] by depriving the applicant access to the courts and of a fair hearing, breached principles of international law, was in contravention of Articles 4(c) and 6(1) of the SADC Treaty, and that the sale was illegal and void since the provisions of the relevant domestic law[95] contravened those Articles. While this case was not expressly argued as an ESC rights case, the conclusions reached by the Tribunal offer a strong legal basis for the protection against forced evictions without recourse to the courts of law in the SADC and the promotion of ESC rights in the SADC in several respects.

First, Zimbabwe was held to be in breach of its legal obligations under Article 4(c) and 6(1) of the SADC Treaty because it acted contrary to the concept of the rule of law which is essential for the protection of all human rights including the justiciability of ESC rights. Second, the sale in execution and subsequent transfer of the applicant's property was held to be illegal and void, and the applicant's title to the property, subject to the mortgage as has been held over it at the time of the sale in execution, was held to remain valid. This protected the applicant's security of tenure. Finally, the State was directed to take all necessary measures to refrain from: (i) evicting the applicant or his family from the property; (ii) interfering with the applicant's use and occupation of the property; and (iii) subjecting the property to any further sale, disposal, transfer, encumbrance or similar limitation of proprietary rights or permitting any other person or body to do so, pending the proper determination of the applicant's debt by an independent and impartial court or tribunal. Despite its significance, the decision remains unenforced because of the lack of political will on the part of Zimbabwe to comply with the Tribunal's judgments claiming that the SADC Tribunal's decisions do not bind Zimbabwe.

1.7 Conclusion

The principles of 'human rights, democracy and the rule of law' were given a central place in the SADC Treaty. Such principles include equality, non-discrimination, participation, accountability, the right of access to the courts, the right to a fair hearing and respect for international treaty and customary international law. The implementation of these principles in the SADC Member States would offer a strong framework for the protection of human rights including ESC rights related to land ownership such as the rights to property, adequate housing, adequate food, work, water and sanitation. Land is a fundamental element in the realization of these human rights.

The decisions of the SADC Tribunal in cases involving compulsory land acquisition without compensation have been progressive in applying the principles of human rights and the rule of law to protect the individual right to property, which is essential for the realization of ESC rights. However, enormous gaps remain in the implementation of the SADC Tribunal's decisions. Therefore SADC Member States should give priority to implementing the SADC Tribunal's decisions and to protecting ESC rights in national constitutions on an equal footing with other constitutional rights. Finally, SADC Member States parties to international human rights treaties protecting ESC rights such as the ICESCR and the African Charter should accord such treaties a legal status that would enable the provisions of these treaties to be invoked directly within the domestic legal system, preferably by incorporating such treaties into the domestic law. These should be utilized as a comprehensive framework and instrument for the development of policies and strategies to achieve equality and to promote the human rights of women, so as to ensure the practical realization of the principle of equality between women and men in access to land.

Notes

* Senior Lecturer in Law, Centre for International and Public Law, Brunel Law School, Brunel University.

1 See International Labour Organization, Convention 169, Indigenous and Tribal Peoples Convention, opened for signature 27 June 1989, available at <http://www.ilo.org/ilolex/cgi-lex/convde.pl?C169> (accessed 13 March 2011), Article 14(1) provides: 'The rights of ownership and possession of the peoples concerned over the lands which they traditionally occupy shall be recognised … ' See also United Nations, Declaration on the Rights of Indigenous Peoples, Article 26(1), adopted 13 September 2007, available at <http://www.un.org/esa/socdev/unpfii/documents/DRIPS_en.pdf> (accessed 13 March 2011).

2 Convention on the Elimination of All Forms of Discrimination against Women, GA res 34/180, UN Doc. A/34/46, entered into force 3 September 1981, Article 16(1)(h).

3 Human Rights Council, *Report of the Special Rapporteur on Adequate Housing as a Component of the Right to an Adequate Standard of Living, and on the Right to Non-discrimination in this Context*, Miloon Kothari, UN Doc. A/HRC/7/16 (13 February 2008), para 67.

4 Adopted 27 June 1981, OAU Doc. CAB/LEG/67/3 rev. 5, 21 ILM 58 (1982).

5 993 UNTS 3, entered into force 3 January 1976.

6 Available at <http://www.sadc.int/index/browse/page/120> (accessed 13 March 2011).

7 Article 4(c) of the SADC Treaty.

8 Article 21(b) of the SADC Treaty which, in addition to enjoining the SADC Tribunal to develop its own jurisprudence, instructs the Tribunal to do so 'having regard to applicable treaties, general principles and rules of public international law'.

9 See *Mike Campbell (Pvt) Limited and Others v The Republic of Zimbabwe*, SADC (T) Case No 2/2007, [2008] SADCT 2 (28 November 2008). See also *Tembani v Republic of Zimbabwe* (SADC (T) Case 07/2008) [2009] SADCT 3 (14 August 2009).

10 Available at <http://www.sadc.int/index/browse/page/171> (accessed 13 March 2011).

11 Article 3(1) of the SADC Social Charter (emphasis added).

12 Adopted by the 2nd Ordinary Session of the Assembly of the Union, Maputo, 11 July 2003, entered into force 25 November 2005, available at <http://www.achpr.org/english/_info/women_en.html> (accessed 13 March 2011).

13 999 UNTS 171, entered into force 23 March 1976.

14 GA res 217A (III), UN Doc A/810 at 71 (1948).

15 *The Case of the Mayagna (Sumo) Awas Tingni Community v Nicaragua (Judgment)*, Inter-American Court of Human Rights, Series C, no 79 (31 August 2001), para 144.

16 *Media Rights Agenda and Others v Nigeria*, Communication Nos 105/93, 128/94, 130/94 and 152/96 (1998), para 77.

17 *Constitutional Rights Project, Civil Liberties Organisation and Media Rights Agenda v Nigeria*, Communication Nos 140/94, 141/94, 145/95 (1999), para 55.

18 See Statement on Social, Economic and Cultural Rights in Africa, Pretoria, 17 September 2004, para 5. This Statement was adopted by the African Commission on Human and Peoples' Rights on 7 December 2004 in its *Resolution on Economic, Social and Cultural Rights in Africa*, ACHPR/Res 73 (XXXVI)04, para 1. See also Draft State Reporting Guidelines and Principles on Economic, Social and Cultural Rights in Africa, adopted by the African Commission at its 48th Ordinary Session (November 2010), paras 45–48.

19 See *Interights, Institute for Human Rights and Development in Africa, and Association Mauritanienne des Droits de l'Homme v Islamic Republic of Mauritania*, Communication 373/2009 (formerly 242/2001), para 44.

20 Ibid.

21 Ibid, para 43.

22 Communication 276/2003, 27th Activity Report.

23 The Endorois are a semi-nomadic indigenous community of approximately 60,000 people, who for centuries have earned their livelihoods from herding cattle and goats in the Lake Bogoria area of Kenya's Rift Valley.

24 Communication 276/2003, n 22, paras 215 and 238.

25 Human Rights Committee, *Concluding Observations: United Republic of Tanzania*, UN Doc CCPR/C/TZA/CO/4, 6 August 2009, para 26.

26 Ibid, para 44.

27 Ibid.

28 *Mike Campbell (Pvt) Limited and Others v The Republic of Zimbabwe*, SADC (T) Case No 2/2007.

29 R. Jenning and A. Watts (eds) (1996) *Oppenheim's International Law* (Vol. I, 9th edn, London: Longman), pp 911–27.

30 See e.g. Article 1(3) of the United Nations Charter; Article 2 of the UDHR; Article 2(1) of the ICCPR; Article 2(2) of the ICESCR; Article 2 of the African Charter.
31 *Kenneth Good v Republic of Botswana*, Communication 313/05, Annex IV, para 218.
32 Ibid, para 219, citing *Marckx v Belgium* (6833/74) [1979] ECHR 2 (13 June 1979); Proposed Amendments to the Naturalization Provisions of the Constitution of Costa Rica, Advisory Opinion Oc-4/84, 19 January 1984, Inter-Am Ct HR (Ser A) No 4 (1984), para 57; Human Rights Committee, *General Comment No 18: Non-Discrimination,* UN Doc HRI/GEN/1/Rev 1 at 26 (1994), para 13.
33 *Kenneth Good v Republic of Botswana*, n 31, para 222.
34 See e.g. *Union Inter Africaine des Droits de l'Homme, Federation Internationale des Ligues des Droits de l'Homme and Others v Angola*, Communication No 159/96 (1997).
35 *Centre for Minority Rights Development (Kenya) and Minority Rights Group International on behalf of Endorois Welfare Council v Kenya*, Communication 276/2003, para 196. Article 18(4) of the African Charter specifically states: 'The aged and the disabled shall also have the right to special measures of protection in keeping with their physical or moral needs'.
36 Ibid, *Centre for Minority Rights Development.*
37 Article 2(d) of the Protocol to the African Charter on Human and Peoples' Rights on the Rights of Women in Africa, available at <http://www.achpr.org/english/_info/women_en.html> (accessed 13 March 2011).
38 *Zimbabwe Human Rights NGO Forum v Zimbabwe*, Communication 245/2002, Annex III, 21st Annual Activity Report at 54, para 170. For similar definitions see, Article 1 of the International Convention on the Elimination of All Forms of Racial Discrimination (ICERD), 660 UNTS 195, entered into force 4 January 1969; Article 1 of the Convention on the Elimination of All Forms of Discrimination against Women (CEDAW), UN Doc A/34/46, entered into force 3 September 1981; and Article 2 of the International Convention on the Protection and Promotion of the Rights and Dignity of Persons with Disabilities, UN Doc A/61/49 (2006), entered into force 3 May 2008. See also the Human Rights Committee, *General Comment No 18: Non-Discrimination,* UN Doc HRI/GEN/1/Rev 1 at 26 (1994), paras 6 and 7; and the Committee on Economic, Social and Cultural Rights, *General Comment No 20: Non-Discrimination in Economic, Social and Cultural Rights,* UN Doc E/C.12/GC/20 (2 July 2009), para 7.
39 See e.g. Committee on Economic, Social and Cultural Rights, *Concluding Observations: Zambia,* UN Doc E/C 12/1/Add 106 (23 June 2005), para 27, 'The Committee is concerned that customary land, which represents over 80 per cent of all land, is traditionally inherited by the man's family in accordance with rules of male primogeniture, to the detriment of widows and, especially, girl children'.
40 Committee on Economic, Social and Cultural Rights, *General Comment No 20,* n 38, para 27.
41 *Zimbabwe Human Rights NGO Forum v Zimbabwe,* n 38, para 169. However, the African Commission refused to grant observer status to the Coalition of African Lesbians allegedly 'because the activities of the said Organisation do not promote and protect any of the rights enshrined in the African Charter'. See 28th Activity Report, para 33.
42 See e.g. *Malawi African Association and Others v Mauritania,* Communication Nos 54/91, 61/91, 98/93, 164/97, 196/97 and 210/98 (2000), para 128. The African Commission stated: 'The confiscation and looting of the property of black Mauritanians and the expropriation or destruction of their land and houses before forcing them to go abroad constitute a violation of the right to property as guaranteed in article 14'.
43 *Zimbabwe Human Rights NGO Forum v Zimbabwe,* n 38, para 171.
44 *Mike Campbell (Pvt) Ltd v Minister of National Security Responsible for Land, Land Reform and Resettlement,* Judgment No SC 49/07, Supreme Court of Zimbabwe, 22 January 2008, [2008] ZWSC 1.
45 SADC (T) Case No 2/2007, [2008] SADCT 2 (28 November 2008).

46 *Gramara (Private) Limited and Others v Government of The Republic of Zimbabwe*, HH 169–2009, HC 33/09, X-ref HC 5483/09, available at <http://www.kubatana.net/docs/landr/high_court_patel_gramara_goz_100126.pdf> (accessed 13 March 2011).
47 Ibid.
48 See Supreme Court of Zimbabwe in *Commercial Farmers Union v Minister of Lands*, 2001 (2) SA 925, stating that ' … it is unfair discrimination … to award the spoils of expropriation primarily to ruling party adherents'.
49 HH 169–2009, HC 33/09, X-ref HC 5483/09 (emphasis added).
50 Ibid.
51 Ibid.
52 Ibid.
53 Article 27 of the Vienna Convention on the Law of Treaties, 1155 UNTS 331, 8 ILM 679, entered into force 27 January 1980.
54 Article 32 of the Protocol of Tribunal and the Rules of Procedure Thereof, available at <http://www.sadc.int/tribunal/protocol.php> (accessed 13 March 2011).
55 See e.g. *Fick and Another v Republic of Zimbabwe*, SADC (T) Case No. 01/2010; A. Chigumira, 'Chinamasa Pulls Zim Out of SADC Tribunal Without Cabinet Approval', *The Zimbabwe Mail*, 2 September 2009.
56 See Communique of the 30th Jubilee Summit of SADC Heads of State and Government, 17 August 2010.
57 See CESCR, *General Comment No 20: Non-Discrimination in Economic, Social and Cultural Rights*, UN Doc E/C 12/GC/20, (2 July 2009), para 25 (which refers to General Comments Nos 15 and 4 respectively).
58 See CESCR, *Poverty and the International Covenant on Economic, Social and Cultural Rights*, UN Doc E/C 12/2001/10 (10 May 2001), para 8.
59 CESCR, *Concluding Observations: Madagascar*, UN Doc E/C 12/MDG/CO/2 (16 December 2009), para 15.
60 CESCR, *Concluding Observations: DRC*, UN Doc E/C 12/COD/CO/4 (16 December 2009), para 29.
61 See UNDP, *Human Development Report 2010: The Real Wealth of Nations: Pathways to Human Development* (New York, NY: UNDP, 2010), pp 143–46.
62 Article 2(e) of the Convention on the Elimination of All Forms of Discrimination against Women (CEDAW), GA Res 34/180, UN Doc A/34/46, entered into force 3 September 1981.
63 Available at <http://www.sadc.int/index/browse/page/465> (accessed 13 March 2011).
64 Article 25 of the Protocol to the African Charter on Human and Peoples' Rights on the Rights of Women in Africa, n 12.
65 Ibid.
66 See e.g. Committee on Elimination of Discrimination against Women, *Concluding Observations: Botswana*, UN Doc CEDAW/C/BOT/CO/3 (5 February 2010), para 39.
67 Ibid. See also Committee on Elimination of Discrimination against Women, *Concluding Observations: Malawi*, UN Doc CEDAW/C/MWI/CO/6 (5 February 2010), para 40.
68 Committee on Elimination of Discrimination against Women, *Concluding Observations: Botswana*, UN Doc CEDAW/C/BOT/CO/3 (5 February 2010), para 40.
69 See Article 25 of the UDHR; Article 11(1) of the ICESCR; Articles 24 and 27 of the Convention on the Rights of the Child.
70 CESCR, *General Comment 12: The Right to Adequate Food*, UN Doc E/C 12/1999/5, (5 December 1999), para 6.
71 Ibid, para 8.
72 Ibid, para 12.
73 CESCR, *Concluding Observations: Madagascar*, UN Doc E/C 12/MDG/CO/2 (16 December 2009), para 12.
74 CESCR, *General Comment 4: The Right to Adequate Housing*, UN Doc E/1992/23, para 8.
75 Ibid, para 8(a) (emphasis added).

76 CESCR, *General Comment 7: The Right to Adequate Housing – Forced Evictions,* UN Doc E/1998/22, annex IV, para 3. The prohibition on forced evictions does not, however, apply to evictions carried out by force in accordance with the law and in conformity with the provisions of the International Covenants on Human Rights.
77 *The Social and Economic Rights Action Center and the Center for Economic and Social Rights v Nigeria,* Communication 155/96, 15th Annual Activity Report, para 60.
78 See e.g. CESCR, *General Comment No 13* (1990), paras 46 and 47, *No 14* (2000), para 33, *No 17* (2005), para 28, and *No 18* (2005), para 22. See also the Limburg Principles on the Implementation of the International Covenant on Economic, Social and Cultural Rights, (1987) 9 *Human Rights Quarterly*, 122–35, para 6.
79 Case CCT 11/00, 4 October 2000, 2000 (11) BCLR 1169.
80 Ibid, para 43.
81 Ibid, para 44.
82 CESCR, *General Comment 7: The Right to Adequate Housing – Forced Evictions,* n 76, para 13.
83 Ibid.
84 CESCR, *Concluding Observations: Angola,* UN Doc E/C.12/AGO/CO/3/CRP 1 (18 November 2008), para 31; CESCR, *Concluding Observations: Madagascar,* UN Doc E/C 12/MDG/CO/2 (16 December 2009), para 27; CESCR, *Concluding Observations: DRC,* UN Doc E/C 12/COD/CO/4 (16 December 2009), para 15 noting that 'numerous cases of peasants [were] expelled from their land due to mining operations in Kijiba, Kaposhi, Ngaleshi, Kifunga and Chimanga (Katanga)'.
85 CESCR, *Concluding Observations: Madagascar,* UN Doc E/C 12/MDG/CO/2 (16 December 2009), para 27. See also CESCR, *Concluding Observations: Angola,* UN Doc E/C 12/AGO/CO/3/CRP 1 (18 November 2008), para 31.
86 CESCR, *General Comment 7: The Right to Adequate Housing – Forced Evictions,* n 76, para 15.
87 SADC (T) (07/2008) [2009] SADCT 3 (14 August 2009).
88 See section 38(2) of the Agricultural Finance Corporation Act (Cap 18:02 of the Laws of Zimbabwe), and section 16(7)(d) of the Constitution of Zimbabwe.
89 See e.g. *Agricultural Bank of Zimbabwe v Luke Manyandu Tembani and Others,* SC 39/07; *John Nyamukusa v Agricultural Finance Corporation,* SC 174/94; *Augustine Runusu Chizikikani v Agricultural Finance Corporation,* Civil Appeal No 567/94, SC 123/95.
90 Under Article 4(c) 'SADC and its Member States shall act in accordance with the following principles: human rights, democracy and the rule of law'.
91 By Article 6(1) 'Member States undertake to adopt adequate measures to promote the achievement of the objectives of SADC, and shall refrain from taking any measure likely to jeopardize the sustenance of its principles, objectives and the implementation of the provisions of this Treaty'.
92 *Mike Campbell and Others v The Republic of Zimbabwe,* SADC (T) Case No 2/2007, n 45.
93 *Chief Lesapo v North West Agricultural Bank and Another,* 2001 (1) SA 409 CC; *Barkhuizen v Napier* [2007] ZACC 5, 2007 (5) SA 323 (CC).
94 Section 38(2) of the Agricultural Finance Corporation Act (Cap 18:02 of the Laws of Zimbabwe), and section 16(7)(d) of the Constitution of Zimbabwe.
95 See section 38(2) of the Agricultural Finance Corporation Act, and section 16(7)(d) of the Constitution of Zimbabwe.

Bibliography

Committee on Economic, Social and Cultural Rights (CESCR) (1992) *General Comment 4: The Right to Adequate Housing,* UN Doc E/1992/23.

Committee on Economic, Social and Cultural Rights (CESCR) (1998) *General Comment 7: The Right to Adequate Housing – Forced Evictions,* UN Doc E/1998/22, annex IV.

Committee on Economic, Social and Cultural Rights (CESCR) (1999) *General Comment 12: The Right to Adequate Food,* UN Doc E/C.12/1999/5.

Committee on Economic, Social and Cultural Rights (CESCR) (2005) *Concluding Observations: Zambia*, UN Doc E/C 12/1/Add 106, 23 June.
Committee on Economic, Social and Cultural Rights (CESCR) (2008) *Concluding Observations: Angola*, UN Do. E/C 12/AGO/CO/3/CRP 1, 18 November.
Committee on Economic, Social and Cultural Rights (CESCR) (2009) *Concluding Observations: DRC*, UN Doc E/C 12/COD/CO/4, 16 December.
Committee on Economic, Social and Cultural Rights (CESCR) (2009) *Concluding Observations: Madagascar*, UN Doc E/C 12/MDG/CO/2, 16 December.
Committee on Elimination of Discrimination against Women (CEDAW) (2010) *Concluding Observations: Botswana*, UN Doc CEDAW/C/BOT/CO/3, 5 February.
Human Rights Committee (2009) *Concluding Observations: United Republic of Tanzania*, UN Doc CCPR/C/TZA/CO/4, 6 August.
Human Rights Council (2008) *Report of the Special Rapporteur on Adequate Housing as a Component of the Right to an Adequate Standard of Living, and on the Right to Non-discrimination in this Context*, Miloon Kothari, UN Doc A/HRC/7/16, 13 February.
International Labour Organization (1989) Convention 169, Indigenous and Tribal Peoples Convention.
Jenning, R. and Watts, A. (eds) (1996) *Oppenheim's International Law* (Vol I, 9th edn, London: Longman).
Limburg Principles on the Implementation of the International Covenant on Economic, Social and Cultural Rights (1987) *Human Rights Quarterly*, 9: 122–35.
Office of the United Nations High Commissioner for Human Rights (OHCHR) International Convention on the Elimination of All Forms of Racial Discrimination (ICERD) (1969).
Office of the United Nations High Commissioner for Human Rights (OHCHR) International Convention on the Protection and Promotion of the Rights and Dignity of Persons with Disabilities (2006).
United Nations (1969) *Vienna Convention on the Law of Treaties.*
United Nations (1981) Convention on the Elimination of All Forms of Discrimination against Women (CEDAW).
United Nations (2007) Declaration on the Rights of Indigenous Peoples.
United Nations Development Programme (UNDP) (2010) *Human Development Report 2010: The Real Wealth of Nations: Pathways to Human Development* (New York, NY: UNDP).
United Nations Refugee Agency (UNHCR) (1984) Proposed Amendments to the Naturalization Provisions of the Constitution of Costa Rica, Advisory Opinion Oc-4/84, 19 January, Inter-Am Ct HR (Ser A) No 4.

2 Genderized land reform and social justice

A gender perspective on the formalization of communal land tenure

Annika Rudman[*]

2.1 Introduction

From the time of de-colonialization the international (donor) community has played a critical role in designing and re-designing post-colonial land tenure schemes in sub-Saharan Africa. Large donor agencies, such as the World Bank, have for many years been interested in identifying the interconnections between land reform, economic development and poverty alleviation. The World Bank has in its policy indicated the benefits of building on communal and customary structures in formalizing land tenure, a strategy that has been believed to support development from the bottom up (World Bank 2003). The analytical point of departure of this chapter is the feminist argument, put forward by amongst others Whitehead and Tsikata (2003) and Ikdahl et al (2005), that in the international and domestic quest to formalize communal land tenure in sub-Saharan Africa, women are likely to end up with less secure land rights than envisaged in international law and national legislation. To reflect on this argument a part of the comprehensive South African land reform is explored serving as an example of domestic legislation that embraces the idea of formalizing communal tenure building on customary structures. This chapter further discusses the theoretical outcomes of this type of reform in relation to security of tenure; and puts this discussion in the context of poverty alleviation and social justice for the women involved. The overall purpose is to explore some of the many aspects of the delicate relationship between women's right to secure land tenure and formalization of land rights along communal and customary lines.

Communal ownership strategies and formalization of communal tenure have great relevance in the larger Southern African Development Community (SADC) region, primarily because the solution to insecure tenure in terms of groups, communities or tribes as connected through customs and traditions are important for a country's overall economic development, internal stability and security. Customary and statutory laws that govern land tenure may differ from country to country, however, women, especially rural women, form a nexus of extreme vulnerability in their relationship with customary law which must be acknowledged in legislation and elsewhere, in order to seek solutions that are suitable for improving women's livelihoods and to further their economic development. From the gendered approach to social justice taken in this chapter it is therefore important to discuss land reform from the perspective of the African feminist legal discourse as represented by African and Africanist feminist lawyers (such as Cook 1991; the WLSA series – WLSA 1992, 1994a, 1994b, 1994c, 1996; Molokomme 1991, 1995, 1996; Whitehead and Tsikata 2003) in order to understand the impact of contemporary, pluralistic African legal systems and the treatment of women by both customary and statutory laws. Embracing this theoretical approach the credibility of land reform based on customary structures as a tool to achieve social justice for women in South Africa and in the wider SADC context is further explored. The analysis focuses on two processes, first, the formalization of old order rights (customary rights) into new order rights and its impact on the security of tenure of women; and second, how customary structures as enforced by new legislation on communal ownership can distort and/or disintegrate women's land rights by introducing traditional, mainly patriarchal, decision-making structures to govern new communal titles. South African statutory law has the potential of revealing key information regarding the effectiveness and justness of formalization strategies as discussed within the broader international community and within the SADC region with the aim of fostering conditions of economic development to boost poverty alleviation in rural settings.

The significance of land reform has been interpreted differently in the different SADC countries. For some, production and the question of privatization or nationalization of assets has been central in land reform, putting issues of expropriation and compensation high on the agenda. For others, such as South Africa, land reform has furthermore taken its point of departure in the racial inequalities of the past and the objectives to achieve reconciliation and social justice. South Africa is with its land reform trying to re-design the very fundament of society in its aim to redistribute, restitute and secure tenure of land. However, the South African government and a larger part of South African society have lately become increasingly aware of the negative impact such an all embracing land reform can have on food production, poverty alleviation and for the purpose of this chapter, women's access to land and social justice.

Any land reform is comprehensive, complex and by its nature often political. Land reform is for example, as put forward by Ntsebeza and Hall (2007: 13) about identity and citizenship as well as security, production and development. The concept of land reform is a political and social arrangement that decisively differs from context to context and country to country. Nevertheless, since the need for a SADC Land Reform Support Facility was highlighted at the 2001 SADC Summit there has been an increased focus, within the region, on identifying land-related issues that bear similarity and to develop and implement pro-poor land and agrarian reform policies and programmes in support of the national development plans of the 15 member states. Furthermore, in 2008 the Deputy Executive Secretary of SADC pointed out that: 'land is the most basic of all resources available for social and economic development and it is a key asset for poverty reduction in the SADC region'. The Deputy Executive Secretary further pointed out that about 70 per cent of the SADC population is rural-based where agriculture and utilization of natural resources are the main economic activities for food security and livelihood support (Caholo 2008). Land reform has a central and powerful role to play within the SADC region not only because of its relevance to gender justice, development and poverty alleviation but also because it embraces a message of emancipation from the colonial (and in the case of South Africa apartheid) legacy that have hindered an all inclusive land development approach for decades. Further, it has relevance to the enforcement of gender equality within the region, as spelled out as a major objective of the member states, in the 1997 SADC Declaration on Gender and Development[1] followed by the 2008 Protocol on Gender and Development.[2] The Declaration initially indicated that all member states committed themselves to promoting women's full access to, and control over productive resources such as land in line with the Convention on the Elimination of All Forms of Discrimination against Women (CEDAW).[3] This message was further strengthened in the Gender and Development Protocol, ensuring gender equality and equity in land reform by 2015 in order to end all discrimination against women in the SADC region with regards to land rights.[4]

2.1.1 Land reform in the SADC region and economic development

The South African Constitution came into force in 1997 and with it a whole new dispensation of rights geared towards giving all South Africans a chance to a dignified life.[5] The Constitution put forward a complex property clause leading the way towards extensive land reform as well as an equality clause prohibiting discrimination on the basis of sex and gender.[6] Furthermore, it set the framework for the coexistence of customary and common law under the ambit of the Constitution and allowed traditional leaders to govern communities living under customary law.[7] Departing from this wide platform it is understandable that land reform has become one of the most politically charged and cumbersome tasks of the post-apartheid governments taking office since 1994; especially in terms of upholding the delicate balance between individual rights and the cultural freedoms of the many traditional communities in South Africa.

Moreover, the aim of economic development and the betterment of the standard of living for the majority of South Africans, as expressed in the socio-economic rights in the Constitution such as the right to human dignity, housing, health care, food, water, social security and education necessitates a further exploration of the theoretical relationship between land reform and economic development. This relationship is explored, within limits, in this chapter by analyzing the basic theoretical standpoints as presented within the scope of what can be referred to as formalization theory. This, and with it related theories, takes its point of departure in the assumption that formalized (from informal to formal) or legalized (from unregistered to registered) titles be it individual or communal will support economic development of either the individual or the group (see e.g. de Soto 2000). The methods of formalization of land rights have historically had a strong international aspect. During the colonial era the push to formalize ownership and possession of land came from the colonial powers. At present it is international organizations like the World Bank together with its bilateral aid donors that are among the actors promoting systems of formalized ownership of land linked to customary tenure.

With its 2003 report on *Land Policies for Growth and Poverty Reduction* the World Bank put the idea of supporting customary land tenure systems through different formalization strategies firmly on the international agenda (World Bank 2003: 32).[8] The report is premised on the idea that the way in which land rights are assigned has important implications for efficiency and economic growth in rural areas (World Bank 2003: xvii–xlvi). The policy discourses, such as the one presented by the World Bank, that advocate formalization of tenure to achieve economic development on a grass root level increasingly envisage that land rights should be assigned to customary structures and that custom can be modified through appropriate intervention. A modified customary system would then have a role to play in local-level land management. As put forward in the report: 'legally recognizing customary land rights subject to a determination of membership and the codification or establishment of internal rules and mechanisms for conflict resolution can greatly enhance occupants' security' (World Bank 2003: xxvii). As interpreted by Whitehead and Tsikata (2003: 94) this policy was put forward to encourage the customary forms of ownership to evolve so that democratically accountable management systems could be introduced building upon what already existed locally, i.e. ownership should be formalized but should still be relevant to the customary structures within which it has to exist. However, the World Bank's thinking pays very little attention to the processes by which evolutionary change is occurring and, as further discussed by Whitehead and Tsikata (2003: 95) it underplays issues of equity in the outcome. The World Bank has indicated, in its policy research, that the same formalization processes that may lead to an increase in the value of land (which is likely to result in an increasing demand for formalization of titles) could also lead to a weakening or even a loss of women's rights to land if women's land rights are not purposely protected and strengthened (World Bank 2003: 58). Still, there has been no revision suggested by the World Bank to the strategy of building land reform on customary tenure and decision-making structures (Whitehead and Tsikata 2003: 94). The World Bank's international formalization policy has been influential in the structuring of communal ownership in South Africa as further discussed below.

Furthermore, regional human rights law has helped develop a strong connection between the enforcement of human rights and development. The SADC countries have focused attention to the interconnectedness between the protection of human rights and the prospect of individuals to escape poverty. In its Declaration on Gender and Development, as discussed above, the countries of the SADC region have committed themselves to, in line with international law, promoting women's full access to, and control over productive resources such as land in order to reduce the level of poverty among women. The member states have further, in relation to the 2008 Protocol, undertaken to repeal and reform all laws, amending constitutions and changing social practices which still subject women to discrimination, as well as enacting empowering gender sensitive laws.[9] This approach, to genderized land reform and development, was put firmly on the international agenda by the UN Commission on Human Rights in 2002, when it acknowledged that the world community recognized that laws, policies, customs and traditions that prevent women from accessing, owning and inheriting land, other property and housing and that exclude women from participating fully in development processes are discriminatory and contribute to the feminization of poverty. It was further recognized that the full and equal participation of women in all areas of life is essential for the full and complete development of any country.[10] The UN Commission on Human Rights has since then, in a number of resolutions on women's equal ownership, access to and control over land, reiterated these statements and highlighted the centrality of women's land rights in economic development.[11] The devastating impact of laws and customs that deny women the right to access, own and inherit land has further been acknowledged and discussed by Grown and Gupta (2005) in a UN Millennium Project report. The report included among its recommendations an urgent call for the promotion of women's land rights. Women's effective land rights were in the report pointed out as an inherent part of achieving the first millennium development goal, to eradicate extreme poverty, and the third millennium development goal, to promote gender equality. The UN's Millennium Project has in line with these targets called for the member states to guarantee women's land rights as one out of seven strategic priorities to reach the third millennium development goal.

As a remedy for the injustice that many women are experiencing in relation to land reform and customary law in Africa and elsewhere, the international and regional African community has further laid down a multifaceted approach to the interrelationship between land reform and development and between development, social justice and customary law and practices. On the international level, CEDAW contains basic rights of special relevance to the protection of women's land rights and the advancement of women's rights in terms of poverty reduction and economic development.[12] These rights emphasize the particular problems faced by rural women and the significant roles which rural women play in the survival of their families.[13] In relation to the effective access to land by rural women, CEDAW further spells out the direct responsibility of the states parties to grant rural women equal treatment in land and agrarian reform as well as in land resettlement schemes. This indicates that the states parties not only have to ensure women's equal status before the law but also in the effective implementation of such laws in the form of resettlement programmes. CEDAW further ensures all rural women the right to participate in all community activities including participation in the decision-making of communal land management bodies.

Furthermore, as a regional contribution to women's rights under international human rights law a Protocol to the African Charter spelling out the specific rights of women in Africa has been introduced by the African Union.[14] It serves as an addition to the protection of women's rights under the African Charter on Human and Peoples' Rights.[15] The Protocol on the Rights of Women in Africa provides a more comprehensive and specific protection of women's rights than the rights spelled out in the African Charter. The Protocol, in line with the 1997 SADC Declaration and 2008 SADC Protocol, firmly relates issues of development with issues of gendered land rights in spelling out that all women should have the right to fully enjoy the right to sustainable development. In this regard, the states parties to the Protocol on the Rights of Women in Africa are legally bound to take all appropriate measures in order to promote women's access to and control over productive resources, such as land.[16]

2.2 Genderized land reform in South Africa

The coming to an end of the apartheid system and the abolishment of infamous acts such as the Land Act[17] and the Group Areas Act[18] paved way for land reform and a new system of land tenure in South Africa. After the first free elections in 1994, a comprehensive land reform programme was introduced to address the massive land dispossessions that took place under the white minority rule. The consequences of the racially determined land dispossession that took place in South Africa during apartheid were multidimensional; they were, amongst others, increased gender discrimination in relation to land, landlessness, insecure tenure and inadequate compensation for the value of property, all contributing factors to the widespread poverty that still plagues South Africa today. The land reform was designed to heal these rifts but, as explored in this chapter, it may entail dramatic and potentially detrimental results for the many women living in rural and customary contexts, being mainly holders of secondary (customary) rights in land. Women's access to land and the protection of their land rights is affected by a wide range of norms. Statutory law and state institutions are far from the only dogmatic authorities (Moore 1999: 33ff). Traditional communities possess the ability to create and implement their own customary laws in line with the ever changing legal, social and economic conditions of these societies. However, at times customary law is so strong that it overrides or changes statutory law creating a conflict between the two systems.

In the view of the history of South Africa adjusting the unequal distribution of land and securing tenure for millions of South Africans have been fundamental objectives of all governments, since 1994. However, the land reform programme needs to be implemented within the ambit of sections 9 (the equality clause), 25 (the property clause) and 36 (the limitation clause) of the Constitution, to secure a gender just and peaceful transformation. Section 25(6) and (9) sets out the parameters for the security of tenure reform seeking to formalize ownership specifically in the rural and semi-urban areas, especially in relation to land held under customary law. All reform as put forward within the wide-ranging reform programme has gender implications and relate in more than one way to the potential for individual and communal development. However, this chapter focuses only on the broader gender implication of the formulation of communal land rights policy building on customary structures and the re-formulation of customary rights in land such as launched through the Communal Land Rights Act of 2004[19] popularly known as CLARA; and the Africanist feminist critique directed against it. The communal land tenure structure, as set up under CLARA, is currently being reviewed and is no longer, as put forward by the Minister for Rural Development and Land Reform, a true reflection of government policy.[20] However, it is mainly the critique as launched by traditional leaders in terms of a survey of the relevant land and allocation of titles, which has bearing on the powers of traditional leaders that has provoked this latest review.[21] The gender issues, such as explored below, mainly remain unsolved and out of the government's focus as was further highlighted in the judgement of *Tongoane and Others v The National Minister for Agriculture and Land Affairs and Others* (*Tongoane* case)[22] as discussed below. A critical reconsideration of women's position within communal land tenure is therefore of great importance for the future development of communal tenure in South Africa and in the wider SADC context; and CLARA has the potential of acting as a significant point of departure for this discussion.

2.2.1 Reforming communal land tenure

In 1999, as an attempt from the government's side to take the conditions of communal customary tenure to a new, more structured level, the government proposed a legislative framework that would allow land to be transferred into the name of a tribe or community occupying a specific portion of land. In this regard the government had three different objectives with the implementation of CLARA. First, the vesting of ownership of communal land in the relevant communities through the different institutions laid down by CLARA and on the terms created by CLARA.[23] Second, some already existing rights in the land, which are referred to in CLARA as 'old order rights' would be converted into 'new order rights'. The effects of the new order rights are to be determined by the Minister responsible for Land Affairs.[24] New order rights are indicated as secondary rights of occupation and use, which are secondary to the communal ownership of the land. These new order rights can be upgraded into freehold ownership through a process prescribed by CLARA. Third, CLARA provides for a land administration committee to represent a community which owns communal land under the ambit of CLARA. This committee has powers and duties conferred to it by CLARA and by the specific rules of the relevant community. The powers include representing land-owning communities, allocating land rights, maintaining records of rights and transactions, liaising with local government bodies in relation to planning and development and various other land administration functions.[25]

The application of CLARA is quite broad, it applies to the land in the former homelands, land that was previously listed in the Schedules to the Natives Land Act of 1913 and the Development Trust and Land Act of 1936 (SADT areas).[26] The target land in the former homelands constitutes approximately 13 per cent of the total area of South Africa (Walker 2002: 82). At least 892 communities will be directly affected by CLARA,[27] and the successful implementation or reformulation of this act will be crucial in the success of the overall land reform programme. According to the Minister for Rural Development and Land Reform, approximately 21,302,413 people or 3,550,402 households occupy and use communal land in the former homelands and SADT areas.[28] Out of a total population of 47.5 million people, this represents approximately 45 per cent of South Africa's population.[29] Furthermore, the former homelands are the poorest parts of South Africa and women constitute 59 per cent of the total population living in these areas (Claassens and Mnisi 2009: 2).

In relation to the question posed in this chapter as to the impact of the formalization of communal titles built on customary structures, CLARA serves as an interesting example of the South African legislators' attempt to merge the relevant constitutional values with the aim of accommodating customary law in legislation to govern the conditions of tenure. During the process of designing CLARA there were intense discussions about the protection of women's rights to land and the problems that many women face in relation to the application of customary land laws. The push for the acknowledgement of women's special needs in the legislation was put forward by, amongst others, the Women's National Coalition. To ensure the pre-emption of the content of the equality clause, the following section was included: 'A woman is entitled to the same legally secure tenure, rights in or to land and benefits from land as is a man, and no law, community or other rule, practice or usage may discriminate against any person on the ground of the gender of such person'.[30] From a feminist perspective the protection, in this part, of women's rights under CLARA seems comprehensive. However, contrary, as it may seem, to the objective of this statement CLARA also introduces a system of translating old order rights, mainly held by men, into new order rights as further discussed below; and it establishes traditional councils as the main governing bodies representing the communities in all issues related to the management of communal land.

As seen from an African or Africanist legal feminist perspective the inclusion of traditional leaders in the procedure of governing the land and their application of customary law and practices is of major concern (Cousins 2002; Walker 2001, 2002; Bohler-Muller Bjuris and Bronwyn 2009). Under CLARA the communities to which the land is transferred will assume juristic personality and will be able to hold rights and incur obligations.[31] The community will be able to govern the land by setting up a special decision-making body called a land administration committee. However, section 21(2) of CLARA spells out that: 'If a community has a recognized traditional council, the powers and duties of a land administration committee of such a community may be exercised and performed by such council'. Further, a recognized traditional council in the context of CLARA is a council defined in section 3 of the Traditional Leadership and Governance Framework Act. This Act requires that a traditional council be comprised of no more than 30 members, a third of which must be women.[32] Of further relevance is section 22 of CLARA which spells out that: 'Subject to section 21(2), the members of a land administration committee must be persons not holding any traditional leadership position and must be elected by the community in the prescribed manner'.[33] The phrasing of section 22 implies that section 21(2) is a dominant section, i.e. when there is a recognized traditional council section 22(2) is not applicable. Consequently traditional leaders will have the right to govern communal land if a council of traditional leaders exists within a specific community. This is the case in the majority of communities within the scope of CLARA, even if it is often far from clear which traditional council should govern over what community in the large number of scattered and fragmented communities in South Africa today.

If there is no traditional council, as spelled out in section 21(2), a land administration committee will govern the land. Section 22(3) of CLARA, similarly to section 3 of the Traditional Leadership and Governance Framework Act, provides that one third of the total membership of the land administration committee must consist of women. Even though the number of women on the committees or in the councils are not a guarantee for the protection of women's interests the fact that women only make up one third of the total seats is not a satisfactory solution in terms of the scope of the equality clause in the Constitution and South African commitments under international and regional African law. Even though it is clear that women has a role to play in the traditional councils and land administration committees, these provisions do not, according to Bohler-Muller Bjuris and Bronwyn (2009: 26), have the effect of freeing women from their oppression and minority status. They argue that rural women will continue to be subjected to patriarchal structures until such time as they have been granted equal representation on such committees and councils, and their voices are heard and valued outside the constraints of traditional stereotypes. To further illustrate the gender implications within the framework of CLARA, Bohler-Muller Bjuris and Bronwyn (2009: 27) put forward the example of section 2(c)(i) of the Traditional Leadership and Governance Framework Act which provides that a senior traditional leader (in most cases a man) will select other traditional leaders to be members of the traditional council and such selection will conform to rules of custom. This senior traditional leader is allowed to select 60 per cent of the membership of the council, which will in most cases have the effect that most councils, which are not democratically elected, demonstrate a male majority.

Thus, equality in representation, in terms of numbers, does not guarantee the consideration of women's needs or interest but, as put forward by Phillips (1995: 82): 'Changing the gender composition of any elected assembly is a major, and necessary, challenge to the social arrangements which have systematically placed women in a subordinate position'. It is unlikely that assemblies composed equally of men and women would behave just as an assembly where women only have a limited position. However, representation is dependent upon so much more than just numbers. It depends on the continuous relationship between representatives and the represented. This is also true in relations to the equality in representation of women in the land administrations committees and the traditional councils. Thus, the shared experiences of women as women can only serve as a promise of shared concerns, there is, as further pointed out by Phillips, no obvious way of establishing strict accountability to women as a group. In other words women's presence in these committees is likely to have an impact, but there is no guarantee.

Partly resting on the arguments presented above and further highlighting the gender implications of CLARA a challenge to the constitutionality of this act was launched in 2006 by the Kalkfontein, Makuleke, Makgobistad and Dixie communities in the *Tongoane* case.[34] The High Court judgment was appealed by the applicants and in their final representation to the Constitutional Court two lines of arguments relating to women's security of tenure, or lack thereof, under CLARA was put forward. The first argument related to the fact that women, who live under a system which derives from customary tenure, seldom have their rights recognized by any written law. In relation to CLARA this has the potential of creating gender inequalities on two different levels. CLARA translates old order rights into new order rights, and entrenches them. However, the vulnerable rights of women, which are not old order rights, are not protected by CLARA, instead they are treated as absent. By entrenching certain (mainly male) rights, and ignoring other (mainly female) rights, CLARA entrenches and strengthens existing insecurity and inequality.[35] As held by the applicants in the case: 'If one starts with a discriminatory system, and then confirms and converts the rights existing under that system into a new system, then self-evidently one will repeat and reinforce the existing discrimination'.[36]

In terms of married couples the legislator tried to remedy the discriminatory nature of the conversion of old order rights by indicating in CLARA that: 'An old order right held by a married person is, despite any law, practice, usage or registration to the contrary, deemed to be held by all spouses in a marriage in which such person is a spouse […] and must, on confirmation or conversion in terms of section 18 (3), be registered in the names of all such spouses'.[37] However, as explained by Nhlapo in the applicants' statement to the Constitutional Court the acknowledgement of the provision in CLARA, which deems old order rights to be held by all spouses in a marriage, will only assist married women living in nuclear families, but does not address the issue of the family-based nature of land rights in extended families. Land rights will, under CLARA, be vested solely in the name of a man and his wife or wives, and will exclude the rights of other family members, such as any widowed mothers or unmarried sisters. CLARA only offers formalization of land rights at two levels, on the community level and the individual level. In this respect it entrenches previous colonial and apartheid distortions that considered land rights as being the property of the male household head.[38] Further, and most importantly, it does not present a structure that will have the capacity to protect the right of those individuals who had vulnerable and insecure so-called secondary rights under the old order, such as single women and widows. It can be argued that by focusing on the creation of individual titles based exclusively on old order rights and ignoring the layered rights which vest in members of the family other than the husband and wife, CLARA fails to protect the already insecure tenure rights of other members of the family or the rights of individuals living mainly outside the nuclear family context. By vesting strong registered rights in the hands of specified individuals, the rights of others are undermined, and they are left with less secure rights. Hence, CLARA strengthens the security of tenure of some individuals, at the expense of those who are more vulnerable.

The second argument highlighted the discussion about the decision-making structures under CLARA. The applicants indicated that by giving traditional leaders undemocratic and unprecedented powers, the application of CLARA has the potential of undermining the security of tenure while section 25(6) of the Constitution requires that tenure rights must be strengthened, protected and guaranteed. The applicants argued that CLARA allows traditional councils (that are not democratically elected) to become land administrators and that CLARA therefore makes the tenure of the majority women in the former homelands more insecure. As further put forward by the applicants: 'Once CLARA comes into operation, groups like the applicant communities will be locked in never-ending struggles to assert and protect their land rights from the claims of traditional authorities cloaked in "customary law"'. As was held in the High Court judgment, some of the existing traditional councils in the relevant communities had not been democratically elected and the interest of women had therefore not been represented in these councils. In these communities the relationship between customary land tenure and the protection of women's rights was further aggravated by the fact that, even though customary law had always had a patriarchal bias, the colonial and apartheid period exaggerated and entrenched it by distorting custom and practice which, in many cases, had been either relatively egalitarian or mitigated by checks and balances in favour of women.[39] In the judgment in the *Tongoane* case handed down by Judge Ngcobo in the beginning of March 2010, CLARA was declared invalid in its entirety. However, this was done on the grounds that the government had failed to comply with specific procedural rules laid down in the Constitution. The judgment did not bring any clarity to the gender issues presented to the court by the applicants.

2.3 Reconciling conflicting customary law with women's rights

Before any conclusion can be drawn about the delicate relationship between women's right to secure land tenure and formalization of land rights along communal and customary lines there is a need to further (briefly) address the dichotomy that is often put forward in international human rights law between the right to culture/custom and the protection of women's rights; and if and how the conflict between women's rights and the customary legal structures can be reconciled. In reality, there is no clear-cut dichotomy between these concepts because these rights overlap and are not each other's opposite as sometimes suggested. Nevertheless, it is of interest to the current discussion to highlight some arguments that have been put forward to voice the different standpoints within this conundrum to frame the formalization discussion as presented above and below.

As indicated, many of the articles in the instruments referred to above and the interpretations laid down by international human rights bodies such as the CEDAW Committee highlights the difficult relationship between women's rights to property on the one hand and customary law on the other. It is of interest to further analyze the tension that is described in both CEDAW and the SADC Protocol, namely between the equality interests/rights of the individual (the woman) and the customary rights of the group (the community living under customary law). The issue at hand is well reflected by the arguments presented by Moller-Okin (1999) and Kymlicka (1989, 1995). They are both, but from different perspectives, concerned with the problem of if /how to protect a group's culture, identity and ethnicity from outer pressure while protecting the individual inside the group from the internal pressure posed by traditional and patriarchal structures. The point of view in favour of group rights as exemplified by Kymlicka's arguments and the response to his arguments by Moller-Okin, questioning the protection of women's basic rights within the group dynamic below can be helpful in identifying the issues that are at hand in the apparent clash between cultural group rights and the basic individual rights of women because it, at least partially, sums up the difficulties in trying to reconcile the often conflicting rights accorded under traditional land tenure and governance arrangements with the international and constitutional requirement of equality. This discussion is further helpful in recognizing the apparent connection between protecting women's property rights and developmental progress such as poverty reduction.

As a point of departure Kymlicka (1995: 89) argues that many minority and indigenous groups (in the South African context relevant to traditional communities) have their own 'societal cultures' which according to him, provide the members of these groups with a meaningful way of life in relation to all aspects of life, not only cultural. According to Kymlicka these cultures should be protected by special rights, i.e. special group rights because societal cultures play such a fundamental role in the lives of the members. If these rights are not protected these groups will largely be assimilated in to mainstream society and their cultural features lost. However, as put forward by Moller-Okin (1999: 12) and in line with the feminist approach discussed above: 'group rights are potentially, and in many cases actually, antifeminist'. Moller-Okin directs critique against the idea of the protection of group rights mainly on the grounds that advocates of group rights fail to acknowledge the differences within the cultural groups and the importance of the private sphere. She presents the argument that the sphere of personal, sexual and reproductive life provides a central focus of most cultures and is a dominant theme in customary rules and practices. Furthermore, personal law, i.e. the laws of succession, division and control of family property as well as inheritance are key elements in the survival of the community. As a consequence the protection of the traditional ways of life is likely to have much greater impact on the lives of women than on the lives of men because far more of women's time and energy goes into preserving and maintaining the personal, familial, and reproductive side of life (Moller-Okin 1999: 13). Hence, customs and traditions are not solely concerned with domestic arrangements, but undisputedly much of customary law and traditions are centred on the private sphere. A person's home is the place where most time is spent and naturally also the place where customs and traditions are entertained and passed on to the next generation. In turn, the allotment of responsibilities and power at home has an important impact on who has the right to participate and who has the influence over the decision-making institutions of the group, where rules and regulations about both public and private life are made.

In approaching this problem from another angle Kymlicka constructs his argument of the importance of the protection of group rights around the rights of individuals, making no distinction between the public/private spheres. Building on the ideas of Rawls, Kymlicka stresses the essential importance of self-respect in every individual's life (Kymlicka 1989: 166). The argument proposes that cultural membership is a primary good and that equal concern for the well-being and rights of individuals can be given within this unit. Kymlicka further argues that the importance of self-respect would have been recognized by the parties in Rawls' original position and that the relationship between cultural membership and self-respect gives the parties to the original position a strong reason to award this membership the status of being a primary good. Kymlicka establishes that without self-respect or as Rawls (1971: 178) puts it the 'sense that one's plan of life is worth carrying out' there is no point in our activities; and without the freedom to examine and confirm our beliefs we cannot achieve self-respect. Kymlicka firmly builds his idea of the cultural rights of groups on the protection of religious and cultural freedoms; and he justifies this by the argument of self-respect and its importance for a person's existence. In essence, cultural minorities (traditional communities) need special rights, because their culture may otherwise be threatened with extinction, and cultural extinction would likely undermine the self-respect and freedom of all group members (men and women).

In opposing these arguments there is, as brought forward by Moller-Okin (1999: 21ff), very little reassurance of the protection of women's rights within the group due to the fact that most discrimination takes place on a personal level inside the group/household. The violations of women's basic rights are actually made possible due to the patriarchal structures and beliefs of the very groups protected by the kind of protection as suggested and advocated by Kymlicka. Relating to this discussion CEDAW and the SADC Protocol clearly express that all member states have an obligation to undertake appropriate measures to modify all customs or practices that discriminate against women. Equally, international and regional human rights law expresses a strong protection of cultural and customary values and the rights for all tribal and indigenous peoples to decide freely on how they want to live.[40] The protection offered is important but the key issue is whether it is possible to reconcile these rights? A potential solution that has been voiced and discussed within the broader international research community could be to try to protect basic rights in terms of women living in a customary context. As long as women's basic rights (question of definition) such as the rights to non-discrimination, life, health and an adequate standard of living are upheld the freedom of cultural and customary practices should be protected and preserved for those women who choose to live within that specific context. However, as soon as these rights are violated, the state should intervene to help modify or abolish harmful practices and stereotypes to protect the rights of the women concerned. The state has, in this regard, an important role to play not only in upholding a negative 'non-infringement' position but to put support structures and mechanisms in place to foster a reconsideration of customary rules and practices in line with national and international human rights standards.

If put in the context of the property rights discussion entertained in this chapter and departing from the standpoints of Kymlicka and Moller-Okin, it is a simple exercise to conclude that there are many different rights and claims that compete in the interaction between women's rights, property rights and cultural or customary rights. But can we, and if so, how do we conclude what claims should prevail; and how does this relate to the broader issues of economic development and social justice? There are a number of ways to approach this issue, and it is not the objective of the present chapter to attempt a concrete answer to these multi-dimensional questions, but if we depart from the feminist legal perspective discussed above and relate this to the idea of a human rights-based approach to development (HRBA) as frequently discussed within this framework, some helpful suggestions can be made and has been made in a number of international scholarly contributions. The HRBA strategy as presented by amongst others Ikdahl et al (2005) has the advantage in the discussion of women's rights *vis-à-vis* cultural/customary rights that it acknowledges legal feminist theories and relates directly to women's property rights. It is further built on the notion that culture is a freedom, i.e. secondary to the rights of non-discrimination and equality. In making this distinction between the individual rights of women as foregoing the protection of the group, the following guiding principles in structuring and understanding women's property rights are put forward by Ikdahl et al. First, all access to land and protection of land rights have to be non-discriminatory. This indicates that formal and informal laws, norms and practices that formally disadvantage women in comparison to men constitute direct discrimination (e.g. inheritance laws that deprive widows of property rights). Further, indirect discrimination relates to norms that appear to be gender-neutral but that actually favour male life situations and as such leave women in a disadvantaged position (referred to by Ikdahl et al (2005: xi) to as for example tenure regimes based on the assumption of household and community unity resulting in de facto inequality). In this regard it is of importance that measures for distribution, formalization and registration are carefully assessed to eliminate both direct and indirect discrimination.

Second, standards for gender-equal and non-discriminatory land reform have to be applied in both the public and the private sphere. As put forward by Ikdahl et al (2005: xi) whether land reform, formalization or registration is based on statutory or customary, individual or communal ownership, mechanisms that protect women against direct and indirect discrimination have to be put in place. Third, equal participation and empowerment of women in land reform and land formalization processes requires that a wide range of national and international human rights instruments address women's rights to participate on an equal basis with men as a substantive right, not only as a formal right. In this regard issues of feminine poverty have to be addressed alongside measures to empower women such as education. And fourth, the applied HRBA sets out procedural requirements that have a bearing on land reform and formalization processes in providing monitoring and accountability procedures in terms of due process and the rule of law. This indicates that rights, such as women's rights in land, must be clear and legally enforceable for individuals. Every state has to provide access to legal remedies in situations where rights have been violated in redistribution and registration processes (Ikdahl et al 2005: xi). This approach clearly creates a hierarchy of rights and identifies some of the problems in the intersection between equality and customary law as further discussed below.

2.4 Women's position under communal tenure reform

International and regional human rights law together with the South African Constitution foster a strong protection of gender equal rights in land reform. This undoubtedly puts forward the question of whether there are any real gains for women in formalizing customary land rights, in terms of accessing land based on customary structures which are predominately structured around the notion of female subordination. Could formalizing land ownership through land reform, building on communal customary structures promote women's economic development to reduce poverty and is this model justifiable from a human rights perspective? If not, what is the alternative? The discussion so far has not covered all the aspects of these wide-ranging questions but it has put the spotlight on a few gender relevant issues to be considered when law and policy is reconsidered and reformed. The latter question of policy reform is considered in Chapters 6, 7, 8 and 9.

A formalization of communal customary tenure has the apparent advantage of creating additional legal certainty. It could be argued that by formalizing land rights into communal titles a stronger legal protection of these rights are created. However, when formalization takes place in a customary context where there is a move from multiple users of the land to multiple owners, women tend to get a less influential role (see e.g. Ikdahl et al 2005; Green 2008; Claassens and Ngubane 2008). In this context women sometimes have to choose between being a second-class citizen under customary law and being completely invisible under the formal system. Individual titles have the capacity of strengthening the individual's tenure security but to protect women's security in land these titles cannot be based exclusively on an old order structure such as customary claims to land. Before colonialization and the impact of apartheid the customary structure had, to a larger extent, the ability to embrace the different needs of the members of a community (tribe, kingdom or clan) (Pienaar 2008: 260–61). However, after the fragmentation of most communities, as a consequence of colonial and apartheid laws, the impact of widespread poverty and the mass movement of people from the rural areas to the major cities the concentration of power around male dominant figures with focus on the extended family responsibility that the customary structure rests on (and by proxy also CLARA) has lost in importance (Rudman 2010: 174–75). The reality is that many people are left to fend for themselves without the overall support of the customary structures. Under these circumstances women are likely to lose out because on the one hand they are not in a position to decide over land because of the influences of customary law that still applies, and on the other hand customary structures providing for the support of for example widows and single women have to a large extent disappeared in a hardened social and economic climate.

Even though the formalization procedure creates structure, legal certainty and lessens the risk of disputes over ownership the most appealing part of the theory of formalization is the promise of economic development, especially for the poor. This is particularly relevant in South Africa, as in the other SADC countries, because the country is still plagued by poverty and inequality regardless of the last 17 years of government policies and budgetary allocations intended to circumvent the legacies of apartheid and support steady economic growth. Today, South Africa has the second highest level of inequality in the world after Brazil, and the gap between rich and poor appears to be widening (Cousins et al 2005: 1). It has further become increasingly clear to all involved parties that growth alone will not reduce poverty and inequality especially with the latest down-turn in the global economy. For some analysts, like de Soto (2000), the main reason behind poverty is the absence of formal property rights to the assets held by the poor. The concept of private property is dominant in the South African context and works well for those South Africans who live in the so-called first economy; but does it work equally well for the women living mainly in the second, informal economy?

Many local (see e.g. Cousins et al 2005) as well as international scholars (see for example Green 2008: 70ff; Ikdahl et al 2005) have pointed to the single-minded focus of formalization theory to secure individual or communal titles in land as solutions to poverty. In de Soto's theory, formalizing property rights has the effect of allowing its owners to create new capital, i.e. it makes assets interchangeable so that they can be used for other purposes. He prescribes a programme to capitalize the poor by legalizing their extra-legal property. However, over the last decade since de Soto's ideas were first presented, serious criticism has been launched against the idea of formalization as a 'cure' for everything, some relevant to the present discussion. The formalization of land rights is, by many, seen as a means of changing the socio-economic reality in which most of the poor people in South Africa live; however, it can be argued that it is this social and economic context itself that would prevent the desirable change, as discussed above.

The central problem with the strategy of formalization of property is the oversimplification of the informal economy and associated land relations such as customary and gender relations. The first fundamental problem with formalizing customary tenure, in the South African context, is that legislation, such as CLARA, frequently has failed to acknowledge the different principles that inform the customary land systems found in rural areas and urban informal settlements, such as customary law. As was discussed above, formalization of land rights in customary settings often means that a portion of land with multiple users (both women and men) becomes the property of a single owner, usually male or a community where the decision-making body is dominated by men. Furthermore, the capital formation function of land is over-emphasized at the cost of other functions such as securing livelihoods or supporting social identity. Land rights, especially in rural communities, are closely related to livelihoods. Women in most developing countries grow between 60 to 80 per cent of the food produced, yet own less than

2 per cent of the land (Green 2008: 74). Women, many of them living outside the nuclear family, in the SADC region and elsewhere in the developing world are often the primary source of the livelihood of the family. The formalization processes, as discussed above, have however, primarily been directed towards formalizing land rights in terms of secure ownership to land, disregarding the protection of informal (secondary) rights to land connected to the livelihoods of many women.

As an alternative to the strict theory of formalization of property rights into individual titles, with all the problems that that entails, a theory of respect and reliance on customary land tenure system in land reform has emerged as the 'politically correct' solution to unsecure and unequal (based on race and ethnicity) access and ownership of land, as discussed above. This theory as promoted by, amongst others, the World Bank is endorsing economic development at the grass root level by supporting customary land tenure systems in reforming ownership. The effects of these ideas are evident in CLARA and in the representations made by the applicants in the *Tongoane* case. In terms of the introduction of customary elements into law aimed at securing communal ownership it has been the objective of the legislator to on the one hand develop customary law through formalizing it; and on the other hand to promote the development of the 'lived law' through encouraging social change in line with the constitutional values. However, the problem with the theory of formalization of land rights based on customary tenure is apparent; putting a concept that by its nature is flexible into a law is dooming it to failure. Just like the colonizers and the apartheid regime failed to capture the 'true' version of customary law, today's legislators will face the same problems. In referring to the traditional leadership in CLARA it is not clear who is to be in control of the land. Is it a traditional leadership supporting its decisions on patriarchal preference or is it a leadership whose thoughts and ideas have been influenced by the constitutional values of gender equality? The government wants to promote the latter vision of South Africa's traditional leadership and change is certainly taking place, but it may be argued that this is not enough to secure the right to equality in land and create legal certainty.

As discussed above, CLARA builds on the communal aspect of ownership but establishes traditional councils in most cases as the bodies that should administer the communal land. The Traditional Leadership and Governance Framework Act requires that 40 per cent of the members of the traditional councils be democratically elected and a third should be women. Changing the gender composition of any elected assembly is a major, and necessary, challenge to the social arrangements which have systematically placed women in a subordinate position; and whether we consider politics as the representation of interest or need (or both), a close approximation to gender parity is one minimal condition for transforming the political agenda (Phillips 1995: 82). In other words, women's presence on these committees is likely to have an impact, but there is no guarantee. In terms of the Traditional Leadership and Governance Framework Act, the requirement that a third of the members of traditional councils must be women should be seen as a step in the right direction but not as fulfilling the minimal condition for transforming conservative traditional councils. Further, the requirement of allocating a third of the seats to women has been met with considerable resistance from the traditional leaders themselves. When CLARA was first introduced in 2004, traditional leaders and their supporters celebrated the way the Act provided for traditional councils to gain power over communal land. As a contrast, many civil society organizations protested that this provision would undermine many of the fundamental democratic rights, such as the right to equality, as set out in the South African Constitution and in international and regional law (Claassens and Ngubane 2008: 161ff).

Conclusively, the main challenge, inherent in CLARA as in any other legislation that intends structuring legal rights and/or building decision-making structures formed around customary law, is to make sure traditional leaders abide by the constitutional principles which are often regarded as alien concepts to their traditional way of living. Will they, as Kymlicka (1989: 196) suggests, adhere to liberal principles of basic rights and therefore have their communal cultural rights protected or will discrimination and oppression of women take place regardless of these prerequisites of protection of basic rights which would then defer the inclusion and protection of customary structures in land reform. There has to be legal certainty in relation to how land will be governed under the communal property regimes, i.e. it has to be possible to predict accurately the outcome of the law in relation to women's security in land tenure. To build any land tenure order on old order rights and include a traditional element in land management will at present not establish such legal security and predictability.

2.5 Conclusions

In light of the discussion above the South African government has for the most part relied on a generalized version of customary law and idealized the role it plays in the fragmented communities in post-apartheid South Africa in reforming communal tenure. Furthermore, its return to the 'traditional' is closely related to the political climate, as in many other sub-Saharan states. The debate about the inherent good in the traditional/old stance and the inherent bad in the individual/new stance is also used to bolster the power of contemporary political leaders, part of whose power base lay within the traditional houses. Added to this is the international push for formal titles, and it is in the crossroad between these arguments that communal titles, based on the traditional structure has gained momentum; a discourse that fails to consider the social realities of the many women either falling outside the social network that traditional societies are built around or living in a context where the traditional structures have been destroyed or not upheld due to dispossession of land, relocation to urban areas, poverty, disease/stigmatization or other societal ills such as drug or alcohol abuse. It further fails to acknowledge the position of some women that within the traditional context lack access to power in the traditional decision-making structures.

Even though many African states display a poor post-colonial women's rights record, especially in acknowledging women's position in land reform there is still hope in democratic reform and state accountability. Thus, there is no need for any modern African state, such as South Africa, to rely so heavily on customary structures in reforming land tenure. As brought forward by Whitehead and Tsikata (2003: 102): 'There seem to […] be too many hostages to fortune in the language of the customary at a national level for it to spearhead democratic reforms and resistance to centralized and elite-serving state power'. Most women, rural or urban, need secure independent control over land, to support a dignified and decent living, for them to realize other human rights such as the right to health and the right to be free from physical and mental abuse.

As discussed above, it has become increasingly popular, both on the international level and within the domestic context, to relate to the social entrenchment and the layered and flexible nature of customary land rights. It is true that land tenure schemes based on a mainly western property regime fail to acknowledge and respond to many of the features held by customary law. In the pluralistic legal reality of South Africa as in many other countries in the SADC region influenced by South African law such as Botswana, Lesotho, Namibia, Swaziland and Zimbabwe, customary law has to co-exist with the other legal sources (common, civil, foreign and international law) under the ambit of a Constitution. However, the question, as asked above, remains how to merge customary law with the rights to equality? Is it at all possible to build a legal land rights regime that allows people to hold land in a communal way and that at the same time upholds women's national and international rights in land?

In this regard there is a need to consider the realities of formal law in its reach, application and acceptance in a traditional setting. Formal law is sometimes unable to provide a coherent response to the issue of women's rights to land, because such laws are a part of a foreign system of governance which has no real link to the social structure of the society in which it is supposed to work. The crucial point here is not to only rely on a set of norms in changing women's position in relation to land in a customary setting, much effort needs to be geared toward changing people's general attitudes toward women and towards women's land rights through education. Furthermore, one of the most visible dangers to women's land rights in South Africa and in the wider SADC region is the apparent incoherence created by the existence of parallel systems of jurisdiction over land rights. The inconsistencies exist both within systems as such, and between different systems in places where older systems of common law co-exist with the modern system of law built on a new constitutional dispensation. The very fact that more than one system exists creates the opportunity for a stronger party to choose the system which serves that person's own ends. This may not be legal under the existing system so far as the law contradicts the Constitution. However, to make this argument access is needed to the modern legal systems (as opposed to the customary one) and it costs money and takes education to be able to use the law, something that many women in South Africa and the wider SADC region do not have access to.

Further, customary (informal) and private (formalized) land tenure systems have advantages and disadvantages. Customary systems facilitate social cohesion and the protection and promotion of culture and tradition. In contrast, private land ownership (on an individual or communal basis) can be argued to give users a sense of security which promotes investment in land. However, from a gender perspective, both systems hold disadvantages for women. The social structure endorsed by custom builds on a patriarchal structure promoting inequality between women and men. While customary systems discriminate on grounds of identity, private systems depend on purchasers having sufficient funds or collateral and therefore by definition only benefit the wealthier in society. De Soto (2000: 142) argues that formalized land and property rights are a primary element in capitalist modes of economic development but it can equally be argued, as was done above that there is a considerable cost to women in land privatization using his theory. Women, in South Africa and elsewhere in the SADC region, are disproportionately numbered among the poorest in society, and therefore enter the land and property market on unequal terms. Government policies, building on de Soto's ideas about formalization of land ownership have been extensively critiqued as leading to growing inequality and poverty as traditional user-rights of marginalized groups are eroded (see e.g. Cousins et al 2005; Ikdahl et al 2005). Economic liberalization, as has been promoted in South Africa, has led to increased and intensified competition over land as a resource. The land market, in South Africa, is not gender-neutral, and excludes poor women by discriminating against them because of their lesser power and resources.

In the latest statement from the Department for Rural Development and Land Reform, the way forward is described as surveying communal land for land use management without giving titles to individuals (Nkwinti 2010). This will possibly move policy away from the gender implications incurred by the transfer of old order rights to new order rights and it could, if designed in such a way, help pinpoint the land use and land needs of women with weaker rights in land. However, it will unavoidably have serious gender implications in line with the arguments supporting a state sanctioned, individualized, tenure structure as further discussed below. In re-designing the communal tenure structure in South Africa (once again) the legislator has to take into consideration the fact that any solution has to be viable within the wider constitutional framework of South Africa. This means that any alternative solution needs to safeguard both gender equality and the survival and respect of customary law.

The discussion about formalization and its effects on economic development and poverty reduction is important as highlighted above. However, it is also imperative to acknowledge that besides the pure 'commodity' value of a title, making it an asset that is interchangeable, a secure title may provide women with other forms of security such as food security if land is used for subsistence farming and it may empower more women to participate in household decisions. Strengthening women's land rights is one avenue towards strengthening vulnerable women's powerbase in the community, keeping women safer at home and preventing girls from leaving for an uncertain future in the urban areas. The discussion above has revealed arguments both in favour and against the theory that formalization brings development and growth. This is an important discussion but it should not overshadow the benefits that women may draw from having formal and secure ownership of land. In the name of gender equality focus needs to be first, on how the titling is structured and, second, what the structure is based on.

There is an opportunity for stronger protection of women's rights in land by formal ownership guaranteed in law. However, the ownership structure is suggested to be individualized and based on surveys of who uses and/or will have use of the communal resources such as land regardless of that person's capacity or position within a specific community. Rather than making use of a right-based and male-power-centred approach a potential solution could be a need-based approach to land reform within the subject area of communal tenure. In moving between different systems of power and law, in the pluralist legal reality of South Africa, it is difficult to distinguish who has a right and easier to pinpoint the needs, especially of vulnerable groups. This approach further fits well with the transformative and reconciliatory objectives of the Constitution and it further supports the justiciability of the socio-economic rights set out in the bill of rights. The exercise of surveying the usage and occupation of land as well as the need of land will possibly rupture old power structures and involve large costs on behalf of the state. However, land reform, including communal tenure reform was supposed to be carried out to put past wrongs right, it could therefore be put forward that it is important and cost efficient to finally make it all-inclusive. Legislation such as CLARA allows for direct patriarchal structures to govern communal land, as discussed above; and even if statutory law appears to be a good vehicle for reforming customary law, the inclusion of old order rights and customary decision-making structures into the law is not the complete answer. Hence, after a need-based assessment has been carried out it will be possible to arrange tenure as either individual, which is arguably the safest tenure regime in regards of upholding and strengthening women's rights or as communal in terms of allocating individual use rights in land that collectively belong to the community departing from needs not old order rights. In this regard there has to be a clear choice, and the parties involved need to have the capacity to make an informed decision. Then, if the choice is made to structure the ownership of land as communal within a specific community it is further possible and advisable to set up communal decision-making structures without relying on existing traditional structures, as has been done under for example the Communal Property Association Act.[41]

To conclude, the scope of international and regional human rights law and the South African Constitution does not justify communal land to be governed by a majority of male traditional leaders. However, since the legislator has envisaged a role for the traditional leadership within the transformation process in South Africa both in land reform and elsewhere it rests upon the state to engage with traditional leaders through their national and provincial associations to come up with mutual strategies on how to revive customary law within the new constitutional dispensation without violating basic rights of women. In land reform a way of reconciling the need for communal tenure structure with the protection of women's land rights is the idea of introducing national policy and structures indicating how the traditional leadership could implement gender equality into the customary structure and how democratic structures can be constructed and become relevant within the community context without building on customary references. This idea is emphasizing the view of the Constitutional Court, that it is the traditional leadership that should be in charge of developing customary law in line with the equality clause in the Constitution.[42] It cannot be expected of the traditional leadership to, on its own, come up with a feasible structure for how gender issues should be implemented into customary structures, but it is evident from the Constitutional Court's jurisprudence that it rests on the traditional leadership to develop customary law in line with the equality clause in the Constitution. Even if changes are made to make ownership structures more gender equal, as suggested above, not much will change until it is required legally and more importantly politically of the traditional leadership to conform to gender equality.

Notes

* PhD, Senior Lecturer, Department of Public Law, University of Stellenbosch, Republic of South Africa.

1 The 1997 SADC Declaration on Gender and Development with its 1998 Addendum on the Prevention and Eradication of Violence against Women and Children.

2 The 2008 SADC Protocol on Gender and Development, signed by SADC Heads of State and Government on 17 August 2008 in Johannesburg, South Africa.

3 Convention on the Elimination of All Forms of Discrimination against Women. Adopted and opened for signature, ratification and accession by General Assembly Resolution 34/180 of 18 December 1979, entered into force on 3 September 1981, 1249 UNTS 13.

4 Ibid, Article 18.

5 The Constitution of the Republic of South Africa, Act 108 of 1996 [/SAPL4] assented to on 16 December 1996 and commencing on 4 February 1997.

6 Ibid, sections 25 and 9.

7 Ibid, sections 39(2), 211 and 212.

8 The 2003 report of the World Bank is the most recent policy report on land reform and poverty reduction and is still relevant to the formalization discourse. The World Bank has, since the report was published, carried out research and pilot project to study different aspects of this policy, see for example its Large Scale Acquisition Study (available at <http://go.worldbank.org/V3UVIDES70> (accessed 23 March 2010)), the Study on the Impact Evaluation of Innovative Approaches to Land Administration (available at <http://go.worldbank.org/347RLEON70> (accessed 23 March 2010)) and the elaboration of a Land Governance Framework (available at <http://go.worldbank.org/HY9RUE0PQ0> (accessed 23 March 2010)).

9 Above, n 2, Articles 2 and 3.

10 UNCHR Res 49 (2002) UN Doc E/CN 4/RES/2003/55.

11 UNCHR Res 22 (2003) UN Doc E/CN 4/RES/2003/22, UNCHR Res 21 (2004) UN Doc E/CN 4/RES/2004/21, and UNCHR Res 25 (2005) UN Doc E/CN.4/RES/2005/25.

12 Above, n 3, Articles 14, 15 and 16.

13 Above, n 3, Article 14.

14 Protocol to the African Charter on Human and Peoples' Rights on the Rights of Women in Africa, Maputo, Mozambique, 11 July 2003, entered into force on 25 November 2005.

15 African (Banjul) Charter on Human and Peoples' Rights, adopted 27 June 1981, OAU Doc CAB/LEG/67/3rev 5, 21 ILM 58 (1982), entered into force on 21 October 1986.

16 Above, n 14, Article 19(c).
17 Native Land Act No 27 of 1913.
18 Group Areas Act No 41 of 1950.
19 The Communal Land Rights Act No 11 of 2004. CLARA has not yet been brought into operation by Presidential proclamation and is currently under review. A Green Paper on Land Tenure Systems Reform is to be submitted for comment and approval by Cabinet before 31 May 2010, including the reformulation of communal land tenure.
20 *Tongoane and Others v The National Minister for Agriculture and Land Affairs and Others*, CCT 100/09 at 40. Referring to the Affidavit filed by the Minister for Rural Development and Land Reform on 18 February 2010.
21 Ibid.
22 Ibid.
23 CLARA further applies to situations where a community has already obtained ownership rights in the land; above, n 19, chapters 7, 8, 9, and chapter 1, section 2.
24 Above, n 19, long title and section 18. Currently this mandate falls under the scope of the Minister for Rural Development and Land Reform.
25 Above, n 19, chapter 7, section 24.
26 Above, n 19, chapter 1, section 2. It also includes land acquired by or for a community, including (but not restricted to) land acquired in terms of the Government's land reform programmes such as land restituted to its owners or occupiers through the restitution process.
27 *Tongoane & Others v The National Minister for Agriculture and Land Affairs & Others* (TPD 11678/06), para 43.
28 Above, n 20. Applicants' Heads of Argument, p 9 at 19.
29 Ibid.
30 Above, n 19, section 4(3).
31 Above, n 19, section 3.
32 Traditional Leadership and Governance Framework Act 41 of 2003, section 3(2)(a) and (b).
33 Above, n 19, section 22(2).
34 Above, n 27.
35 Above, n 20, p 133 at 368.
36 Above, n 20, p 133 at 369.
37 Above, n 19, section 4(2).
38 Above, n 20, p. 133 at 373 (34).
39 Above, n 20, p. 131 at 361 (14).
40 See for example the International Covenant on Civil and Political Rights, of 19 December 1966, adopted and opened for signature, ratification and accession by General Assembly resolution 2200A (XXI) of 16 December 1966, entered into force on 23 March 1976, UNTS 171, the African (Banjul) Charter on Human and Peoples' Rights, adopted 27 June 1981, OAU Doc CAB/LEG/67/3rev 5, 21 ILM 58 (1982), entered into force on 21 October 1986, and United Nations Declaration on the Rights of Indigenous Peoples, GA Res 61/295, UN Doc A/RES/61/295 (13 September 2007), 46 ILM 1013 (2007).
41 Communal Property Association Act No 28 of 1996.
42 *Shilubana and Others v Nwamitwa*, CCT 03/07 [2008].

Bibliography

Bohler-Muller Bjuris, N. and Bronwyn, D. (2009) 'Does the Communal Land Rights Act Really Protect the Rights of Rural Women to Own Land?', *Africagrowth Agenda*, 26–27 April–June.

Caholo, S. (2008) Department of Land Affairs, SADC meeting of ministers responsible for land, opening statement by Dr João Samuel, Deputy Executive Secretary, Southern African Development Community (SADC), Secretariat at the SADC meeting of

Ministers Responsible for Land and Land Reforms, Sandton Convention Centre, South Africa, 27 March, available at <http://www.sadc.int> (accessed 4 February 2010).

Claassens, A. and Mnisi, S. (2009) 'Rural women redefining land rights in the context of living customary law', unpublished article (Cape Town: Programme for Land and Agrarian Studies (PLAAS), School of Government, University of the Western Cape).

Claassens, A. and Ngubane, S. (2008) 'Women, land and power: the impact of the Communal Land Rights Act', in A. Claassens and B. Cousins (eds) *Land, Power and Custom: controversies generated by South Africa's Communal Land Rights Act* (Cape Town: UCT Press), pp 154–83.

Cook, R. (1991) 'Guest Editor's Introduction', *Third World Legal Studies*: vi–ix (special edition).

Cousins, B. (2002) *Reforming Communal Land Tenure in South Africa – Why Land Titling is not the Answer – Critical comments on the Communal Land Rights Bill 2002* (Cape Town: Programme for Land and Agrarian Studies (PLAAS), School of Government, University of the Western Cape), available at <http://www.oxfam.org.uk/resources/learning/landrights/downloads/saclrb.rtf> (accessed 20 March 2010)

Cousins, B., Cousins, T., Hornby, D., Kingwill, R., Royston, L. and Smit, W. (2005) *Will Formalizing Property Rights Reduce Poverty in South Africa's 'Second Economy'? Questioning the Mythologies of Hernando de Soto*, Policy Brief Debating land reform, natural resources and poverty, No 18 October 2005 (Cape Town: Programme for Land and Agrarian Studies (PLAAS), University of the Western Cape).

de Soto, H. (2000) *The mystery of capital: Why capitalism triumphs in the West and fails everywhere else* (London: Bantam Press).

Green, D. (2008) *From Poverty to Power: How Active Citizens and Effective States can Change the World* (Dorset: Oxfam International).

Grown, C. and Gupta, G. (2005) *Taking Action: Achieving Gender Equality and Empowering Women, United Nations Millennium Project Taskforce on Education and Gender Equality*, available at <http://www.unmillenniumproject.org/documents/Gender-complete.pdf> (accessed 19 March 2010).

Ikdahl, I., Hellum, A., Kaarhus, R., Benjaminsen, T. and Kameri-Mbote, P. (2005) 'Human Rights, formalization and women's land rights in southern and eastern Africa', Studies in Women's Law No 57, Institute of Women's Law, University of Oslo; Revised version of Noragric Report No 26 June 2005, Norwegian University of Life Sciences.

Kymlicka, W. (1989) *Liberalism, Community, and Culture* (Oxford: Clarendon Press).

Kymlicka, W. (1995) *Multicultural citizenship* (Oxford: Oxford University Press).

Moller-Okin, S. (1999) *Is Multiculturalism Bad for Women?* (Princeton: Princeton University Press).

Molokomme, A. (1991) *Children of the fence: The Maintenance of Extra-Marital Children Under Law and Practice in Botswana, Research report 41* (Leiden: University of Leiden).

Molokomme, A. (1995) 'Women's Rights to Land and property in Southern Africa', paper presented at the NGO Forum for Women 4th World Conference, Beijing, September 1995.

Molokomme, A. (1996) 'State Intervention in the Family: A Case Study of the Child Maintenance Law in Botswana', in R. Palriwala and C. Risseuw (eds) *Shifting Circles of Support: Contextualising Kinship and Gender in South Asia and Sub-Saharan Africa* (London: Sage), pp 270–301.

Moore, S. (1999) 'Changing African land tenure: Reflections on the incapacities of the state', in C. Lund (ed) *Development and rights, negotiating justice in changing societies* (London: Portland Press), pp 33–49.

Moyo, S. (2008) *African land questions, agrarian transitions and the state: contradictions of neo-liberal land reforms* (Dakar: Council for the Development of Social Science Research in Africa).

Nkwinti, G. (2010) *Government Communications, transcript of economic sectors and employment cluster briefing*, 2 March 2010, available at <http://www.info.gov.za/speeches/2010/10030311251002.htm> (accessed 12 March 2010).

Ntsebeza, L. and Hall, R. (2007) *The Land Question in South Africa: The Challenge of Transformation and Redistribution* (Cape Town: HSRC Press).

Phillips, A. (1995) *The politics of Presence* (Oxford: Clarendon Press).

Pienaar, G. (2008) 'The inclusivity of communal land tenure: a redefinition of ownership in Canada and South Africa?', *Stellenbosch Law Review*, 19(2): 259–77.

Rawls, J. (1971) *Theory of Justice* (Cambridge, MA: Harvard University Press).

Rudman, A. (2010) *Equality before custom? – A study of property rights of previously disadvantaged women under land reform and communal tenure in post-apartheid South Africa*, unpublished thesis, University of Gothenburg, available at <http://gupea.ub.gu.se/dspace/handle/2077/21378> (accessed 19 March 2010).

Walker, C. (2001) 'Piety in the Sky? – Gender Policy and Land Reform in South Africa', in S. Razavi (ed) *Agrarian Change, Gender and Land Rights* (Oxford: Blackwell Publishing), pp 113–48.

Walker, C. (2002) *Land Reform in Southern and Eastern Africa: Key issues for strengthening women's access to and rights in land*, Report on a desktop study commissioned by the Food and Agriculture Organisation, Sub-regional office for Southern and Eastern Africa, Harare, Zimbabwe, March 2002.

Whitehead, A. and Tsikata, D. (2003) 'Policy Discourses on Women's Land Rights in Sub-Saharan Africa: The Implications of the Return to the Customary', in S. Razavi (ed) *Agrarian Change, Gender and Land Rights* (Oxford: Blackwell Publishing), pp 76–112.

Women and Law in South Africa (WLSA) (1992) *Maintenance Law in Botswana* (Botswana, Gaborone: WLSA).

Women and Law in South Africa (WLSA) (1994a) *Inheritance in Swaziland: Law and Practice* (Swaziland, Mbabane: WLSA).

Women and Law in South Africa (WLSA) (1994b) *Inheritance Law in Lesotho* (Lesotho, Maseru: WLSA).

Women and Law in South Africa (WLSA) (1994c) *Women, Marriage and Inheritance* (Botswana, Gaborone: WLSA).

Women and Law in South Africa (WLSA) (1996) *Inheritance in Zimbabwe: Law, Customs and Practices* (Zimbabwe, Harare: WLSA).

World Bank (2003) *Land Policies for Growth and Poverty Reduction – A World Bank Policy Research Report* (Washington, DC and Oxford: World Bank and Oxford University Press).

3 Framing women's rights and citizenship within the Southern African Development Community land reform discourse

A feminist critique

Lyn Ossome

3.1 Introduction

Women's right to land is a critical factor in determining social status, economic wellbeing and empowerment. Their right to property is unequal to those of men in many African countries, and their right to own, inherit, manage and dispose of property is under constant attack from customs, laws and individuals. Institutions that ought to affirm this right and guarantee them secure tenure remain constrained by outdated laws inimical to the principles of gender equity. The emerging regime on land reform in Africa, largely directed by the World Bank and bilateral donors has now peaked at its financialization,[1] creating further constraints on accessibility of land to women. Across the Southern African Development Community (SADC), particularly prominent is the demand to deal with the skewed patterns of land ownership against women, including extensive privatization of land and foreign appropriation. Although widely regarded as a shared concern, arriving at a common organizing principle among SADC member states grappling with land reform issues is, however, a complex endeavour, stemming from diverse colonial legacies, often contradictory post-colonial development trajectories, and varied political and economic interests and views to globalization. Southern African women have proactively engaged states and the international community at all these junctures, asserting their right to participation and inclusion as full citizens in various reform projects, including land reform. Moreover, the women's movement and specifically feminist concerns encompass significant issues within the land reform discourse despite a decidedly tenuous relationship between states and women's movements across the continent. Using Zimbabwe, South Africa, Tanzania and Mozambique as examples, and laying emphasis on rural economies, the aim of this chapter is to discursively examine the manifestations in law, culture, policy and globalization of contemporary land reform issues in the SADC, and to critique from a feminist perspective the prospects, if any, of unifying interests among SADC countries with regards to a gender-equitable land reform process. I shall argue that far from the benefits that are claimed to accrue to women as a result of formalization of tenure, the yoke of cultural limitations and the ambivalence of law with regards to mitigating these limitations may in fact result in the opposite, further circumscribing women's enjoyment of full citizenship.

3.2 Women's citizenship and land in post-liberation southern African economies

Many feminist theorists have argued that abstract theories of democracy ignore the way citizens' gendered lives mean men and women experience political institutions differently. Rather than treating citizenship as a universal relationship between (ungendered) individuals and the state, they suggest that democratic theory must acknowledge the way gender dynamics affect both individual political participation and the impact of state policies on individuals (Jensen 1995; Phillips 1991; Young 1990; Pateman 1989).

The question of access to and enforcement of rights is one that is distinctly tied to that of citizenship – a notion which as Yuval-Davis (1997: 6) contends can throw light on some of the major issues which are involved in the complex relationships between individuals, collectivities and the state, and the ways gender relations (as well as other social divisions) affect and are affected by them. Liberation movements in Africa notoriously prided nationalist goals like dismantling race and class biases over equally pervasive gender discriminations in their struggles against colonial regimes. In South Africa, this tendency to subsume gender concerns under concerns about racial equality had long been visible in the anti-apartheid movement. Until the mid-1980s, leaders in the anti-apartheid movement had generally remained silent on gender issues or, at most, had pointed to the way that apartheid prevented women from fulfilling their tasks as wives and mothers.

By the early 1990s, increasingly, feminist intellectuals, mainly women, began to argue that unless gender concerns were considered during the course of democratization, new political institutions would recreate and reinforce inequality (Hassim 1991; Hassim, Metelerkamp and Todes 1987; Horn 1991; Serote 1991).[2] However, despite accessing civil and political rights, real political and economic autonomy remained inaccessible to women as substantive rights to land, in which power resided, remained elusive. The reasons for this lay variously in the structures of these economies that confined women to informal citizenship, and processes through which women were able to access land rights excluded them. In Tanzania for example, a land audit done in 1991 by the Presidential Commission of Inquiry into Land Matters[3] failed to recognize the land problems faced by women as being capable of distinct analysis, and led to their marginalization in debate and policy.[4] The subsequent National Land Policy and The Land Act (1999) also failed to address gender issues.

Convincing scholarship has been put forward linking (land) rights to democracy and citizenship, one strand of thinking being that in a liberal democracy, rights *inter alia* protect individuals against government. However, widespread economic dependence on government largesse can interfere with the exercise of these rights. New democracies are especially vulnerable to systematic compromise by opportunistic politicians who can use their unchecked power over people's subsistence and control of government largesse to get re-elected. Thus the thinking that privatizing land by giving people ownership in fee simple to the public land they occupy will inject a dose of independence into patronage-infested democracies.[5] Land titling transforms a person's tacit license to reside on government lands into a property interest in fee simple, and property rights attained through land titling provide a measure of economic independence so that individuals are less vulnerable to political reprisals. Other scholars differ, arguing that selective and coordinated state intervention is a necessary condition for economic growth and social development (Tsie 1996: 75).

By the former position, land titling has been argued to have particular significance for African women's participation in democratization and enjoyment of citizenship rights. Malawi, Zambia, Mozambique, South Africa, Namibia and Tanzania have all passed wide-ranging new land laws. The main thrust of the new legislation is to liberalize land tenure and to facilitate the creation of land markets in Africa. In this context, attention now appears to be focusing at the international level on the role which land might play on the wider macroeconomic plane by promoting economic growth and good governance.[6]

This particular strand has been strongly promoted by the World Bank, most recently in its Policy Research Report[7] which however observes in relation to the potential of titling as a key determinant of formal credit access, that formal titles may not have an effect on access to credit in situations where: (a) the option of foreclosure is not feasible; (b) the necessary financial infrastructure and/or banking system that will lend to small producers is not available; or (c) the profitability of projects by potential users of credit is low. In addition, at low levels of income and in the absence of other mechanisms for social security, land serves as a social safety net. Foreclosing on the land of households that have defaulted on credit would deprive them of their basic means of livelihood and may not be socially desirable, which is essentially the reason for customary systems in restricting the marketability of land. Even where formal law decrees that land should be fully tradable, such legislation may be impossible to implement. Because banks are unlikely to lend under these circumstances, expected credit market effects will not materialize.[8]

The fact that the pattern of land reform has not been uniform in all areas and has not happened in neat sequence across the continent should not be taken to mean that the main thrust of the changes is not remarkably similar everywhere. The main idea behind the new land laws, to reiterate, is to liberalize land tenure to enable land to be held individually rather than communally. The aim is to provide for and encourage foreign investment in land. Shivji has, however, argued that the outcome of this process will be 'displacement and marginalization' (Shivji 1998: 105).[9] Women particularly stand at the vanguard of such potential disenfranchisement, given past experience with neo-liberal economic policies like the Structural Adjustment Programmes of the 1980s that impacted on African women in extreme ways.

Of interest here then is how have southern African women fared under democratization and decentralization of land, and what factors are influencing their claims to land (rights)? Because of its primary concern about class, the democratization approach fails to consider the role of patriarchal power in influencing women's participation and representation in political activity. Other questions which remain unanswered include how successful women have been in influencing policies and decisions on land; what structural constraints they face in organizing and lobbying for land access and rights; how women's interests in land differ according to class, ethnicity, and race; and whether democratization and decentralization in different contexts revive and reinforce traditional authorities, or lead to new democratic institutions, which address gender issues.[10] The sections that follow expound on these subjects, applying a feminist critique to land reforms in the SADC and its meanings for women's rights and citizenship.

3.2.1 Tensions shaping women's rights to land in southern Africa

Broadly speaking, African land questions can be distinguished by region. Whereas North Africa has experienced severe shortages of arable land, in West Africa the problem is predominantly one of land administration and conflict between the state and local communities. In settler colonies, the land questions arising can be seen to be connected with the concentration of resources and therefore with the issue of redistribution,[11] formally conducted by the state. State involvement in the allocation of land through formal registration and titling has so far impacted negatively on women's access to land. Women, whose access to land has historically been guaranteed through customary channels, have generally been denied access through formal titling and registration. In the titling process, express norms against women 'owning' land trumped their rights to the use of land through marriage or kin. Furthermore, men gained new kinds of rights: the right to go before the formal apparatus of the state and trump formal claims to land. Under formal titling women are dually condemned; land is no longer available through customary channels and women are severely restricted in their financial and social ability to gain land through government or market routes.[12]

Indigenous land tenure has changed over time due to various factors, including population pressure, commercialization of agriculture, increasing land sales, opening of investment opportunities in land, urban expansion, AIDS, and land grabbing. In areas of acute land shortage, where the value of land has increased, women tended to lose their customary rights (Lastarria-Cornhiel 1997: 1325). Economic liberalization seems to have further accelerated such processes, both in pace and in scale. In many contexts, liberalization has opened new opportunities for investment in land, leading to increased and intensified contests over land. As land gains value as a commodity for investment, land-grabbing by political elites, appropriation of village land by the state, and allocation of land to investors – both nationally and locally – have become common phenomena (Moyo 1998; Kanyinga 1998). On the other hand, the poor are selling land as a desperate act for survival as poverty deepens. Retrenchment, unemployment and declining real wages due to high inflation are forcing urban workers to search for rural land in order to produce food to supplement their low income. The pressures on women, to dispose of land and at the same time gain maximum utility from the land that is available for their use is shaping into a crucial nexus between women's economic vulnerability, voidance of their citizenship claims and rights, and economic growth in southern Africa.

In the context of such arrangements, gender and women's rights activists have tended to support reforms in land legislation, viewing this as an important strategy for mitigating not only the liberal market sweep and issues of competition and conflict over land set out above, but also ensuring that new laws take into account women's roles as producers and reproducers, and particularly their central role in agricultural production. The section that follows briefly examines the mode and impact of the legislative route on women's land rights in some SADC countries.

3.3 What does land *law* reform mean for southern African women?

Law is a critical arena within which African women have sought to challenge patriarchal domination, access (civil, political, economic, cultural) rights, and to actualize their citizenship claims. Its efficacy for women outside the *real* ambits of power, however, remains captive of patriarchal and elite political and economic interests. Indeed it has been rightly observed that 'as a political arena, law represents a montage of compromises, defeats and victories of past struggles. As a battleground, it is perceived as defining the means through which change can be effected – or existing arrangements protected by beneficiaries of existing arrangements. Alternatively, it may be seen to legitimize the existing injustices experienced by marginalized individuals and groups in society' (Ooko-Ombaka 1979). The discourse around the extent to which the law has served in the interests of women in securing land rights is largely grounded upon the tensions between dual legal systems, where it is read to favour women in cases where for example traditional dispute resolution mechanisms are seen to capture the spirit of formal legislation.

In most southern African states, customary law is seen as part of the national legal system receiving constitutional recognition and protection. The difficulty that arises is in determining what to do when laws within a state are in conflict and in particular what should happen when personal laws violate principles of equality.[13] Although most constitutional bills of rights include prohibition of gender or sex-based discrimination, not all do. That there is a potential for conflict between some aspects of personal law, and the non-discrimination or equality before the law provisions are recognized in the constitutions of Namibia, Malawi and South Africa.[14] These constitutions make clear that in the event of a conflict, the non-discrimination or equality provisions are there to rank above the custom or culture under consideration. These 'women friendly' constitutions are generally found to have been drafted after 1990. They reflect and acknowledge the sacrifices made by women during the struggles for liberation which led to independence. The Constitution of Mozambique gives specific recognition to the sacrifice of women in the war against the Portuguese.[15] This group of constitutions reflects an understanding of the fact that women, and African women in particular, have experienced multiple and intersecting discrimination based on grounds of sex, race and class.

The next group of constitutions include that of Tanzania, which while recognizing the existence of customary law as well as containing an equality before the law provision, is silent about what is to happen in the event of conflict between personal laws and the constitutional guarantee of equality. The final group of constitutions illustrated by Botswana, Lesotho, Zambia and Zimbabwe all ring-fence customary law, meaning that customary law is exempt from the scrutiny demanded by the women-friendly constitutions discussed earlier. What distinguishes the constitutions is the historical framework within which they were drafted. The progressive constitutions arose as a result of internal negotiation with substantial input from women. By way of contrast, the last group of states have merely kept the gender provisions that they were given in British-drafted constitutions at the time of political handover.

Attendant to this is the push towards land *law* reform whose methodology, rather than reinforce women's access to land resources, threatens to further marginalize them. The idea that law should be brought 'back in'[16] to land reform is one that has steadily taken root, with the faith that the law will achieve equity, efficiency and certainty in land relations. McAuslan contends that land reform in South Africa must include land law reform because it seeks to change the nature of the legal regime and legal culture that applies to African-held land. In Tanzania the same reasoning pertains: 'land reform is pre-eminently land law reform: the substitution of a law to facilitate the right of citizens to access and hold land, for a law which had facilitated the state's administrative control over the citizens' access to land'.[17] Critiquing this approach, Manji (2006: 98–118) has laid bare its underlying assumptions, laying the blame on states that have uncritically tied their reform agenda to that of the international financing institutions at the expense of women. She also acknowledges the role that civil society plays in marginalizing gender considerations in land reform, observing that 'gender-progressive' groups (such as women's advocacy groups and non-governmental organizations concerned with reducing or eliminating the social, economic and political inequalities facing women in relation to men) in Tanzania rarely challenged the emphasis placed by international financial institutions, donors, governments and technical legal consultants on law as the solution to the problems of land relations, arguing that their engagement in the land reform process has affirmed rather than questioned the use of law to bring about development. They tended to adopt a technical, instrumentalist approach to law that has limited their scope for action.[18] This technocratic approach was an important factor in the failure of the women's movement in Tanzania to address the crucial issues facing women in relation to land. The preoccupation with the details of legal formulations in the draft land bills limited the ability of women's groups to formulate their basic demands.[19]

Law's ability to harness gains for women is in many ways dependent on the contexts and realities of women's lives, and thus should not be taken for granted; uniting feminist legal scholars is the view of law as a patriarchal institution, often arguing for attention in legal advocacy to particular contexts, and that situations generating conflicts should be analyzed in light of larger patterns of political, economic and social inequalities along gender, race and class lines.[20] The UN Economic Commission for Africa has in this vein lamented the continued presence of strong cultural and traditional practices constraining progress in achieving gender parity in ownership of property and land, noting the need to find ways to support well functioning customary systems while engendering and strengthening the channels for change in those that are not. While recognizing the need to review, reform and harmonize customary and statutory laws and legislation to address sources of discrimination against women owning land, it should, however, be noted that the removal of legal clauses that discriminate against women cannot change cultural and social behaviour (UNECA-SA, 2003). As such, following an equality approach it might be useful to specifically identify the types of land utility (economic) activities in which women are involved, and the importance attached to these activities. Valuations of women's contribution to production activities are an important guide to the sort of outcomes that might accrue to them as a result of land law reform.

Such an analysis goes beyond the scope of this chapter, but as Izumi (1999: 15–16) has suggested, two particular areas for attention are the gaps between statutory institutional reforms at national level, informal institutional changes, and actual practice at local level. This is because formal and legal rights to land do not necessarily provide women secure rights in reality, if such rights are not made socially legitimate and enforceable. At present, women in Zimbabwe have legal rights to land, but in many contexts they are without secure access. Institutions that govern women's relationship with land cannot be seen simply as a set of rules, norms, policies and laws: it is the social legitimacy of these which constitutes institution. Because of this, women's access and rights to land is indeed a question of social change.

3.3.1 Contemporary versus cultural valuations of women's land rights

Whether land is subject to hierarchically ordered claims and the meaning of social embeddedness are very important in understanding the gender aspects of land access. Women have long had access to land in sub-Saharan Africa, but men and women have rarely, if ever, had identical kinds of claims to land, largely because the genders have very differentiated positions within the kinship systems that are the primary organizing order for land access.[21] As part of land reform projects, many African countries have recently given legal recognition to customary tenure as well as to the institutions administering it. However, implementing these laws remains a challenge, well exemplified by the process in South Africa. As Hassim (2009) points out in the case of South Africa, the Constitution upholds both cultural recognition as well as recognition of women's rights, but leaves the precise working out of these to legislative processes and political debate. In approving the Constitution, the Constitutional Assembly was clear that recognizing customary law did not mean a return to the past. Rather, it called for 'harmonization' between customary law and the constitutional value of equality. This recognition is valuable in directing debate away from the binary tension of 'good' modern law and 'bad' tradition, but it offers few pointers as to where the reform process should focus. Feminist legal advocates have taken on a number of cases in which customary family and inheritance law has been challenged, but the legal challenges have not been accompanied by political contestation in the broader political sphere.[22] Thus although potentially carving out spaces for the interpretation of customary variations of the law in favour of women, the lack, failure or insufficiency of mutual, intervening interests at the interface of customary law and formal law has meant that implementation has fallen short of this promise. In other words, the prerequisite neat fit between formulation and articulation of demands envisioned on the one hand mostly by feminists and the active intervention this requires from the political establishment (including legislative/ state and traditional power structures) on the other to actualize them remains elusive, and mostly idealized. This owes partly to the danger of over-rating the ability of women political representatives to articulate feminist ideals and follow them through. In South Africa, under party leadership pressure and the belittling of the importance of gender, many (female MPs) did not identify openly with feminist agendas, and male dominance and patronage inhibits the articulation of feminism (Hassim 2006: 199).[23]

Despite its limited success to date, the emphasis on a feminist approach here underscores the thinking that achieving harmony between traditional and formal authority over land tenure is often an additional and complex project in pursuit of substantive post-legislative changes in the lives of women, and requires a more radical exposure of underlying tensions, which conventional gender approaches that do not significantly challenge the status quo may not achieve. Hassim speaks to this contention by noting that the real test of whether increased representation would work is to consider what would happen if women's organizations were to push for legislative changes that would directly challenge entrenched patriarchal interests – that is, if women's organizations were to demand changes on the basis of their strategic gender interests rather than women's needs. One key clash in the (South Africa) Constitution making period, for example, was between traditional leaders and feminists, when some traditional leaders' opposition to gender equality set the stage for a protracted conflict. The Constitution itself validated both equality and cultural autonomy while ensuring that equality will prevail when the two areas are in conflict. In legislation proposed by the African National Congress (ANC) in 2003 (the Traditional Leadership and Governance Framework Bill, and the Communal Land Rights Bill), concerns about gender equality once again came up squarely against concerns of traditional leaders. At issue in this particular debate was the extent of traditional leaders' formal authority over land allocation in rural areas. The Communal Land Rights Bill was set to become the biggest test of the extent to which a constituency of (rural) women could successfully defend their policy claims against other powerful interests. The bill recognized 'communities' as juridical persons and proposed to transfer state land to communities. For the traditional leaders, however, the bill did not go far enough in securing traditional authority, as 'communities' would now have rights. For women, on the other hand, the emphasis on communities reinstated the power of traditional leaders as they became the officially recognized representatives of community interests (Hassim 2006: 202–3). The compromise draft that was passed, which handed over powers of land administration, allocation and ownership in communal areas to traditional councils, provided for 30 per cent representation of women on traditional councils, but still left the issue of women's rights unresolved. In brief, the key objections related to the failure of the bill to protect the rights of rural women, the undemocratic nature of traditional councils, and the entrenchment of the control of chiefs over key aspects of women's lives.[24] This case demonstrates a complex yet not insurmountable aspect of translating legislation in ways that favour and uphold the rights of women.

Acknowledging the importance of law in social change and the impact of custom in resisting that change, the SADC Declaration on Gender and Development borrows from the Convention on the Elimination of all forms of Discrimination against Women (CEDAW) by providing that states undertake to engage in 'repealing and reforming all laws, amending constitutions and changing social practices which will still subject women to discrimination, and enacting empowering gender-sensitive laws'.[25] This is particularly important because most of the SADC countries have plural legal systems, aspects of which discriminate against women. Indeed, some countries' constitutions are in contravention of the SADC Declaration so that the Zimbabwe Constitution continues to ring-fence customary personal law from the non-discrimination provisions in the Constitution thus allowing the continuation of discrimination against women 'in matters of adoption, marriage, divorce, burial, devolution of property on death or other matters of personal law'.[26] Similarly, Zambia has a legal foundation for gender inequality, with the Constitution ostensibly protecting the equal rights of men and women but also allowing for the application of customary laws and cultural norms which are heavily biased towards patriarchy (World Bank 2004).

Understanding this tension within plural legal systems is significant if the full length of the impact of land (law) reform is to be exposed and not allowed to 'mask the fact that alternative forms of tenure are deprecated and undervalued by advocates of formalization'.[27] Communal and informal tenure arrangements are characterized as 'passive', 'defective' and 'extra-legal', and as belonging to 'the grubby basement of the pre-capitalist world'. The legal centralist assumptions that underpin contemporary land reform efforts have thus remained largely unexposed. Legal centralism has been described as the idea that 'law is and should be the law of the state, uniform for all persons, exclusive of all other law, and administered by a single set of state institutions. To the extent that other, lesser normative orderings exist, they ought to be and in fact are hierarchically subordinate to the law and institutions of the state'.[28] There is a subliminal relegation of informal tenure within this discourse that is problematic when regarding the limitations of formal laws in guaranteeing women's tenure of land. Women's continued recourse to informal tenure cannot simply be wished away: as Manji (2006) points out, empirical research among women urban farmers who work small plots of land within the borders of many third world cities under informal arrangements has demonstrated how, even in the face of undeniable uncertainty as to their continuing access to land, they wish to retain the advantages of informal arrangements. This allows them to evade the payments of rates and taxes and avoids the revelation of important sources of independent income to male members of their family.[29] Real social and economic imperatives compel women to seek to circumvent the bureaucracy of the law and formalization, and at the same time demonstrate the need for laws that mesh with the actual contexts of women.

What is demonstrated here is the need to align the contemporary drive towards formalization of land, with its emphasis on 'bringing in' the poor (and women) into the system of formal credit, with the recognition of already existing informal networks which account for the actual spaces within which women negotiate social and economic capital. Returning to the discussion about citizenship and inclusion, the significance of such an undertaking is that it would enable a more substantive engagement between the state and women. Some feminists have argued that rights alone are not sufficient to bring about substantive citizenship for women. While it is recognized that substantive equality is required to take account of social and economic status, Gouws (1999) argues that this leads to citizenship based on rights claims, which oversimplify complex power relations: rights discourses are often blind to social and economic disparities between groups and, therefore, access to social and economic rights also needs to be recognized. She notes that in South Africa rights discourses have failed to transform gender relations and construct equal political, social and economic citizenship for women. What this suggests is that while 'rights' have accrued to southern African women, through legislative and constitutional means, there, however, remains the need to extend the meaning and reach of democracy and citizenship to deliver more concrete gains for women, as is explored below.

3.4 Application of substantive equality in land reforms

In southern Africa in general, land redistribution to peasant households is firmly on the political agenda, and campaign for land rights for women can receive separate attention from that of men. Compared to land reform programmes in other countries, many of which are focused more on productive development, the South African programme for instance places a strong emphasis on equality and the redress of historical inequities. In the formulation of policy, attention has been paid to the interests of the rural poor generally, and the interests of rural women in particular.[30] The ANC Freedom Charter called for redistribution rather than nationalization of land and ensured that land would remain under private ownership, yet experience shows that this ostensible entrenchment of women's interests in political arrangements such as these should not be taken for granted as guaranteeing equity in access and control of land resources. These promises, guided by deep post-liberation political sentimentalism have nonetheless fallen short in reality.

3.4.1 Land reforms as contested spaces for gender equity

At the basic level, demands for gender equity face a number of key challenges. These vary from a lack of awareness amongst populations potentially affected by land reform processes and its significance; the need to ensure that such programmes support women's interests; making sure that women find themselves in conducive work environments in which they are treated with equal respect to men; and overall a revamping of social and cultural attitudes which tend to hold women rather than the political machineries that formulate land-related policies responsible for the promotion of gender equity. Moyo and Yeros (2005) note that with regards to gender specifically, rural movements in the late 1990s have adopted a conscious policy of equity, which, in turn, has been bearing fruit in terms of mobilization and internal democratization, as well as in terms of lobbying effectively against the state for the inclusion of gender-specific legislation in the agrarian reform process. In Zimbabwe, by contrast, the land occupation movement has fallen short of a gender-sensitive politics, despite the fact that women have participated in the occupations in large numbers. In this case, the strong patriarchal currents of the nationalist movement remain dominant.[31]

A number of other factors hinder gender-equitability in land reform, not the least of which are the assumptions upon which such reforms are now being based. The inbuilt assumptions regarding the availability and the appropriation of women's labour and resources have particular implications for women's interests and rights to land. The World Bank has over the last three decades substantially influenced a particular strand of thinking around land reform in developing countries through a series of policy publications on land issues. The World Bank Policy Research Report, *Land Institutions and Land Policy* (World Bank 2003) identifies four main issues which can have an adverse effect on land-related and general economic growth in rural areas. First, in terms of what it calls 'production outcomes' the report asserts that, to the extent that owner-operated farms are more efficient than those which are wage-labour operated, the distribution of land between these types of farms is important. Second, the Report asserts that secure land tenure is essential in order to provide 'investment incentives' both at the level of the household and of the economy. Third, the frequency of disputes and situations of insecure tenure are seen as disincentives to invest in land and thus as undermining the entire rural economy by discouraging domestic and foreign investment in both land and related non-agricultural ventures. Fourth, the inability to use land as collateral for accessing credit is perceived to have far-reaching effects on households in terms of their ability to make 'indivisible investments'. It also inhibits the emergence and efficiency of rural credit and other factor markets.[32]

Manji (2003) identifies a number of problems with these conclusions drawn by the Bank. She criticizes the way in which the World Bank seemingly unproblematically links labour and capital by means of the notion of productivity advantage, through the promotion of 'non-contractible' labour which she shows assumes availability of women's flexible and unremunerated labour. As she points out, there has long been a considerable literature available, much of it dealing specifically with the Third World, which has revealed the ways in which the family 'functions as an ideological and economic site of oppression'. The availability of women's unwaged labour within the family, which is closely coupled with male control over women's reproductive capacity, has been the central focus of these feminist analyses,[33] which insist on the need to disaggregate individual interests at stake in the household. Further, she questions the 'equitability' of the World Bank's objectives of redistribution of land to small owner-operators from larger operators so that the poor have 'significant landholdings as part of their optimal asset portfolio', and whether transfers can be equity-enhancing if they are founded on the freely available labour of women. Also drawing attention to the Bank's promotion of indivisible expenditure, that is, the social use value of credit and the idea that such credit will enable the household to invest money in public goods such as schooling and healthcare, she recalls the Bank's disastrous experiment with Structural Adjustment Programmes in Africa in the 1980s, and argues that far from contributing to efforts to reduce poverty, the promotion of rural credit can only ensure that it remains a persistent reality.[34]

In light of the above arguments, the question can be posed whether market-driven land reform can be compatible with the goal of equitable distribution of land among women and other dispossessed groups. Given that, whether deliberately or not, cooptation of women's movements across Africa has notoriously been exercised with regards to benefiting from 'hard' legislative amendments, and that contemporary land reforms in southern Africa fall short of endorsing rights discrimination, how much then, can women reasonably expect from the state, and to what extent can they rely on sub-regional organizations such as the SADC to mediate equitability in land issues between the market and the state?

3.5 The SADC as mediator

The foregoing discussions have touched on a number of issues regarding the status and location of women within contemporary land reform processes of various countries in the SADC, and have also raised a number of questions which shall now be directed towards the institutional mechanisms of the SADC to gauge whether it offers any opportunities for addressing these questions. The SADC comprises 14 countries, namely Angola, Botswana, Democratic Republic of Congo (DRC), Lesotho, Malawi, Mauritius, Mozambique, Namibia, South Africa, Seychelles, Swaziland, Tanzania, Zambia and Zimbabwe. It was formed on 1 April 1980 and was originally known as the Southern African Development Co-ordination Conference (SADCC). At its formation there were nine member states. In 1992 a meeting was held in Windhoek, Namibia which led to the signing of the Declaration and Treaty which established the SADC. The objectives of the Community include poverty alleviation, employment creation, the promotion of self-sustaining development through self-reliance and interdependence of member states. The SADC Treaty also provides that the community seeks to 'evolve common political values, systems and institutions' and 'to strengthen and consolidate the long-standing historical, social and cultural affinities and links among people of the region'.[35]

As Fareda Banda contends, given the diversity of countries within the SADC grouping, this is indeed a tall order. The countries range from the very small, in terms of population, like Namibia, to the very large like the DRC; from economically strong countries like Botswana and South Africa to some of the poorest countries in the world such as Mozambique and Malawi; from post-socialist states like Tanzania to aggressively capitalist states like South Africa; and from conflict ridden Angola and the DRC, to, peaceful Mauritius and Seychelles. However, although many things divide the states, there is much that unites them, not least the position of women. In all SADC countries, women are, relative to men, disadvantaged, socially, economically, culturally, politically and legally.[36] This despite the fact that Article 6(2) of the SADC Treaty prohibits discrimination on the basis of sex. SADC countries have shown a formal commitment to gender equality in that all of them have ratified CEDAW.[37] Indeed, the SADC bloc was influential in getting the Optional Protocol to CEDAW adopted. During Namibia's presidency of the Security Council it helped to push through Security Council Resolution 1325 on Women, Peace and Security.[38] All SADC countries have ratified the African Charter on Human and People's Rights 1981 together with the UN Convention on the Rights of the Child, 1990. Still there appears to be a gap between promise and practice. Reasons for this are many. Ongoing civil wars in Angola and the DRC mean that all but the elite are subject to poverty and deprivation. The AIDS pandemic is having a monumental impact on the economies and populations of the entire region. Where women's rights are concerned, there is of course the barrier of the broadly defined 'culture', which is often put forward as the reason for their inferiority treatment.[39]

The elimination of gender discrimination has been on the agenda of the SADC since its formation. At least in principle, the SADC Protocol on Gender and Development stipulates directly or indirectly with regards to land in Article 18 that State Parties shall, by 2015, review all policies and laws that determine access to, control of, and benefit from, productive resources by women in order to: (a) end all discrimination against women and girls with regard to water rights and property such as land and tenure thereof; (b) ensure that women have equal access and rights to credit, capital, mortgages, security and training as men; and (c) ensure that women and men have access to modern, appropriate and affordable technology and support services. It is clear that the Protocol envisions fluid mobility between its categorization of factors of production that State Parties ought to develop in order to ensure that women benefit from land reform projects. These include land itself, labour specialization and skills training, ready access to capital markets and a generalized dedication of women's productive roles towards development based on land tenure. These assumptions, however, belie the fact that as shown by history, women's participation in all these projects, access to and control of these resources have largely been rhetorical and externally motivated rather than being indicative of states' dedication towards changing women's social and economic position.[40]

Arguing as we have the limitations of the state on the one hand, and challenges of the market on the other to deliver secure land tenure for women, what recourse then, could the (SADC) economic bloc, roughly situated in between these two positions hold? The preceding analysis points to the fact that women's access to land has benefited to a great extent from state intervention, through constitutional and legislative amendments to laws to allow redistribution of land and circumvent customary prohibitions to women's enjoyment of land rights, including opening up of markets for their products. Uniting the SADC has been its gradual shift towards a neo-liberal leaning, critiqued by a number of scholars, some of whom reckon it can be fairly concluded that the development policy pursued by the SADC during the 1990s has fallen into line with international financial institutions' and donors' approach to economic regionalism among developing countries (Schiff and Winters 2002). Others critically view this trajectory as an extension of structural adjustment programmes (SAPs), arguing that the immiseration embodied (in them) is incompatible with empowerment and popular democracy, and are in essence technocratic 'solutions' to what are fundamentally political problems such as poverty, land reform and gender inequalities (Tsie 1996: 80).

There is a fine line here characterized by the tensions brought on by globalization, pressures from increased regional and international competition and the global recession, and the need to protect developing economies. Women sit neatly in the crosshairs (again recalling the trauma of SAPs), and their struggles for land rights in a very real sense dramatize the urgency for clear and effective interventions at regional level where recourse to national solutions fall short. However, the SADC is limited by a lack of synergy between national and regional concerns and interests – its legal structure does not compel members to enact the necessary legislation at a national level, and implementation of SADC decisions may not be guaranteed. The SADC countries have retained their sovereignty and decision-making functions under the Treaty, meaning that national governments have reserved their positions – they reserve the right to weigh treaty commitments against national interests and will probably subordinate the former to the latter (Tsie 1996: 85).

3.5.1 Arenas for feminist engagement with policy and legislation

The failure to understand gender concerns in land reform as having economic and social ramifications for society as a whole reinforces the risk of relegating impacts on women altogether. It is important to understand the economic as well as political ramifications for women from this perspective. As noted by Manji (2006: 83), that tenure reform rather than redistribution has come to characterize land reform in the present day is the result of a series of political and economic choices, among them the choice to prioritize a functioning market economy over the provision of secure livelihoods and to promote the idea of land as a form of collateral rather than as a means to tackle landlessness and poverty. Feminists have long argued this point: the economic opportunities that women get (such as agricultural activities related to land ownership) can have a decisive influence on the working of the economy and the related social arrangements. Indeed, 'a field of one's own' can be a major influence on women's initiative and involvement, with far-reaching effects on the balance of economic and social power between men and women (Agarwal 1995).[41]

But neo-liberal orthodoxy dominates land and agrarian reform policy making in many African countries, due in part to their dependence on aid from and resulting dictation of policy interests by the West, which are not always concerned with making sure that women's interests are taken into consideration. Recourse to funding for women's land projects sought from clearly defined feminist funding organizations in Africa is thus notably a positive step.[42] The real impact of years of feminist-driven funding towards equity-enhancing projects, however, still ought to be documented. Indeed, despite efforts by the African women's movement funding machinery to define among its core agenda the financialization of women's agricultural enterprise, hard core financing of land remains captive of and defined by bilateral and multilateral donors, and thus their interests rather than the real needs of rural African women.

Recourse for women in accessing land has so far been directed towards the state, through which women have legitimated their claims to land use and ownership using constitutional and legislative means. Indeed, as noted by some feminists, in the fight for gender equality, activist feminist lawyers are oriented towards the international conventions and instruments and a rights perspective and have a generally positive stance towards the role of the state and statutory law to deliver the rights of women (Butegwa 1994; Cook 1994).[43] However, Manji (2001) has argued that the capacity of the state to carry out land reform is severely limited, and has pointed out an altogether different set of actors involved in the land reform process; private citizen implementors to whom new laws and policy is directed. In the absence of state action to carry out the new policy, private citizens take it into their own hands to bring about change. As such, they may be judged to have conformed with or abided by the goals of the policy on land reform. Private citizen implementors have altered land relations without the interventions of government, and have been able to do so by using the procedures set out in government-enacted legislation.[44] Private citizen action has also been greatly enhanced by the Millennium Development Goals (MDG) campaigns across the continent which seek citizen rather than state-centric solutions to poverty reduction. If, as has been argued in the case of South Africa, 'non-governmental interventions will actually constitute the shaping force in the process of land reform',[45] then this suggests the need to recast and re-focus areas of feminist engagement towards spaces that are actually now being shown to be more effectual. In other words, in the absence of formal, legal mechanisms to deliver the land needs of the (rural) population,[46] which alternative avenues should be explored by the women's movements in southern Africa to secure substantive land rights for women? A substantial and crucial constituency with this regard already exists in rural women.

Experience has also shown that process matters. In some countries women were marginalized from land reform processes through a failure of women's movements to foreground a land rights agenda. In Tanzania for example, Manji (1998: 661) has argued that the preoccupation with employment as an indicator of women's status led to a failure to recognize the importance of land as their most valuable asset in a predominantly rural economy. In consequence, in the early 1990s women's groups in Tanzania did not sense the importance of the nascent land debate. Second, once they did become involved in the debate, their approach was largely technocratic and legalistic. This meant that they were not in a position to set the agenda on women's land rights, but rather found themselves playing a reactive role to reports and draft legislation. Third, the origins of feminist groups and their membership of largely urban-based, middle-class women had limited their ability to engage with the issues which most concern rural peasant women. Fourth is that the land issue in Tanzania had crystallized a conflict which was potentially inherent in the class constitution of the dominant women's groups. This was the potential conflict of interest for women who may benefit from the liberalization of the land market, either as business people in their own right or in conjunction with their families.[47]

The lingering question thus seems to be how should disparate interests among women and other groups, and potential class conflicts be circumvented in order to marshal the support of grassroots women and enable a more concerted campaigning around women's basic demands for land rights in their countries and region? The foregoing criticisms indicate a lack of core presence of women at the critical decisive stages of planning, and suggest that an increased critical mass would be useful in galvanizing the objectives of women's resource networks around more transformative agendas. This is only possible when there is meaningful consultation among women's networks that seek to build bridges between funding, legislation and implementation of land reform processes.

3.6 Conclusion

This chapter has highlighted a number of arguments and discussions on the land discourses in the SADC, touching specifically on the relationship of women as citizens to land and the various manifestations of the ongoing land reform process. In placing the state at the centre of this discussion, it is clear that culpability for the seeming disenfranchisement of women from this process is the collective result of an eschewing of the interests of women's rights from actual processes of reform; for instance the nominal representation of gender concerns in legislation, the marginal participation of women's and gender-progressive organizations in (land) reform processes, and the limited accountability mechanisms available both within countries and the SADC. One issue particularly strides the formalization of land tenure; the practical complexities associated with easing tensions between traditional power structures that regulate communal land, and the formal legislation of equality. This chapter critiques, from a feminist perspective land reform processes in the SADC region, its main contribution being to analyze the ways in which various aspects of land reform programmes in the region are undermined by the lack of a unifying notion around what equality in, and equitable land distribution should resemble were it to truly benefit rural women in the long term. It argues for a determinedly feminist approach within decision making as one that can prioritize women's strategic needs, yet also remaining cognizant to the mostly political challenges that beset this approach both within and outside the women's movement. Moreover, the impact of greater participation by women in processes of defining and shaping law reform and policy initiatives is still debated. Increased representation of women across the board, whether in legislative bodies, traditional authorities, or on other decision making bodies, has been shown in this chapter as being insufficient in forestalling the short-changing of women as they clamour for land resources, due in most part to the deep-seated socio-economic power inequalities that remain hidden, often couched in a narrow 'rights' discourse, even as women ostensibly access political mileage.

Second, these observations underscore the importance of maintaining a critical eye on the prevailing compulsion to frame women's rights to land within the wider discourse of citizenship, various narrow notions of which women are often forced to conform to – in particular the fact that women, though belonging to communities, are often forced to access their rights as citizens through other groups in the community, their own passageways circumscribed by powerful patriarchal structures in society. This vigilance is important, given the fact that land laws like the South African one with a market bias clearly violate the constitutional right to gender equality. As argued by some critics of the South Africa market-based land reform programme, 'it is only those who are already in positions of power in communities who will be heard and who will have the wherewithal to exercise their rights, while those who are currently voiceless and marginalised will be shunted further to the peripheries of access and development' (Tilley 2002: 41).

A third observation, which builds on the second, relates to the question of citizenship, where there is an apparent conflation of the gains that have materialized from states' experiments with this liberal democratic concept, to the detriment of women in southern Africa. On the one hand, women in South Africa, Zimbabwe, Mozambique, Tanzania and other countries in the region have ostensibly gained greater access to legal recourse and a demonstrable visibility of their needs in the land reform discourse, espoused through civil and political rights, but at the same time been exposed to the rigours of market-based land policies towards which the law is also now being bent, which interfere with their enjoyment of social rights, and by extension, the full realization of the civil and political rights. Added to this is the unclear resolution of the tensions between customary law and formal laws guaranteeing gender equality. The ongoing wholesale liberalization of land threatens the survival and livelihood particularly of rural women, whose yet under-valued contribution towards Africa's food security denies the legitimacy of their claims articulated through various activist platforms, international conventions, national legislation and local partnerships. As Giddens points out, to the extent that citizenship rights remain the object of political struggles to defend, reinterpret and extend them, who is involved in these struggles, where they are placed in the political hierarchy and the political power and influence they can yield will help to determine the outcomes. Citizenship thus emerges as a dynamic concept in which process and outcome stand in a dialectical relationship to each other. Such a conceptualization of citizenship is particularly important in challenging the construction of women (and especially minority group women) as passive victims, while keeping sight of the discriminatory and oppressive male-dominated political, economic and social institutions which still deny them full citizenship (Giddens 1991 in Lister 1997: 9). From the foregoing analysis in this chapter, the proliferation of legislation governing land reform in the region, based at times on universalizing assumptions about rural women's social, political and economic ability to benefit from them, may in fact, have the inverse effect of concealing bottlenecks, and thus fail to materially benefit women.

This chapter straddled the discourses of land tenure and redistribution in southern Africa and in its feminized critique of specific aspects within these processes sought to demonstrate the fallibility of land reform programmes that detach from the real contexts particularly of rural women, and which end up leaving them exposed to the vagaries of the market. If this be the case, the challenge for the SADC as an organizing force should be the pursuit of strategies that seek to mitigate the social, political and economic threats potentially posed by privatization of land in southern Africa, which include destruction of social structures and communities, alienation of land, loss of crucial water catchment areas to large plantations of food and agro-fuels, and entrenched poverty, not to mention the gender-specific impacts of such disenfranchisement. It remains to be seen what impact market-driven land reform in the region shall have on women in the long run.

Notes

1 See Manji, A. (2006), *The Politics of Land Reform in Africa: From Communal Tenure to Free Markets* (London and New York, NY: Zed Books), p 62.
2 See Seidman, G. W. (1999) 'Gendered Citizenship: South Africa's Democratic Transition and the Construction of a Gendered State', *Gender and Society*: 292.
3 Widely referred to as the Shivji Commission.
4 Manji, A. (1998) 'Gender and the Politics of the Land Reform Process in Tanzania', *The Journal of Modern African Studies,* 36(4): 648.
5 Atuahene, B. (2006) 'Land Titling: A Mode of Privatization with the Potential to Deepen Democracy', *Saint Louis University Law Journal,* 50: 770.
6 Manji, A. (2003) 'Capital, Labour and Land Relations in Africa: A Gender Analysis of the World Bank's Policy Research Report on Land Institutions and Land Policy', *Third World Quarterly,* 24(1): 97.
7 *Land Policies for Growth and Poverty Reduction – A World Bank Policy Research Report,* June 2003.
8 Ibid.
9 Above, n 1, pp 45–46.

10 Izumi, K. (1999) 'Liberalization, Gender, and the Land Question in Sub-Saharan Africa', *Gender and Development*, 7(3) (Agriculture): 11.
11 Above, n 1, pp 41–42.
12 Gray, L. and Kevane, M. (1999), 'Diminished Access, Diverted Exclusion: Women and Land Tenure in Sub-Saharan Africa', *African Studies Review*, 42(2): 24.
13 For example, in early 1999, the Supreme Court of Zimbabwe decided against the claim of Venia Magaya, the eldest child of her father's senior wife, who had been appointed heir to her father's estate in Harare by a community court. The court argued that under Zimbabwean customary law, which has coexisted with civil law since the colonial period, women are juveniles, and only men can inherit from a father (Supreme Court of Zimbabwe 1999).
14 In Banda, F. (2006) 'Women, Law and Human Rights in Southern Africa', *Journal of Southern African Studies*, 32(1) (March): 16.
15 Ibid.
16 McAuslan, P. (2003) *Bringing the Law Back In: Essays in Land, Law and Development* (Aldershot: Ashgate).
17 Ibid.
18 Above, n 1.
19 Above, n 1, p 103.
20 The most important writings and practical applications of feminist legal theory have primarily occurred in the family law, criminal law, reproductive rights, and employment law arenas. These areas of the law tend to have the most immediate and extensive relationships to the general population of women. Important theoretical feminist work has also been done in legal disciplines such as property law, tax law, and corporate law. See <http://feministlawprofs.law.sc.edu/?p = 1227> (accessed 24 February 2010).
21 Whitehead, A. and Tsikata, D. (2003) 'Policy Discourses on Women's Land Rights in Sub-Saharan Africa: The Implications of the Re-turn to the Customary', *Journal of Agrarian Change*, 3(1) and (2): 77.
22 Hassim, S. (2009) 'Democracy's Shadows: Sexual Rights and Gender Politics in the Rape Trial of Jacob Zuma', *African Studies*, 68(1) (April): 70.
23 Hassim, S. (2006) *Women's Organisations and Democracy in South Africa: Contesting Authority* (Madison, WI: The University of Wisconsin Press).
24 While earlier versions of the bill had explicitly provided for the right to gender equality in respect of ownership, allocation, use of, or access to land, this provision disappeared from the final version of the bill. There was no longer any provision clearly banning discriminatory practices. Similarly, it did not require that rules devised by communities to govern the administration of communal land comply with the equality clause in the Bill of Rights, although earlier versions of the measure did make provision. See Hassim, ibid, pp 202–9) for an in-depth analysis of these issues.
25 SADC Gender and Development Declaration 1997, H(iv), cf CEDAW, Articles 2(f), 5.
26 Constitution of Zimbabwe 1979, as amended, s. 23(3).
27 Above, n 1, p 20.
28 Quoted in Manji, above, n 1, p 20.
29 Above, n 1, p 21.
30 May, J., Stevens, T. and Stols, A. (2002) 'Monitoring the Impact of Land Reform on Quality of Life: A South African Case Study', *Social Indicators Research*, 58(1/3) (June): 294.
31 See Moyo, S. and Yeros, P. (eds) (2005) *Reclaiming the Land: The Resurgence of Rural Movements in Africa, Asia and Latin America* (London and New York: Zed Books), pp 49–50.
32 Above, n 6, p 99.
33 Above, n 6, pp 103–4.
34 Above, n 6, p 108.
35 As quoted in SADC Gender Monitor (1999) at 44.
36 Banda, F. (2002) 'Going It Alone? SADC Declarations and the Gender Debate', *Journal of African Law*, 46(2): 259–60.

37 Convention on the Elimination of All Forms of Discrimination Against Women, 18 December 1979, 1249 UNTS 13.
38 Security Council Resolution 1325, 2000.
39 Above, n 36.
40 From the 1980s for example, the Women in Development (WID) discourse challenged set assumptions about the accrual of benefits to African women from a development perspective, while the 1990s heralded a transition towards deeper thinking around gender and development (GAD). Both of these shifts in policy approaches towards women were highly captive of competing interests at the global level on Africa's development (see Tinker 1990; Boserup 1970).
41 See Sen (1999: 202).
42 The African Women's Development Fund (AWDF) and the Urgent Action Fund-Africa are two such autonomous feminist funding bodies.
43 Above, n 21.
44 Manji, A. (2001) 'Land Reform in the Shadow of the State: The Implementation of New Land Laws in Sub-Saharan Africa', *Third World Quarterly*: 337.
45 Ibid, pp 338–39.
46 Ibid.
47 Above, n 6.

Bibliography

Agarwal, Bina (1995) *A Field of One's Own* (Cambridge: Cambridge University Press).

Atuahene, B. (2005–06) 'Land Titling: A Mode of Privatization with the Potential to Deepen Democracy', *Saint Louis University Law Journal*, 50: 761–81.

Banda, F. (2002) 'Going It Alone? SADC Declarations and the Gender Debate', *Journal of African Law*, 46(2): 259–64.

Banda, F. (2006) 'Women, Law and Human Rights in Southern Africa', *Journal of Southern African Studies*, 32(1): 13–27.

Boserup, Esther (1970) *Women's Role in Economic Development* (London: Allen & Unwin).

Butegwa, Florence (1994) 'Using the African Charter on Human and Peoples' Rights to Secure Women's Access to Land in Africa, in R. J. Cook (ed) *Human Rights of Women: National and International Perspectives* (Philadelphia, PA: University of Pennsylvania Press), pp 495–514.

Cook, Rebecca J., (1994) 'State Accountability Under the Convention on the Elimination of All Forms of Discrimination Against Women', in R. J. Cook (ed.) *Human Rights of Women: National and International Perspectives* (Philadelphia, PA: University of Pennsylvania Press), pp. 228–56.

Giddens, Anthony (1991) *Modernity and Self-Identity* (Cambridge: Polity Press).

Gouws, A. (1999) 'Beyond Equality and Difference: The Politics of Women's Citizenship', *Agenda*, 40: 54–8.

Gray, L. and Kevane, M. (1999) 'Diminished Access, Diverted Exclusion: Women and Land Tenure in Sub-Saharan Africa', *African Studies Review*, 42(2): 15–39.

Hassim, Shireen (1991) 'Gender, social location and feminist politics in South Africa', *Transformation*, 15: 65–81.

Hassim, S. (2006) *Women's Organisations and Democracy in South Africa: Contesting Authority* (Madison, WI: The University of Wisconsin Press).

Hassim, S. (2009) 'Democracy's Shadows: Sexual Rights and Gender Politics in the Rape Trial of Jacob Zuma', *African Studies*, 68(1): 57–77.

Hassim, Shireen, Metelerkamp, Jo and Todes, Alison (1987) '"A bit on the side?": Gender struggles in the politics of transformation in South Africa', *Transformation*, 5: 3–31.

Horn, Patricia (1991) 'What about women's emancipation?', *Transformation*, 15: 25–39.

Izumi, K. (1999) 'Liberalization, Gender, and the Land Question in Sub-Saharan Africa', *Gender and Development*, 7(3): 9–18.

Jensen, Jane (1995) 'Extending the boundaries of citizenship: Women's movements in Western Europe', in Amrita Basu (ed) *The challenge of local feminisms: Women's movements in global perspectives* (Boulder, CO: Westview).

Kanyinga, K. (1998) 'The Land Question in Kenya: Struggles, Accumulation and Changing Politics', PhD dissertation, International Development Studies, Roskilde University.

Lastarria-Cornhiel, S. (1997) 'Impact of privatization on gender and property rights in Africa', *World Development*, 25(8): 1317–33.

Lister, R. (1997) 'Citizenship: Towards a Feminist Synthesis', *Feminist Review*, 57: 28–48.

MacDonald, C. (2003) 'The Value of Discourse Analysis as a Methodological Tool for Understanding a Land Reform Program', *Policy Sciences*, 36(2): 151–73.

Manji, A (1998) 'Gender and the Politics of the Land Reform Process in Tanzania', *The Journal of Modern African Studies*, 36(4): 645–67.

Manji, A. (2001) 'Land Reform in the Shadow of the State: The Implementation of New Land Laws in Sub-Saharan Africa', *Third World Quarterly*, 22(3): 327–42.

Manji, A. (2003) 'Capital, Labour and Land Relations in Africa: A Gender Analysis of the World Bank's Policy Research Report on Land Institutions and Land Policy', *Third World Quarterly*, 24(1): 97–114.

Manji, A. (2006) *The Politics of Land Reform in Africa: From Communal Tenure to Free Markets* (London and New York, NY: Zed Books).

May, J., Stevens, T. and Stols, A. (2002) 'Monitoring the Impact of Land Reform on Quality of Life: A South African Case Study', *Social Indicators Research*, 58(1/3): 293–312.

McAuslan, P. (2003) *Bringing the Law Back In: Essays in Land, Law and Development* (Aldershot: Ashgate).

Moyo, S. (1998) 'The Impact of Structural Adjustment on Land Uses in Zimbabwe', paper presented at the synthesis conference on Structural Adjustment and Social and Political Contexts in Sub-Saharan Africa, Copenhagen, 3–5 December.

Moyo, S. and Yeros, P. (eds) (2005) *Reclaiming the Land: The Resurgence of Rural Movements in Africa, Asia and Latin America* (London and New York: Zed Books).

Ooko-Ombaka, Oki (1979) 'Law and the Limits of International and National Reform', SJD dissertation, Harvard Law School.

Pateman, Carol (1989) *The disorder of women* (London: Polity).

Phillips, Anne (1991) *Engendering Democracy* (Philadelphia, PA: Pennsylvania University Press).

SADC (2008) *Protocol on Gender and Development*, available at <http://www.sadc.int/index/browse/page/465> (accessed 20 December 2009).

Schiff, M. and Winters, A. (2002) 'Regionalism and Development: The Implications of World Bank Research for ACP and Latin American Countries', *Journal of World Trade*, 36(3): 479–99.

Seidman, G. W. (1999) 'Gendered Citizenship: South Africa's Democratic Transition and the Construction of a Gendered State', *Gender and Society*, 13: 287–307.

Sen, A. (1999) *Development as Freedom* (New York, NY: Anchor Books).

Serote, Pethu (1991) *The quest for democracy: South Africa in transition* (London: Penguin Books).

Shivji, I. G. (1998) *Not Yet Democracy: Reforming Land Tenure in Tanzania* (London: International Institute of Environment and Development).

The Sixth Africa Development Forum (ADF VI) (2008) *Achieving Gender Equality and Women's Empowerment in Africa: Progress Report*, November, available at http://www.uneca.org/adfvi/documents/ADFVI_Progress_Report_ENG.pdf (accessed 9 and 10 March 2010).

Tilley, S. (2002) 'An Examination of Market Assisted Agrarian Reform in South Africa', Discussion Paper 2, paper for the International Union of Food, Agricultural, Hotel, Restaurant, Catering, Tobacco and Allied Workers' Associations (IUF) Land and Freedom Project.

Tinker, Irene (ed) (1990) *Persistent Inequalities: Women and World Development* (New York, NY: Oxford University Press).

Tsie, B. (1996) 'States and Markets in the Southern African Development Community (SADC): Beyond the Neo-liberal Paradigm', *Journal of Southern African Studies*, 22(1): 75–98.

United Nations Economic Commission for Africa (2003), Land Tenure Systems and Sustainable Development in Southern Africa, Southern Africa Office, ECA/SA/EGM. Land/2003/2.

Whitehead, A. and Tsikata, D. (2003) 'Policy Discourses on Women's Land Rights in Sub-Saharan Africa: The Implications of the Re-turn to the Customary', *Journal of Agrarian Change*, 3(1) and (2): 67–112.

World Bank (2003) *Land Policies for Growth and Poverty Reduction – A World Bank Policy Research Report* (Washington, DC and Oxford: World Bank and Oxford University Press).

World Bank (2004) *Zambia: Strategic Country Gender Assessment* (World Bank, Washington, DC), available at <http://siteresources.worldbank.org/EXTAFRREGTOPGENDER/Resources/ZambiaSCGA.pdf> (accessed 10 March 2010).

Young, Iris (1990) *Justice and the politics of difference* (Princeton, NJ: Princeton University Press).

Yuval-Davis, N. (1997) 'Women, Citizenship and Difference', *Feminist Review*, 57: 4–27, available at <http://www.jstor.org/stable/1395799> (accessed 2 February 2010).

4 Land and resource rights, tenure arrangements and reform in community-based natural resource management in the Southern African Development Community

Munyaradzi Saruchera and Sibongile Manzana

4.1 Introduction

This chapter highlights the need for Community-Based Natural Resource Management (CBNRM) to be used as a platform to lobby and secure tenure reform, pro-poor rights-based policies and spur social movements to capture resource rights at the local level. Intermediaries in the CBNRM sector may also need to participate in realigning institutional arrangements for resource management to ensure downward accountability and ensure rights to land and resources for local people. At the same time, there is a need to establish mechanisms for surveillance and lobbying state and local authority structures to ensure tenure and resource rights of the poor are maintained. As argued later in this chapter, land administration provides a challenge that needs to be transcended in order for resource rights and CBNRM governance reform to be enshrined in the beneficiation and governance processes.

The chapter is organized as follows: this section provides some background understanding to the land question, tenure and resource rights, and resource rights and governance in order to locate the interaction between land reform and CBNRM in southern Africa. This is followed by a discussion in section 4.2 that locates the status of CBNRM in the different countries under review before exploring the connections between land reform and CBNRM in section 4.3. Then section 4.4 discusses the policy and legal frameworks surrounding CBNRM in the region, while section 4.5 examines the issue of rights. The land reform constraints on CBNRM and challenges of land administration are discussed in section 4.6. Then section 4.7 presents thoughts on the role for CBNRM in land reform and section 4.8 poses some questions for thought and finally section 4.9 draws out some conclusions emerging from the discussion.

4.1.1 Background to land issues in southern Africa

Southern Africa's land question has yielded more or less similar issues and challenges in a variety of socio-economic, political and spatial settings, and the more prominent one has generally been the reclamation of freehold farmland from colonial and private control to local or community ownership. This is especially pertinent for Namibia, South Africa and Zimbabwe. The assertion of historical land claims and title; reform and modernization of tribal or customary forms of land tenure and administrative arrangements; regulation of self-provisioning and the accommodation of equity, gender, sustainable use and environmental concerns in the allocation and distribution of land and the accompanying rights are arguably some of the most prominent challenges facing the region.

Given the centrality of land and the aforementioned issues to livelihoods, the discourse on land reform and resource rights in southern Africa is invariably about community livelihoods and informs the rural development strategies. Land reform and the applicable rights form the foundation of local economies and inform access arrangements to other resources such as wildlife, forestry products and water that occur on the land. As such, land reform policy (that is redistribution, tenure and restitution) has a direct bearing on the performance of CBNRM arrangements, and more significantly on the rules and laws of access and for those people who derive benefits from a variety of natural resources.

Moyo (2000a) argues that the southern African land question is characterized by contradictory and sometimes irrational land-use patterns of over-utilization in communal areas and under-utilization in the commercial sector. The author further asserts that throughout the region, land distribution and ownership have remained largely skewed in favour of the rich and powerful social class, often white and emergent black elites, in countries such as South Africa, Namibia and Zimbabwe, whilst in Botswana, Malawi and Zambia the debate is often around tenure rights and land utilization. The obtaining landholding pattern reflects colonial and after-independence land and agricultural policies across the region.

Against a background where land remains the basic source of livelihood for the majority of people, the importance of land as a key political, economic and social resource and its governance cannot be over-emphasized. The colonial nature and history, as well as the decolonization process of each country, inform the nature of land reform for a particular country. By and large, land reform programmes have either been government-led or market-based and in some cases attempts to mix both approaches have been made.

Zambia has been independent for 46 years, Botswana 44 years, Malawi 45 years, Angola and Mozambique 35 years, Zimbabwe 30 years, Namibia 20 years and South Africa 16 years. The land reform experience and path followed by each of these countries is partly related to the period they have been implemented and also influenced by the global political environment and ideology. For example, the land problems experienced by Angola and Mozambique are different from those faced by Zimbabwe, Namibia and South Africa.

According to Manjengwa (2006), in the case of Mozambique, this is largely because all land was nationalized at independence and the focus was on tenure reform, thus avoiding many of the present land problems facing Zimbabwe and other countries. Mozambique's Land Law of 1997 was developed after wide research and consultations with a broad range of stakeholders. To this extent, the law is viewed by the World Bank and Oxfam, among others, as progressive and among the best on the continent, as it offers significant opportunities for poverty alleviation and stability in rural areas. The Mozambican Land Law retains the principle that land is state property that cannot be sold or mortgaged and the constitution recognizes land rights of direct users and producers. The Land Law also protects customary rights of existing occupiers on communal land and strengthens the rights of private entities wishing to acquire access to land and natural resources for commercial purposes (Lahiff 2003).

The customary rights of access and management are equivalent to the state-allocated land use and benefit rights (DUAT – *a direito de uso e aproveitamento de terra* – which is commonly translated as a 'right of use and benefit'). Land debates in Mozambique often focus on productive use and ownership of land, and the Land Law is viewed as devolving authority and autonomy to local holders of rights. However, there are also debates for privatization of land being pushed by donors and others who regard the Land Law as not having a clear legal framework for private property and a free land market. The push for privatization is undermining the progress of the Land Law and many stakeholders contend that it is unnecessary to privatize land as the Land Law sufficiently protects investors and prevents conflict (Manjengwa 2006).

According to Marongwe (in Saruchera 2004), Botswana was least affected by colonialism and has now been independent for 45 years. Arguably, it has stood out as one of the successful land reform cases with clear land tenure and resource rights arrangements, even though it has also been criticized by some as denying many local users their resource rights and favouring large-scale capture by elites. In Malawi, the expansion of estate agriculture for export cash crops (tobacco, tea and sugar) occurred at the expense of communal land. This resulted in high localized population pressures in the southern and central regions of the country, where 78 per cent of households in the smallholder sector owned less than one hectare of land while leasehold land was abandoned and under-utilized according to the 1992/93 national sample survey of agriculture. The high land pressures saw an encroachment onto gazetted forests, national parks, private land and protected areas by smallholder producers across Mulanje, Thyolo and Kasungu (Marongwe in Saruchera 2004).

Following the attainment of independence, Mozambique, Namibia and Zimbabwe embarked on resettlement policies to cater for both individual and group land holdings. For Zimbabwe and Mozambique cooperative[1] resettlement was part of a socialist transformation aimed at redistributing natural wealth. However, the cooperative resettlement model failed for a variety of reasons, and key among them were a lack of group cohesion, inappropriate beneficiary selection and tenure insecurity. This chapter argues that the failure of the cooperative model indicated that cooperative resource ownership, especially land, is inappropriate in southern Africa.

The shift from government-led land redistributive land reform to a market-based approach was largely influenced by the adoption of economic structural adjustment programmes (ESAP) that were driven by the World Bank and the International Monetary Fund. ESAP shaped the land reform dynamics and livelihoods in

Zambia and Zimbabwe, following the removal of exchange rate controls, subsidies and the relaxation of regulatory policies. The wildlife-based land use option was a major outcome of ESAP that saw some local communities entering the tourism sector, resulting in the conceptualization of wildlife-based land reform models (Moyo 2000b).

4.1.2 Tenure and resource rights

The main tenure systems currently obtaining in southern Africa are communal property, state property and private or freehold. Most land tenure systems in Africa are communal in character which Cousins and Classens (in Saruchera 2004) argue is a misnomer in many respects because communal is generally understood to mean common ownership of all resources and collective[2] production. This is rarely the case though. In the context of African communal tenure, there is a degree of community control over who is entitled to accessing resources and thereby qualified for allocation of land for residence and cropping, as well as rights to common property resources under the group's control. In these circumstances, the group seeks to maintain the identity, coherence and livelihood security of its members.

Marongwe (in Saruchera 2004) notes that the notion of private property rights is viewed as the ideal tenure system, and as a result, land tenure arrangements have remained fixed and to this extent, private property is too exclusive and insensitive to the changing social, economic and environmental realities of the region. Exclusion also applies to state property, both of which tenure systems have negatively affected livelihood opportunities available to rural communities that are most dependent on natural resources. Some environmental management issues such as water, biological and ecological diversity, however, transcend individual property boundaries and thus challenge the supremacy and efficacy of individual rights for land and natural resource management (NRM) and decision making.

Owing to the rigidity of both private and state property rights systems, resource-sharing arrangements and opportunities among state, private and communal farmers have not been exploited, thus compromising the livelihood opportunities available to communal land dwellers. To this end, private and state resource tenure systems continue to operate as closed systems that deprive communal area residents of livelihood opportunities. Typical examples include collection of timber and non-timber forestry products, from state and private forests, for firewood and consumption in the case of honey, wild fruits, herbal medicines and mushrooms and lease of unused farm and grazing land that could enhance rural communities' livelihoods. Parameters that could be considered in working out usufruct rights would include agreements that stipulate rules and regulations guiding exploitation of natural resources and incentives, and disincentives that promote sustainable resource utilization.

In many circumstances, access to land automatically determines access to natural resources such as wildlife, forestry products and biological resources. However, the same does not apply to mineral resources which belong to the state, and any revenue accruing from the exploitation of such minerals also belongs to the state. This is the case in all the countries under review, and particularly in South Africa where cases of some foreign platinum mining houses, in partnership collusion with the government's Department of Minerals and Energy (DME), have been engaged in eviction battles against local communities that are resisting to be moved from their tribal land endowed with platinum deposits. The Mineral and Petroleum Resources Development Act 2002 of South Africa is permissive towards mining companies, at the expense of community rights to social justice, land and mineral wealth. The Act merely requires the mining houses to 'consult' communities and report back the outcome to the DME upon which they can get issued with a mining right that entitles them to start mining without the consent or permission of the land owners or occupiers (Curtis 2008).

However, it is not clear under what circumstances land rights are inclusive of mineral rights and the due processes for adequate community compensation for relocation and loss of mineral rights in the case of South Africa. While communities are being forcibly removed from their tribal land to make way for Anglo Platinum's Portgietersrus Platinums Limited Mine (near Mokopane) because they have no claim to the mineral wealth, the same law allows traditional authorities such as the Bafokeng, the Bakwena Ba Magopo and the Bakgatla Ba Kgafela to exercise mineral rights over their land and receive royalty income used for community development, and account to the national government for the income every five years. The latter case points to an innovative potential for minerals to play a role in resource-based community development, once management and distribution issues are clarified.

Land registration in communal areas has been tried, with varied levels of success. For example, Mozambique experimented with land registration by villagers in northern parts of the country that is under customary management, and in the case of Malawi, legal provision was made for identification and registration of community rights over water access and traditional grazing areas (Marongwe 2000). Thus far, it appears that freehold or private land rights are a dominant tenure system in Namibia, South Africa and Botswana while in Mozambique, Zimbabwe and Zambia, long-term nationalization of land by the state is preferred. However, in Mozambique, Malawi, Botswana, Zambia and South Africa, measures to secure customary land rights are common and so to an extent community resource rights are comparatively secure. An operative rationale in these contexts is that community livelihoods depend on natural resources access, as such resource rights that include land, water, fisheries, wildlife, forests and minerals do provide opportunities for poverty reduction.

The Zimbabwean case has notably been dominated by policy reversals, revisions and contradictions over the last ten years. Currently, the pronounced policy position is that all farmland belongs to the state and users can lease it over a 99-year period, and yet even in this situation property rights are highly insecure given the political and socio-economic instability of the country at present. In Zambia, an integrated approach to the conservation, management and utilization of forests and woodland resources and the participation of local communities, traditional institutions and the private sector is provided for in the Forestry Act 1999. The same Act does, however, still place forests under the control of government, which brings about tension and conflict between land tenure and tree ownership according to Simuunza (1999). He states that 69 per cent of the forests fall under what was known as trust land, 18 per cent on customary land (previously reserve land), and 13 per cent on state land.

According to the Zambian National Environmental Action Plan 1994, this means that 87 per cent of protected forests fall within land rights of customary law, a situation that could cause traditional authority, local communities and the state forestry department to conflict. Interpretation of the Zambian Land Act would mean that although planted trees belong to the planter, cutting any trees for sale can only be done with a licence from the Forestry Department. In real terms, the government is not able to monitor the process, resulting in unlicensed decimation of forests (Marongwe, in Saruchera 2004).

With respect to Mozambique, at independence all land was nationalized and managed by the state on behalf of the people. For those who so wished, they could convert their earlier freehold rights into the new state-allocated right of 'use and fruition' or DUAT. The underlying principle of property in land vested in the state has remained despite Mozambique's embracement of multiparty politics and other basic pillars of a liberal market economy. The right of ownership is vested in the state and so no land may be sold, mortgaged or alienated. However, local traditional structures and land management systems have remained intact, resulting in the formal recognition of customary land systems and the rights attributed to rural people in the 1995 National Land Policy and the 1997 Land Law (Norfolk and Tanner 2006).

Occupation remains the principal means by which the rural poor access land rights and the rights are duly recognized in law as equivalent to the state DUATs. However, recognizing poor people's rights is one thing and protecting and making them in favour of an equitable system is another. Despite the political assurances guaranteeing access to land for all as a poverty reduction strategy, there are clear signs that a classical enclosure process is underway in high tourism potential areas, argue Norfolk and Tanner (2006).

The 2004 Constitutional revision reasserts the basic principle of state land ownership. Effectively, this means that the constitutional right to use land shall be enjoyed by all Mozambicans while the state determines the conditions under which citizens may exercise that right. Even though all land belongs to the state, the Constitution recognizes the right to private property and improvements or constructions made on or to the land over which a private person or organization has a DUAT are private assets of such person or organization. The assets can be bought and sold while the DUAT is administratively transferred to the new asset owner. Technically, selling land is illegal, but attributing value to basic structures provides a legal basis to an unregulated and open land market (Norfolk and Tanner 2006).

According to the Land Law 1997 of Mozambique, there are three ways in which a DUAT may be acquired. First, through the occupancy of land by individual persons and by local communities in accordance with customary norms and practices, so long as these do not contradict the Constitution. Second, a DUAT may be acquired through the occupancy of land by individual national persons who have been using the land in good faith for at least ten years, and finally, through the authorization of an application submitted by an individual or corporate person.

4.1.3 Resource rights and local governance

Whiteside (1998) contends that local-level institutions and organizations are at the centre of land governance and resource rights, given their central role in defining household user rights over resources, and influence norms of behaviour that determine sustainability and are responsible for access to common pool resources. Devolution of authority, decentralization and democratization of resource rights is only meaningful when local-level organizations are centrally involved in community participation. Effective local-level institutions in charge of land and natural resources rights issues remains a major challenge that confronts most southern African countries. Many governments have not decentralized resource rights to local communities for a variety of reasons, mainly due to insufficient capacity, state failure to perform the function and illegal and unsustainable resource utilization has continued unchecked.

According to Marongwe (in Saruchera 2004), good governance is located within the framework of sustainable NRM debates, and as such attempts of good governance should necessarily focus on rights, facilitation of local processes, enhancing access to the law, capacity building and development of relevant conflict management systems. To this end, traditional authorities in southern Africa have been accused of failing to meet the criteria for good governance in the current socio-economic order. This is due to the reasons that they are not democratically elected, often lack transparency and accountability and tend to favour clan members in the allocation of land and other resources. Ntsebeza (1999) questions the ability of traditional leadership to embrace democratic principles and gender equality in the discharge of their function, and even argues that the institution of traditional leadership is at variance with the South African Constitution that requires elected local government structures across the country.

Customary land makes up about 96.5 per cent of Zambia and traditional chiefs and village headmen are responsible for administering it. Once allocated land by traditional leadership, individual ownership is perpetual through continuous cultivation and can be inherited upon death of owner. Traditional leadership is therefore central to local level administration of land, and in an effort to improve tenure security of customary land, the Land Law 1995 proposed freehold title on customary land. Marongwe (in Saruchera 2004) refers to this new arrangement as a fusion of revised customary land tenure system which traditional leadership view as an erosion of their power. However, although land conflicts are ultimately subject to magistrates' courts, cases rarely go that far before they are resolved in traditional areas.

South Africa's land reform is demand-driven and implemented through a decentralized approach. Several pieces of legislation and a new set of institutions were established to deal with various aspects of land reform. Examples are the Communal Land Rights Act 2004 and the Restitution of Land Rights Act 1994 which provides for the Commission on Restitution of Land Rights and the Land Claims Commission that are responsible for implementing the restitution programme. At local level there exists a legislative framework for the development of communal property associations and trusts to take care of the community's land affairs on a basis agreed by members in terms of a written constitution. Communal Property Associations (CPA) do acquire rights in their own right and have perpetual succession. The KwaZulu Natal Ingonyama Trust Act 1994 saw the establishment of the Ingonyama Trust that is administered for the benefit, social well-being and material welfare of the Zulu tribes and communities. These types of local-level institutions are new phenomena that came with the new political dispensation and hence the extent to which they contribute to good governance and effective resource management is still to be explored fully and proven.

The Land Board model in Botswana and Namibia has been viewed as the best approach to local-level land allocation and administration. The model's main advantage is that it fuses both customary and formal tenure systems and also proffers a strategy for decentralization of land policy implementation. However, despite its relative success, the land board approach has been criticized for not being democratic and dominated by local elites at the expense of wider local community groups. The other issue is that the ability of Land Boards to solve problems of overlapping land rights and multiple needs of different groups has been questioned. Another weakness with this approach is that it only recognizes certain land use types as legitimate in allocation, for example arable and grazing land, but not hunting areas or land for gathering resources. There is need for clarification of the place of Land Boards within a broader spectrum of devolved local-level governance and the development planning process (Quan 2000).

In Mozambique, land reform was informed by a socialist ideology that gave rise to new institutions known as secretaries who are effectively heads of zones responsible for implementing the land law and have vast knowledge about vacant and unallocated land. The Land Law 1997 and the Regulations of 1998 thereof stressed the importance of community representation. A legal mandate to enable local communities to participate in natural resources management and the allocation of new DUATs was introduced in the Land Law. Article 24 of the Law stipulates that the customary norms and practices of local community groups are part of the formal systems of NRM and local conflict resolution. Local communities are effectively recognized actors within the institutional environment and have a legally recognized role in the management and administration of land and land rights registration (Norfolk and Tanner 2006).

4.2 CBNRM in southern Africa

In response to the growing need for improved community livelihoods and enhancement of community resource rights, many southern African countries developed a strategy for sustainable NRM – CBNRM – over the last two decades or so. While some of the countries have a formalized CBNRM policy, others practice it without a specialized legislative framework.

The rationale of the CBNRM programmes is that, historically, inappropriate colonial development policies led to projects and protected areas that displaced local communities and undermined their livelihoods, leading to human and environmental insecurity. Botswana, Malawi, Mozambique, Namibia, Zambia, Zimbabwe and South Africa implement different forms of CBNRM programmes at different scales. Many of the CBNRM programmes have focused on wildlife conservation and management in conservation areas and on communal lands. However, other resources such as forests, fisheries and rangelands have been managed by communities and the state. Environmental and livelihood benefits derived from CBNRM vary widely between projects that include conservation objectives linked to eco-tourism and the management of resources for consumption and sale.

The CBNRM approach was arguably intended, by many implementers, as a way to co-opt community groups into more efficient and sustainable ways of environmental conservation and management while improving local incomes at the same time (Jones and Murphree 2004; Dzingirai and Breen 2005). However, Katerere (in Benjaminsen et al 2002) states that the CBNRM approach was intended to focus on strengthening the human rights of local communities by enhancing their control over their natural resources, recognizing their priorities and supporting their participation in higher level decision-making.

The success of CBNRM initiatives in southern Africa can be attributed to the efforts of non-governmental organizations (NGOs), state and donor funding which funded and facilitated implementation of the CBNRM programmes. The approach emphasizes local institution building, capacity development, organizational innovation, experimentation and research that in turn promoted productive, competitive, equitable and sustainable resource use for local benefit.

Shackleton and Campbell (2000) argue that while donors and NGOs have been instrumental in driving the CBNRM agenda towards local control over natural resources, the transfer of rights to local actors, which rests with the state, has been partial and designed to diffuse tension and conflict between the state and often impoverished and restless rural communities. The reasons for this are varied. The colonial and independent states have, historically, manipulated and disempowered community institutions and concentrated power in the state. There also seems a lack of commitment by the state to release power to local institutions despite numerous policies for devolution. At best, CBNRM is about decentralization of governance or deepening democracy at the local level and yet this goes against the motives of states that generally have centralizing tendencies. Against this background, the CBNRM approach can effectively be empowering or disempowering for local communities.

The International Resource Group (2008) highlights the following indications of the scale and impact of CBNRM programmes in the sub-region:

- Namibia established 50 registered communal conservancies on 10 million hectares of land, with documented increases in wildlife, particularly in the northwest region and a net national income and increased wildlife capital value of about US$60 million, almost matching total donor and government investment of about US$66 million from 1990 to 2003. However, by 2005 conservancy-related income was just over US$3 million and the #Khoadi / / hoas and Nyae Nyae conservancies generated higher income and related benefits. Long (2004) says that CBNRM has contributed to the protection and recovery of wildlife species in communal areas, established institutional structures (conservancies) that offer development decision-making and action fora and enhanced livelihoods;
- Zimbabwe established the Communal Areas Management Programme for Indigenous Resources (CAMPFIRE) in 37 districts (63 per cent of the rural districts in the country, of which 51 per cent were participating fully in CAMPFIRE programmes) across five natural regions covering 4 million hectares, and elephant and buffalo populations increased in the participating areas. Household income from the programme were modest and the bulk of the dividends were used for community infrastructural development whilst rural district councils retained a huge portion of the generated income;
- Botswana developed the CBNRM Programme (CBNRMP) which covers the entire country over 100 villages with 135,000 people involved. A total of 94 legal CBNRMP entities exist, 35 of which generate income. US$3.2 million was generated from commercial use and US$2.7 million from in kind income. The CBNRMP has allowed the communities to move from cattle management to wildlife-based incomes with associated benefits to the habitat. A decrease in poaching and human-wildlife conflict has been noted. The Marula tree planting CBNRMP in the Kgetsi ya Tsie project, however, demonstrated constraints of resource management in open access areas and problematic tenure systems;
- Malawi has over 3,000 Village Natural Resources Management Committees. CBNRM is based on other forms of natural resources that have value to the local communities, given that the country does not have extensive wildlife outside reserves. The Sustainable Management of Indigenous Forests (SMIF) project resulted in increased household livelihoods and income although charcoal production did not decrease. A total of 63 tonnes of raw baobab material for oil and powder production was supplied to a processing plant facility and the generated income went directly to the local community. About 350 hectares of extensive woodlots were established in the BERDO project to mitigate against deforestation, and rivers are becoming perennial once more while animal species are starting to move back into the forests where they had been extinct. From the Community Partnerships for Sustainable Resource Management (COMPASS) phase 1 (from 2000 to 2004), US$511,000 worth of community benefits were generated, and in 2005 fish farmers produced metric 500 tonnes of fish. Beekeeping was expected to increase production of honey from 40 tonnes to 800 tonnes in 2009, and US$25,000 was generated

from conservation enterprises such as guinea fowl rearing, tamarind and baobab juice production, and tree, seedling and timber sales; and

- South Africa is implementing different programmes in nature reserves, communal areas and resettled land. Most of the land claims on conservation areas were settled in a way that allows the conservation status of the land to be maintained through partnership arrangements such as the Makuleke land claim in northern Kruger Park, Mkambati on the Wild Coast, the Kalahari Gemsbok Park and the Richtersveld National Park in the Northern Cape. The Makuleke community receives modest dividends from leasing their tourism rights in the Kruger. The Mkambati and Dwesa/Cwebe communities have struggled to set up ventures with private sectors due to land tenure issues and other factors. Some reserves have been established on communal areas, for example the Tembe Game Reserve, the Madikwe Game Reserve, the Mawewe cattle-game project and Mahushe Shongwe Nature Reserve. Collapse of communal institutional structures and power struggles have flared up in CBNRMPs that were created by the land reform process. Dispute and low tourism revenue characterize the Richtersveld contractual national park partnership between the local community and the South African National Parks. Land Care programmes on soil and water conservation as well as rangeland management and other unique CBNRMPs where the state pays individual community members to engage in resource management (Working for Water and other Public Works programmes) and the then Department of Environmental Affairs and Tourism's CBNRM projects such as the Masifundise small-scale traditional fishers in Cape Town are under implementation.

There are more than 58 CBNRM interventions in Mozambique, many of which have land rights components. However, most of the initiatives are donor-driven and external resources and their long-term sustainability and empowerment of local communities is questionable. If successfully implemented, land reform under the Land Law could secure tenure rights for communal people and strengthen property rights for investors. Private investors are currently benefiting the most from land and valuable resources, with little or no return to local communities who hold nominal user rights over the natural resources. Mozambique's land reform places communities at the centre of NRM through its requirement of community-level NRM plans and the formation of NRM committees. Formalizing community-based management of natural resources in Mozambique has not been without its challenges.

The interest and optimism of the CBNRM approach has led to the development of different CBNRM models linked to specific resources, and Shackleton and Campbell (2000) provide an insightful discussion and classification of these in their report. Zimbabwe's CAMPFIRE, Zambia's Administrative Design for Game Management Areas (ADMADE), Botswana's controlled hunting areas and Mozambique's Tchuma Tchato are the most popular and publicized CBNRM approaches in southern Africa. Malawi, Namibia and South Africa developed their own CBNRMPs that were informed by their contexts and needs.

Conservancies that are controlled and managed by groups of villagers who operate eco-tourism enterprises with support of relevant NGOs and the national tourism authority were established in Namibia, with relative success.

In the case of Botswana, a community forms a legally recognized trust which develops a land use plan while in Namibia communities are required to demonstrate administrative capacity and commitment to run a conservancy. The market-driven land reform of South Africa resulted in communities entering into partnership arrangements and contractual agreements with the private sector. However, in Namibia and Zimbabwe, CBNRMPs do not automatically transfer land ownership to communities as the state reserves the right to expropriate any piece of land, including conservancies.

The notion and conceptualization of community has been a challenge in CBNRM (see Kepe 1998) despite its appeal to professional and community development practitioners, planners and resource managers alike. The notion offers manageable units comprising identifiable resource users. Like most development interventions, CBNRM initiatives treat communities as homogenous without due consideration of complex dynamics, difference, multiplicity of competing interests and power struggles located in many community settings that should be understood in planning. Local elites in many communities often have the capacity to link with outsiders (state agents or private sector) to capture/privatize resources and cease to be accountable to their own community structures.

4.2.1 CBNRM typologies in southern Africa

There are three distinct types of CBNRM models that can be identified as operative in southern Africa, namely imposed, assisted and organic.

Imposed: Community empowerment processes are viewed as incomplete and power remains with local government structures in this model. This arrangement can be referred to as de-concentration of central government power to line ministries and lower-levels of state institutions such as district councils or municipalities. Zambia's ADMADE and Zimbabwe's CAMPFIRE CBNRMPs are typical examples. Invariably, the lower-level state agencies are poorly funded and so they inevitably use CBNRM initiatives as revenue generation sources. There is often little community involvement in planning and decision making and a larger portion of the generated revenue is captured by the state. Imposed CBNRM models are usually driven by the state, donors or NGOs and eventually communities question the purpose and value of the programmes. Donor policies play a role in shaping local CBNRM approaches and the governance and macro-economic policies that determine local NRM (Leach et al 1999; Fakir 1998). Imposed CBNRM models can graduate to assisted or organic models with more involvement of community participation.

Assisted: Assisted CBNRM models build on initial community efforts and power shifts to the community through the establishment of village-based management structures. Where village structures are accountable at the local level, credible external support is rendered and high devolution, this form of CBNRM tends to be successful. Examples of village forest committees and village natural resource committees from Malawi fit into the assisted model. However, while credible external support can help set a CBNRM agenda, the views of external facilitators tend to be informed by their own agendas and theoretical frameworks as opposed to the community's local history, values, priorities and practice, and subsequently undermine community interests.

Organic: The organic forms of CBNRM exist in contexts where communities own the ideas, implementation and resource beneficiation processes. In other words, the locus of power is the community and decisions and power over resource use and allocation are devolved to the community. There are few such models, if at all, in southern Africa at the moment. The closest case is that of the Makuleke community of South Africa that successfully reclaimed its rights to land that was previously under the control of and was forcibly incorporated into the Kruger National Park during apartheid.

While CBNRM proponents hail the Makuleke case as a successful and effective devolution model, it is the view of this chapter that real rights of this community were not realized. The reasons for this argument are that the reclaimed land has remained as a park and the community is forced into a 'partnership' with the park authorities. Attempts by the community to exercise its full rights of ownership were not entertained by the South African National Parks and a compromise for partnership was effectively forced on them. It therefore follows that communities in this situation can only realize their rights through a forced partnership with the state, its agent or preferred partner.

CBNRM initiatives in the region should be premised on holistic land reform processes that address all the mechanisms for expropriation (social, economic and political) bases of existing land distribution and communal tenure arrangements to be sustainable in the long-term. As already pointed out in this chapter, the CBNRM models being implemented in the sub-region are either imposed or assisted. Zimbabwe's CAMPFIRE programme has super structures that are managed by Rural District Councils and Village and Ward Wildlife Management Committees, while Zambia's ADMADE and Botswana's CBNRMP reinforce the power and positions of chiefs and other local elites. For this reason, the CBNRMPs have had minimal impact on community livelihoods, and the programmes continue to be resisted by poor people interested in accessing more and better land.

4.3 CBNRM and land reform

Land is Africa's key natural resource that is centrally linked to the continent's development and all aspects of common property resource management. As such, land has been at the centre of liberation struggles in southern Africa, given that the countries share a common history of land dispossession, dual land tenure systems and creation of rural labour reserves/homelands. Ownership of land in the reserves was vested in the colonial state and residents enjoyed usufruct rights as regulated by the local authorities that were either created (native administration) or co-opted (in the case of traditional leaders) by the state. A separate legal dispensation for the native administration areas that was ostensibly based on customary law to legitimize the cooption of traditional leaders and governance of the natives was thus created.

It is within the above historical context that communal tenure, which effectively determines resource rights, was established in order to deny indigenous people property rights. Today, independent southern African states are still grappling with land tenure reform programmes or developing new land laws to redress this past. A mix of approaches has been adopted and varied results have been achieved from the different land reform programmes.

Besides the ambiguous communal tenure system on state land, nowhere else do communities exist as legal entities, in their own right, in any legal system in southern Africa in the same way as individual actors. It is against this background that in the communal tenure regimes absolute rights over land and other natural resources invariably are held by a local government entity on 'behalf of the community'. As the land and natural resources appreciate in value, the local government entities tend to enclose the resources. To this extent, communal tenure implies that communities can only control the resources with negligible value, hence throughout the region the rights to trees depends on their intended use and not the tree itself per se.

Examples of Zimbabwe's Communal Forest Produce Act 1987 and the Forest Act 1982 give individuals the right to harvest trees for their own use without a permit, yet the 1987 Act vests management of common forests in the rural district councils that have the right to grant concessions to outsiders to utilize the same communal forests commercially without necessarily consulting local residents. Just like timber, the granting of hunting concessions and fishing permits in communal areas is also controlled by state agents or its preferred agent (Murombedzi 1999).

The above illustration demonstrates that the locus of power, authority and rights to resources that continues to inform CBNRMPs across the region remain in the state. Thus, legal powers that do not recognize community rights and interests undermine local management arrangements, including CBNRM. Land and natural resources in southern Africa remain in the hands of powerful elites and so communities continue to be constrained by entitlement failure from enjoying meaningful and full rights of their resources.

4.4 CBNRM policy and legislative framework

Across southern Africa, the policy and legislative frameworks impacting on CBNRM are wide-ranging and contained in various separate statutes, national and sectoral policies dealing with the general environment (land, agriculture, forestry, fisheries, wildlife), planning, tourism, small enterprise development, regional government and traditional authorities and, by reference, to customary laws. These frameworks are both facilitative of CBNRM and a hindrance at the same time. Historically, legislation and policy in this area have had ideological biases towards powerful actors with vested interests. In practice, this has meant that legislation and policy focused primarily on the formal commercial sector at the expense of rural communities that were excluded from its operations. The communities were provided with a separate and inferior set of rights that were often collective in nature as opposed to individual rights, resulting in further marginalization and underdevelopment of these communities. However, the legislative and policy frameworks, and post-independence reforms, have provided legal parameters for positive development of CBNRM in some contexts (Corbett and Daniels 1996).

Specific legislations from selected countries are discussed, albeit not comprehensively in this chapter, but they are sufficiently discussed to impart some insights and appreciation for purposes of analysing CBNRM and land rights within the context of the region's land reform. The countries under review have varying degrees of CBNRM policy and legislative frameworks that are determined by overall national environmental policies, acts and sectoral policies, National Environmental Action Plans and Biodiversity Strategy and Action Plans on forest, wildlife, water and fisheries. The implementation of these policies and plans is also varied, with many of them still unfulfilled for a variety of reasons despite the good intentions.

Many of the countries have also signed up and ratified international environmental agreements such as the Convention on Biological Diversity (CBD), the Convention on International Trade of Endangered Species (CITES) and the United Nations Convention to Combat Desertification (UNCCD) under which they have committed to meet requirements towards poverty reduction, sustainable development and NRM. To this end, the CBNRM strategy is one leading approach for securing communal property rights, enhancing tenure security, local governance and grassroots institutions and sustainable livelihoods.

With respect to Namibia, Long (2004) states that the essential policy framework for CBNRM is found in the Ministry of Environment and Tourism documents on wildlife management, utilization and tourism in communal areas as well as the establishment of conservancies and the promotion of community-based tourism policies and laws. The most significant factors that led to the development of CBNRM policy and legislation in the case of Namibia were the following:

- concerns of rural residents over better management of wildlife;
- experiences of conservation NGOs in the north-west of the country;
- experiences and lessons learned from elsewhere in the sub-region and from the freehold farming sector; and
- the development of common property resource management theory.

The above factors led to the eventual development of policy and legislation, notably the Wildlife Management, Utilisation and Tourism in Communal Areas Policy of 1995. The policy states the right to utilize and benefit from wildlife on communal land should be devolved to a rural community that forms a conservancy in terms of the Ministry's policy on conservancies and the Nature Conservation Amendment Act of 1996. The Act confers the rights of communal area residents over wildlife and tourism as commercial farmers. As opposed to setting up fences and the size of farm determining ownership over exploitable game and the right to use other species, the Nature Conservation Amendment Act of 1996 sets the formation of a conservancy as a condition for granting ownership and use rights over game to communal area residents (Long 2004).

Once a conservancy has been declared in the Government Gazette, the Act gives the conservancy committee, on behalf of the community, rights and duties for consumptive and non-consumptive use and sustainable management of game in order for the community members to derive benefits from such use and management. The same Act makes provision for communal area residents who do not form conservancies to benefit from wildlife indirectly, through the formation of Wildlife Councils that are formed by the Minister after consultations with a local community. Whilst the Wildlife Council may not include any conservancy, game park, nature reserve or land subject to lease, it effectively gains the same rights and obligations as a conservancy.

Sustainable use of natural resources forms a basic principle of the Mozambican National Land Policy. The Ministry of Environmental Coordination developed several environmental laws, including forest and wildlife laws and the new Territorial Planning Law that impinge on the Land Law. The laws are premised on the same principle as the Land Law, that is all natural resources are state property and licences are granted after consultation with communities. The land, forestry and wildlife laws recognize local communities' participation in the sustainable use and management of natural resources which effectively entrenches common property rights.

Local resource management councils that are composed of state, community, private sector and NGOs were created to promote sustainable use under the forest and wildlife laws. Communities retain traditional use rights for hunting, firewood, forest plans, water for cattle and small-scale irrigation even where titles are issued to other land users (Manjengwa 2006). She further states that a key legal tenure change provided by Articles 10 and 12 of the Land Law is a requirement that communities participate in the administration of natural resources. The Land Law facilitates community management of natural resources and the delimited communities can adopt appropriate organizational structures such as associations to respond to specific situations.

Even though Mozambique's legal framework is arguably favourable to local community participation in NRM, implementation and interpretation constraints continue to be experienced. For instance, while the Wildlife and Forestry Law 1999 foresees the delegation of state powers for natural resource management to local communities, there is no complementary generic law on the distribution of delegated powers and how local authorities and communities feature. The net effect is that CBNRM initiatives are implemented with procedural uncertainty and progress dependent on the willingness of the government agent in charge at a certain time and place. The Ancuabe, Sanhote and the Tchuma Tchato CBNRM projects are examples where government agents maintain enormous influence and authority in regulating access to the resources and marginalizing customary institutions and the local people's rights in the process.

In Malawi, policy formulation is a top-down phenomenon where sectoral policies have been developed in isolation. Because the various national policies dealing with a variety of sectors (fisheries, forestry, wildlife, land) interfacing with CBNRM contain provisions for community-based management of resources, Malawi has no specific CBNRM policy currently. The sectoral policies that are often developed in isolation often result in policy conflict and frustrate implementation efforts. NRM policy and strategies are outlined in the National Environmental Policy 1996, the National Environmental Management Act 1996, the National Environmental Action Plan 1994, the Forestry Act 1997, the Fisheries Conservation and Management Act 1997 and a series of completed or evolving sectoral policies. The forestry policy has recently been reviewed to address pricing of forest products and the role of traditional authorities and communities in co-management of forest resources. Land resources and irrigation policy, parks and wildlife management policy and fisheries policy have been considerably reviewed but implementation is either slow or negligible in most cases (<http://www.compass-malawi.com> (accessed June 2008)).

The above policies incorporate significant provisions in support of CBNRM such as giving Ministers or Directors authority to negotiate co-management agreements with communities. The Land Use Planning Policy and several policies outside mainstream environment have either been approved or are under consideration, all of which have a bearing on the way natural resources are managed and used in Malawi.

Botswana's CBNRM policy was adopted in 2006 with the intention to guide and facilitate the strengthening of and support to existing and future CBNRM activities. It has ten objectives that provide for: land tenure and natural resource rights devolved to communities, a framework for community incentives to manage natural resources sustainably, community participation, protection of community intellectual property rights, community participation and monitoring, community capacity building, institutional support framework for CBNRM implementation.

The policy serves to guide implementation of CBNRM activities on communal and state land and gives communities incentives to engage in conservation activities leading to sustainable development and poverty reduction. It also seeks to establish an institutional, regulatory and participatory framework for CBNRM implementation and promote responsible, accountable and transparent decision-making. Botswana's CBNRM originated from nation-wide land use planning and inevitably the policy interfaces the Tribal Grazing Land policy, Wildlife Conservation policy of 1986 and the 2002 Revised National Policy for Rural Development. CBNRM is further identified as one of the six sustaining livelihood programmes of the National Strategy for Poverty Reduction of 2003.

4.5 Rights to land and resources

Whilst government policy usually allocates procedural rights, as opposed to substantive rights, the regimes for allocating and managing substantive rights are poorly administered at community level. In this context, CBNRM has a potential role to play in developing scope for substantive rights allocation and administration at community level across southern Africa's community-based natural policy and legislative frameworks. Rights-based and sustainable livelihoods approaches are at the centre of CBNRM philosophy and form a basis for resource-poor and landless communities to claim and assert their rights, and compel the state to accede and formalize the demands for resource rights.

The constitutions of many southern African countries employ obscure legal concepts in protection of property guarantee clauses and rights around land. Ng'ong'ola (in Saruchera 2004) identified three main functions served by the property guarantee clauses in the constitutions. The first function is an affirmation of the right to have or hold property as a fundamental right equivalent to the first-generation political and civic rights such as the right to life, freedom of expression and others. The constitutional property clauses are premised on Article 17 of the Universal Declaration of Human Rights which gives everyone the right to own property, either alone or in association with others.

The second function of the clauses attempts to regulate loss of property rights as the behest of government. The main property guarantee in most constitutions is restriction on the circumstances and possibility of loss. Third, the constitutions may provide the assurance that certain basic needs will be provided for those who have no property to lose. It seems in the ambit of this function that CBNRM was crafted for communities who effectively had no property to lose. For this reason, this chapter argues that CBNRM has failed to be an instrument for meaningful and effective political change, and it is unable to address the fundamental challenges associated with the structure of rural economies and meaningful rights to individually-owned property. Against this view, it is rather curious that the issue of the 'collective' arises time and again when dealing with CBNRM.

4.5.1 Does CBNRM give communities real and effective rights beyond welfare projects that seek to cushion and postpone poverty and property ownership?

There are two important aspects with respect to rights that are derived from policy and associated legislation governing CBNRM in the southern African countries discussed in this chapter. The first is that in order for communities to gain rights legally over natural resources, especially wildlife and forests, they need to fulfil certain conditions, which means that the rights are conditional and dependent on the authority of the state. For example, in the case of Namibia, communities should form a conservancy or Wildlife Council in order to gain legal rights over wildlife and tourism. The second aspect is the recognition that the rights gained on the formation of an organizational structure (village committees in the case of Zimbabwe, Malawi, Zambia and Mozambique; community conservancy in the case of Namibia; community-based organization or a representative and accountable entity in Botswana and a communal property association in the case of South Africa) are limited. In addition, rights are only legally vested in these structures and not more broadly in the rest of the community.

4.5.2 And so what does it mean in practice when rights are conditional and limited?

Long (2004) argues that specific legislations dictate that communities form organizational structures in order to gain rights over natural resources and in order to register the organizational structures there are specific conditions set out in the legislation to be met. In addition to meeting the various and onerous conditions, the regulations accompanying the legislation stipulate that certain specific further conditions be covered in the organizational structure's constitution. Legislation further provides for actions of the organization's management committee to be guided by the constitution that sets out the relationship between the committee and the community members. These limitations and conditionalities apply to Namibia, Botswana, Zimbabwe and South Africa and the rest of the countries implementing CBNRM activities.

Dzingirai (1999) adds that many rural peasants lack full awareness of their basic rights as citizens and participants in community-based natural management. Owing to past repressive governance and, in some instances, ongoing disenfranchisement from policy processes, those who may be aware of their rights fear engaging the state.

The rights conferred on communities are conditional to government officials who can withdraw the rights of the community organization, and the legislation does generally not specify the grounds on which rights can be withdrawn or refused. However, the CBNRM policy and programmes of many communities are rights-based in that the rights and obligations of the community over resources are entrenched in legislation. Although legislation gives 'ownership' of resources to communities and or private players in Namibia and South Africa, it is not entirely accurate in describing the rights actually held. In the case of Botswana and Zimbabwe, legislation however explicitly leases usufruct rights and does not give ownership rights.

For example, ownership of wildlife only confers the right to use a specified number of defined species, and for any other form of utilization a permit or quota is usually required from the respective government ministry. Use of the notion of ownership is however a useful and significant legal tool in the sense that the state alienates the state resources from it and thus removes the need to seek treasury approval every time state property (resources) is used by non-state entities. Any mechanism that removes red tape and place decision-making closer to the resource users is welcome in the capture of resource rights.

The Botswana CBNRM policy confers a range of land tenure and natural resource user rights to communities. Subject to an approved land use and management plan for a specific area to be leased, an annual land rental payable to the Land Authority and a resource utilization royalty payable to the Ministry of Environment, Wildlife and Tourism, communities may obtain a 15-year NRM lease from the relevant Land Authority for commercial use of natural resources. The communities may receive benefits from the use of natural resources and also sub-lease or transfer any commercial natural resource user rights to one or more joint venture partners with prior written permission of the Land Authority. Financial benefits deriving from the sale of natural resources or hunting quotas will see a portion paid to the National Environmental Fund held by the Ministry of Environment, Wildlife and Tourism.

In Botswana, qualifying communities are eligible for natural resource user rights and related benefits derived from such resources within their defined and designated areas. However, to enjoy such user rights, a community must establish a community-based organization as a Representative and Accountable Legal Entity whose performance will be regularly monitored by the community and accountability defined by the existing laws of the land. A community must also comply with the requirements to develop and implement various plans and strategies intended to ensure appropriate and sustainable use of land and natural resources. As discussed earlier in this section, the user rights are limited and subject to a variety of conditions within conditions, and thus making it such an onerous task for communities to access and manage.

Of interest in the context of Botswana CBNRM policy is that when allocating exclusive natural resource user rights, needs of subsistence users residing in the defined geographic area must be recognized and provided for within ecological limits. The allocations should be monitored to determine the limits of subsistence use and commercial exploitation. Official quota setting practices apply where commercial exploitation is identified. It is, however, not clear how commercial and subsistence is distinguished and what mechanism is used to determine the needs and limits of subsistence users and use. As is the case with the rest of the countries, government, as custodian of the land and its resources, retains the ultimate authority to determine, monitor and regulate use and protect the resources, yet another case of nominal rights and the presence of powerful elites with vested interests!

4.6 Land reform constraints on CBNRM

By and large, the conceptualization and implementation of land reform programmes in southern Africa were not premised on a community-based NRM rationale. Redistributive policies and strategies primarily aimed at equity, poverty alleviation or redress of historical injustices are not necessarily the same policies aimed at conservation and sustainable use of natural resources. Concerns of food security and productive agriculture are generally a central basis for most land reform programmes.

Jones (2003) identified the following land reform constraints to CBNRM in the context of Namibia, some of which are generally applicable across the region:

- governance issues are often ignored in new resettlement areas and decision-making is often done by government project managers. There is usually no traditional leadership among the land reform beneficiaries who originate from different backgrounds;
- land reform and resettlement programmes are largely managed in isolation from other ministries that usually support sustainable NRM;

- many resettlement projects are unlikely to be sustainable unless they have been supported for a long period due to lack of skills on the participants and lack of infrastructure;
- in the long term, many resettlement farms are not large enough to sustain the number of people settled on them and any hope of viable resource management depends on cooperation between the residents yet joint resource management institutions are not promoted from the onset;
- the ecological aspect of land reform is often missing and the environmental viability of resettlement projects is usually not investigated, nor is the capability of the land matched to appropriate use.

Against the above background, there is no attention paid to the development of joint decision-making to govern the affairs of the newly resettled or to manage their land and resources.

The post-colonial settlements in the sub-region were dominated by interests of the colonial settler class, resulting in the entrenchment of property protection clauses in many southern African countries' constitutions. The bills of rights of Zimbabwe, Namibia and South Africa have property protection clauses which effectively made land reform a legal and cumbersome process. The protection of property clauses in the respective constitutions employs obscure and legal concepts that give rise to complicated legal disputes and copious and inaccessible academic commentary (Murombedzi 1999; Ng'ong'ola 2004).

As a result, land reform remains unfinished business as it has either been temporarily halted, bogged down by complex concerns over foreign investment or continues on a snail's pace, with the result that the landless are gradually growing impatient or have resorted to self-provision through invasion, squatting or poaching.

Although the Mozambican Land Law 1997 has been hailed as progressive, the land reform process has not fundamentally changed property relations that remain highly unequal and dualistic in nature. Land reform has not delivered significant benefits to the rural population and natural resources remain in the hands of a few elites. Much as the Land Law has offered significant opportunities for alleviating poverty due to its customary rights guarantees and the strengthening of investors' property rights, in practice implementation has been difficult. High value land and valuable natural resources are in high demand and the interests of communities and private enterprises are in perpetual conflict. This has partly been due to delimitation processes that raised high expectations among communities, only to bring few tangible benefits.

Quite often, valuable natural resources are not included in the areas for community delimitation as happened in the Chadzuca and Nhakwanika communities in Manica District where state authorities refused to include the valuable IFLOMA (Manica Forestry Industries) plantation. The plantation will remain in the hands of a private investor even though it is an integral part of the land of the local communities. Similarly, in Macossa District also in Manica Province, Coutada 9 (a hunting area) was zoned rather than delimited, and the largest and lucrative portion remains with the private safari operator whilst the local community controls a buffer zone next to their settlement (Durang and Tanner 2004).

Competition for land and natural resources between locals and outsiders is high despite the clear provisions of the land law. According to the Land Law, communities should be consulted and involved in the negotiations of new private investments, and yet despite the provided mechanisms, in practice, consultations are inadequate and the resulting partnership arrangements are often inappropriate, unequal and with little community benefit. Consultations are rushed to facilitate private sector land rights at the expense of communities. The community groups are often not aware of the legal implications of the agreements they enter into regarding their land.

The power imbalance between the private sector and communities and government does not help the situation much by rushing to allocate forestry licences and concessions without due consideration to the details of community involvement and understanding. As a result, millions of hectares of land have been allocated to private entities for agriculture, livestock, forestry and human activities without meaningfully engaging communities. For example, white Zimbabwean and South African farmers have been allocated huge tracts of land under long leaseholds. Long history of resource extraction by colonialists, rebel movements, party officials, the private sector and the state has seen few benefits accruing to the rural poor (Manjengwa 2006).

Tenure laws and policies in Namibia, South Africa and Mozambique provide for communities, associations and individuals to register as legal entities that can own land in their own right. However, the key issue with land administration is the extent to which official sanctions apply to different forms of tenure. CBNRM initiatives on communal lands where communities rely on natural resources tend to be affected by the dysfunction of local-level management, lack of power to regulate access by outsiders and insecure tenure over communal land.

When CBNRM participants access more and better quality land or diversify into non-farm income and services, they tend to move away from CBNRM-dependent livelihoods and group-based arrangements into private livelihood options where they make individual decisions and are not subjected to group processes. CBNRM activities also tend to be concentrated in marginal lands with the least access to water infrastructures and markets.

In contexts where property rights have been conferred to individuals such as owners of wild resources on private land, this has served as an incentive for the owners to manage the resources effectively. This has been the case with wildlife and agro-tourism on private land. At least 10 per cent of the total land area is under private game farming in South Africa, at least 50 per cent in Namibia and 5 per cent in Zambia. It is the success of private land ownership that has motivated the extension of the same model into rural areas under CBNRM. Unfortunately, there has not been a comparable transition of strong property rights to own, use and dispose productive resources in the communal areas.

Organizationally, communal areas are complex entities with the result that there are separate laws and policies dealing with the management of wild resources on public, private and communal lands and, for as long as land reform does not tackle these issues, the CBNRM constraints remain. The dualistic approach that is present in the formal and informal economic spheres and commercial and subsistence farming sectors is replicated in the treatment of private versus communal land and thus undermining the potential of CBNRM. The nature of land and resource distribution presents a major challenge for CBNRM in this regard.

4.6.1 Land administration: the missing link

The reviewed land reform literature alludes to the big challenges of land reform across southern Africa and yet few authors critically analyze the weaknesses in land administration and causes of slow implementation in the current land reform programmes. Land administration is at the heart of land policy and almost in all countries the state has been accused of irresponsible land delivery.

Land administration systems in southern Africa, and beyond, have generally failed to perform the functions they were designed for. With the exception of Botswana where land administration was addressed 30 years ago, land administration remains incidental in many countries. Land reform in South Africa and Namibia is very slow in implementation due to a number of structural, policy and technical challenges, namely land market constraints, weak capacity or reluctance to navigate the administrative and political machinery of market transactions, market power and influence of the elites holding the land, high land prices for good quality land, delays in processing and resolution of land claims, inadequate funds for land acquisition and support.

According to Okoth-Ogendo (in SARPN undated), land administration comprises five components, namely: conflict resolution, fiscal, cadastral, juridical and regulatory. A central feature for most of the post-settler societies is that the juridical and regulatory components, while highly rated in the standards and quality of implementation, they were designed to serve minority interests that hold property. South Africa has gone furthest in its attempts to redress past legislation that was racially imbalanced, but implementation has been painstakingly slow and very little progress has been achieved in making regulatory and cadastral functions affordable for the majority. The attributes and premise that supported large-scale capital intensive farming of the past is difficult to extend to the poor because of limited land delivery services and steep costs.

For the 'non-settled' state, government inherited limited skills and public infrastructure at independence, and in some cases whatever capital existed was destroyed by internal strife. Therefore there is need to redesign land administration functions with a simplified legal framework, user-friendly dispute handling and better business practices. Responsible land administration should be community-based and citizen-led in order to decentralize land administration to the local level.

Land policy development that is delivery-based should consider what is practical and able to be done in terms of the legal and regulatory mechanisms because in many cases, impractical land policy has resulted from legal tools that were not designed to deliver the desired and appropriate approaches.

4.7 Role for CBNRM in land reform

The resettlement model of land reform was implemented in Namibia, Zimbabwe and Mozambique and resulted in some challenges. Resettlement often meant uprooting resource-poor and unskilled people and placing them on pieces of land that were either too small or environmentally unsuited for more than subsistence living. They were also usually resettled in areas with no social services, market and physical infrastructures, and with no decision-making in governing the affairs of the resettled or to manage their land and natural resources. In several ways, the resettlement schemes have considerable potential for promoting sustainable use of land and natural resources given the number of people on these schemes is usually quite small. They have defined, accepted and enforceable rights to the land and have opportunities to gain rights over other resources through sectoral legislation and policies.

Under resettlement schemes are clear land and resource boundaries and those that have a right to use the land and resources are clearly defined. Quite often, the adverse environmental conditions require cooperation between residents in the resettlement schemes to ensure sustainable natural resource use. The cooperation could be easily achieved through land use zoning into managing grazing land, farmland, timber products, water and other services. Cooperation may, however not be easily fostered among the newly resettled given they would have no prior history of working together and may have different ethnic backgrounds.

In southern Namibia, the Oskop conservancy provides an illustrative point with regards to the potential of resettlement scheme. The conservancy was the first to be registered in a resettlement scheme and is quite different from most conservancies in the country. The conservancy is small (9,573 hectares) and was previously a freehold farm bought to consolidate a communal area under the colonial homeland policy. The conservancy had 14 households and 120 people and lacked significant wildlife resources and other tourist attractions. Livestock farming is the mainstay of the local economy whilst wildlife constitutes additional income for the community. Local-level institutional development evolved and saw the water point committee merging with the conservancy management committee and jointly administering conservancy affairs, controlling the resettlement of farmers, water management, use and allocation of land through an agreement reached with the Witbooi Traditional Authority, which is the custodian of the land. Members of the committee feel that having such authority has localized land management and reduced competition for land between farmers, livestock and wildlife (Jones 2003).

Conservancy development in Namibia has generally been accompanied by well-developed and specific support to local communities, including institutional development, governance, capacity building in committee and financial management, wildlife monitoring and negotiating with the private sector. The same approach and support would be required by most land reform resettlement scheme beneficiaries. With lessons and the experience from Oskop conservancy, land reform programmes in Namibia and other countries in the region can be replicated. It would be inadequate for government to resettle people without addressing issues of how the land and its resources would be managed and used, and how the resettled people can run their affairs.

There is also a substantial role for CBNRM to provide a scope and tool for formulating land reform policy prior to the resettlement stage, through planning and redistributive stages to sustain livelihoods. CBNRM can also be potentially used as an effective tool to lobby for tenure reform through establishing conservancies and eco-tourism enterprises, which in turn provide an institutional framework for strengthening land claims and establishing natural resource rights. Given the increasing clamour for environmentalism and pro-poor rights-based policy, CBNRM has the potential to spur on a regional social movement that will capture resource rights for the grassroots.

In the case of South Africa, where land reform provides for land claims and restitution in policy and legislation, there is scope for integrating CBNRM and land reform as was the case in Makuleke, Mkambati and Richtersveld, notwithstanding the challenges and 'forced' partnership that have resulted in Dracula tendencies to swallow the community through conditions and limitations imposed by the state. Similarly, traditional authorities can facilitate tenure reform by asserting community resource rights on mineral wealth, securing agreements with the state and claiming royalty income rights from or partnering with mining companies engaged in mineral resources extraction found on tribal and community land. Through such arrangements, community-based NRM initiatives can be undertaken to address poverty, sustainable livelihoods and community development.

4.8 Issues for thought

There are important issues and lessons emerging from the survey of literature on land rights, tenure arrangements and the implications for CBNRM in southern Africa, and the following are some to ponder.

The first issue concerns the dependence of CBNRM on primary utilization of natural resources that limits the choices available to communities. Beyond CBNRM, there is need for a broad comprehensive and diverse rural development strategy that encompasses social, economic and political development and takes into account secondary activities in value addition.

Second, there is a need to continue rethinking and in some instances revisiting the appropriateness of the current institutional arrangements for reforming, claiming or capturing and then maintaining resource rights by the resource-poor communities, delivery mechanisms and the administrative capacity to promote downward accountability and representation of poor classes in order to protect their land and resource rights.

The third issue concerns decision making over the allocation of rights and the accompanying resources. In our view, it is crucial that mechanisms for determining who should decide on what and which rights go to who, be further investigated and built into resource, peace and security policies within community and national organizations. The role of the state and traditional authority institutions in formulating rules and mediating over tenure and resource rights requires ongoing scrutiny to determine relevance and need for creative alternatives.

Fourth, the CBNRM programmes in southern Africa have been severely constrained by the failure to adequately address resource rights. In order to be successful, maybe CBNRM should be complemented by appropriate national policies, political and administrative decentralization and devolution of authority over natural resources, and supported by the development of rights for such change.

Fifth, the degree to which a CBNRM initiative is imposed, assisted or organic largely depends on the specific role of the stakeholders involved. Hence, the multiplicity of stakeholders, that is NGOs, the private sector, donors, the state and communities should be recognized and their respective roles fully addressed in practice.

The sixth issue hinges on the big question of whether partnerships and CBNRM are feasible without addressing the issues of inequity with respect to land and other key resources. In addition to this is the issue of rights and obligations of communities over land and natural resources. Currently, community rights are limited by the rights of other users and institutions, including the state.

Seventh, current CBNRM policies tend to favour community benefits over individual benefits thereby reducing the effectiveness and poverty alleviation effect of CBNRM and creating the risk that individual households are not motivated to get involved in sustainable natural resources and land management. Much as it is necessary to mobilize community participation, people could be more committed on an individual level of ownership where use rights are clear and well defined for accruing benefits to individuals, as is the case in Malawi and Botswana where CBNRM projects on veld and forest products provide higher incentives and members are rewarded in proportion to their inputs.

Eighth, capacity building of local institutions for sustainable land and NRM is crucial for CBNRM, given that the projects need long-term and continuous support to be successful. Older community organizations generally seem to perform better than young ones.

Ninth, there is the need for documenting the impacts of CBNRM on the degradation status of the resource base and preventing desertification as well as the environmental benefits in order to integrate CBNRM in holistic land management where appropriate and challenge land reform mindsets. There is also the need for documentation, dissemination and learning from cases regarding the importance of CBNRM in promoting local-level governance and political organization at community level in order to improve governance of natural resources.

Finally, it would be necessary to devise strategies for bridging policy, legislation and practice between land tenure and CBNRM, which is critical.

4.9 Conclusion

In conclusion, the role of land and other resource rights is central to the development of many communities and unequal distribution of resource rights has often been a cause or precipitation for conflicts as shown in Zimbabwe (over land, wildlife and forestry resources), South Africa (over land, fisheries, veld products such as hoodia and minerals) and Botswana. Among other factors, equitable resource rights could therefore play a role in building social cohesion, stability and peaceful co-existence in communities.

In order to secure and maintain the security of community resource rights, there is the need for comprehensive and inclusive tenure reforms. With respect to tenure security, there arises the need to clearly distinguish customary tenure and rights from statutory tenure and rights in land reform processes. There is still an important role for customary tenure in land and resource rights among rural and traditional communities of virtually all the southern African countries discussed, especially because it is a potential solution for landlessness and resource rights struggles in the region. The colonial distortion of many traditional customary practices and systems requires and necessitates further investigation of the optimal role of customary tenure.

Under international law, states represent important property rights holders and are granted sovereignty over their natural resources. For this reason, states are in a strong position as local and international grantors and guarantors of resource/property rights. Besides, states can also own, control and use natural resources in their own right or through any of their administrative structures or grant user rights to preferred beneficiaries.

Social movements and other non-states actors are emerging as important players for agitating, lobbying and even capturing of important political space and community rights through land occupation and resource capture. These outfits often act within and outside policy in their rapid response, and many times have led the state, as opposed to following it, on radical policy shifts. Examples of radical social movements that have brought about resource rights policy shifts and champion the cause of the poor are Via Campesina and the Masifundise Development Trust. Given the slow pace of land reform in Namibia and South Africa, and resource enclosure by the powerful elites in other contexts, maybe an emergence of more radical local social movements as has been witnessed in Nigeria's Niger Delta and self-styled war veterans in Zimbabwe or sophisticated abalone poachers in South Africa's Western Cape province could be an undesirable, but logical, option if the state does not effectively respond to and resolve long-standing resource rights demands.

The evolution of CBNRM policy has been issue-based, largely premised on wildlife or some other high-valued resource, and proved effective in the short term. However, the issue-based approach has its limitations in that it neglects the complex interaction between different aspects of the environment. An integrated CBNRM approach that encompasses all resources, guaranteed full tenure rights and management capacity, among other factors, is necessary.

As argued in this chapter, despite the land and tenure reform programmes and new natural resource laws and rights, the exclusive land and resource rights of the poor remain under threat from inappropriate policies and institutional arrangements. The unequal socio-economic and political relations and the actions of powerful vested interests as well as the weakness of community or grassroots organizations continue unabated. Colonialism and institutionalized racism may have ended, but segregation remains deeply entrenched, occasioned by the same economic and political hegemonic development models that cater for the rural and the urban, the poor and the rich, and between men and women with consequences for the marginalized and downtrodden.

Notes

1 The United Nations Institute for Namibia (UNIN) defines cooperatives as higher forms of political and economic organization in which the means of production are owned collectively and used for the benefit of the community as a whole.
2 Collective production is an organization of agricultural production in which the holdings of several farmers are run as a joint enterprise. A collective farm is essentially an agricultural production cooperative in which members-owners engage jointly in farming activities.

Bibliography

Benjaminsen, T., Cousins, B. and Thomson, L. (eds) (2002) *Contested Resources: Challenges to the Governance of Natural Resources in southern Africa* (Cape Town: Programme for Land and Agrarian Studies, University of the Western Cape).

Corbett, A. and Daniels, C. (1996) *Legislation and Policies Affecting Community-Based Natural Resources Management in Namibia* (Windhoek: University of Namibia).

Cousins, B. and Classens, A. (2004) 'Communal Land Rights, Democracy and Traditional Leaders in post-apartheid South Africa', in M. Saruchera (ed) *Securing Land and Resource Rights in Africa: Pan-African Perspectives* (Cape Town: Programme for Land and Agrarian Studies, University of the Western Cape).

Curtis, M. (2008) *Precious Metal: The Impact of Anglo Platinum on Poor Communities in Limpopo, South Africa* (Johannesburg: Action Aid and the Netherlands Institute in South Africa).

Durang, T. and Tanner, C. (2004) 'Access to Land and Other Natural Resources for Local Communities in Mozambique: Current Examples from Manica Province', Green Agric Net Conference on Land Registration in Practice, Denmark, 1–2 April.

Dzingirai, V. (1999) 'Land Reform and Community-Based Natural Resource Management', *Common Property Resource Digest*, 50, on file with author.

Dzingirai, V. and Breen, C. (2005) *Confronting the Crisis in Community Conservation: Case Studies from Southern Africa* (Pietermaritzburg: University of KwaZulu Natal).

Fakir, S. (1998) 'Is Community-based Natural Resource Management Possible Without Land Reform? Some Issues for Consideration', paper on file with author.

Government of Botswana (2006) *Draft Community-Based Natural Resources Management Policy* (Gaborone: Ministry of Environment, Wildlife and Tourism).

Government of Malawi (2000) *Land Policy of the Republic of Malawi* (Blantyre: Ministry of Lands, Housing, Physical Planning and Surveys).

International Resource Group (2008) *Creating Synergies Between Community-Based Natural Resources Management and the United Nations Convention to Combat Desertification (UNCCD):*

Lessons Learned from a Regional CBNRM Assessment in the Southern African Region (New York, NY: United Nations Commission on Sustainable Development).

Jones, B. (2003) *Selected Natural Resources Management and Limited Rural Development Assessment Report* (Windhoek: USAID/Namibia Programme Strategy for 2004–2010).

Jones, B. T. B. and Murphree, M. W. (2004) 'Community based natural resource management (CBNRM) as a conservation mechanism: Lessons and Directions', in B. Child (ed) *Parks in Transition: Conservation, Development and the Bottom Line* (London: Earthscan).

Katerere, Y. (2002) 'Community-Public-Private Partnerships in CBNRM: The Real Challenges', in T. Benjaminsen, B. Cousins and L. Thomson (eds) *Contested Resources: Challenges to the Governance of Natural Resources in southern Africa* (Cape Town: Programme for Land and Agrarian Studies, University of the Western Cape).

Kepe, T. (1998) *The Problem of Defining 'Community': Challenges for the Land Reform Programme in Rural South Africa* (Cape Town: Programme for Land and Agrarian Studies, University of Western Cape).

Lahiff, E. (2003) *Land and Livelihoods: The Politics of Land Reform in Southern Africa* (Brighton: Institute of Development Studies).

Leach, M., Mearns, R. and Scoones, I. (1999) 'Environmental Entitlements: Dynamics and Institutions in Community-based Natural Resources Management', *World Development*, 27(2): 225–47.

Long, S. A. (ed) (2004) *Livelihoods and CBNRM in Namibia: The Findings of the WILD Project*, Final Technical Report (Windhoek: Ministry of Environment and Tourism).

Manjengwa, J. (2006) 'Natural Resource Management and Land Reform in southern Africa', Commons Southern Africa, Occasional Paper Series No 15 (Harare/Cape Town: CASS/PLAAS).

Marongwe, N. (2000) *A Review of Existing Policy/Framework for Management of Land, Forests, Water and Fisheries in Mozambique, Zambia and Zimbabwe*, Report for IUCN-Regional Office for the Southern Africa Networking and Capacity Building Project (Harare: IUCN).

Marongwe, N. (2004) 'Land and Resource Rights in Southern Africa', in M. Saruchera (ed) *Securing Land and Resource Rights in Africa: Pan-African Perspectives* (Cape Town: Programme for Land and Agrarian Studies, University of the Western Cape).

Metcalfe, S. and Kepe, T. (2008) 'Dealing land in the midst of poverty: Commercial access to communal land in Zambia', *African and Asian Studies*, 7: 235–57.

Moyo, S. (2000a) *Neo-Liberal Policy Perspectives: The Major Constraint to Land Redistribution Programmes* (Harare: Southern African Regional Institute for Policy Studies (SARIPS)).

Moyo, S. (2000b) *Land Reform under Structural Adjustment in Zimbabwe: Land Use Change in the Mashonaland Province* (Uppsala: Nordiska Afrikainstitutet).

Murombedzi, J. (1999) 'Land Expropriation, Communal Tenure and Common Property Resource Management in southern Africa', Common Property Resource Digest Number 50 (Bloomington, IN: International Association for the Study of Common Property).

Ng'ong'ola, C. (2004) 'Constitutional Protection of property and contemporary land problems in Southern Africa', in M. Saruchera (ed) *Securing Land and Resource Rights in Africa: Pan-African Perspectives* (Cape Town: Programme for Land and Agrarian Studies, University of the Western Cape).

Norfolk, S. and Tanner, C. (2006) *Mozambique Country Case Study on Improving Tenure Security for the Poor* (Maputo: Food and Agriculture Organization).

Ntsebeza, L. (1999) *Land Tenure Reform in South Africa: An Example from the Eastern Cape Province* (London: IIED).

Quan, J. (2000) 'Land Boards as a Mechanism for the Management of Land Rights in southern Africa', in C. Toulmin and J. Quan (eds) *Evolving Land Rights, Policy and Tenure in Africa* (London: International Institute for Environment and Development).
Saruchera, M. (ed) (2004) *Securing Land and Resource Rights in Africa: Pan-African Perspectives* (Cape Town: Programme for Land and Agrarian Studies, University of the Western Cape).
Shackleton, S. and Campbell, B. (2000) 'Re-empowering Communities to Manage Natural Resources: Where does the Power Lie? Case Studies from southern Africa' (unpublished paper).
Simuunza, I. (1999) *An Analysis of Policy and Legislation Governing Selected Natural Resources in Zambia*, A Report for the Zimbabwe Environmental Research Organisation/IUCN Regional Office for Southern Africa (Harare: Zimbabwe Environmental Research Organisation/IUCN Regional Office for Southern Africa).
Southern African Regional Poverty Network (SARPN) (undated) *Integrating Land Issues and Land Policy with Poverty Reduction and Rural Development in Southern Africa* (Pretoria: SARPN).
Whiteside, M. (1998) *Living Farms: Encouraging Sustainable Smallholders in Southern Africa* (London: Earthscan).
WWF Southern Africa Regional Programme Office (2006) *Regional Community-Based Natural Resource Management Capacity Building Project, Southern Africa*, Final Project Report 2003–5 (Harare: unpublished document).

Websites

<http://www.affirm.dk/unite/docs/press_statement_111206.html> (accessed June 2008).
<http://www.compass-malawi.com> (accessed June 2008).

5 The land question in southern Africa

A political economy perspective

Edward Lahiff

5.1 Introduction

As clearly demonstrated by the other contributions to this volume, the 'land question' continues to be a major political, economic and social issue within virtually all the countries of southern Africa and, in recent years, has become a priority for the formal structures of the Southern African Development Community (SADC) as well. At the outset, however, it should be said that no single 'land question' can capture the wide range of conditions prevailing in the region, but rather a set of interconnected questions with strong regional commonalities but also distinct national and local characteristics.

Central to these questions are the shared history of colonialism and widespread dispossession of indigenous populations, as well as the continuing centrality of agriculture and other land-based livelihoods to the economy of the region. Tanzania, for example, depends on agriculture for 42.5 per cent of its gross domestic product (GDP) and 80 per cent of employment, among the highest rates in the world; at the other end of the regional spectrum, South Africa depends on agriculture for just 3.2 per cent of its GDP and 10.3 per cent of its employment.[1] The racial imbalance in landholding that has persisted long after the formal ending of settler-colonialism in countries such as Zimbabwe, Namibia and South Africa, and attempts to address it, have been the most prominent expression of the land question in the region. Other key questions persist, however, even in those countries where farmers of settler origin are no longer a significant presence. These include the question of how to broaden access to land in the context of growing populations and enduring poverty (heavily concentrated in the rural areas). Also, how to balance the drive for a modern, export-oriented and efficient agricultural sector that contributes to macro-economic development with the livelihood and food security needs of the rural population, especially smallholders. Finding the appropriate balance between private enterprise and State intervention and support especially in the eras of structural adjustment and neo-liberalism, presents particular challenges for the region. And finally, how to deal with the millions of households being squeezed out of the agricultural economy and facing an uncertain future in urban and peri-urban areas – what Bernstein (2002) has aptly termed 'the agrarian question of labour'.

Despite the enduring importance of these issues for the region, the nature of the 'land question' (or, more accurately, land *questions*) has also evolved over time, as has the political importance attached to them. Land featured prominently in independence struggles across Africa from the 1950s to the 1970s but the first wave of post-colonial land reforms effectively came to an end with the downturn in the global economy of the mid-1970s and the subsequent imposition of severe structural adjustment programmes in the 1980s. Land reform came back onto the political agenda in the 1990s, as South Africa, always something of an exception to continental and regional norms, attempted to address its extreme mal-distribution of land by constitutional, and market-based, methods, and more forcibly with the adoption of 'fast-track' land reform in Zimbabwe from 2000. Elsewhere in the region, the era of neoliberal globalization has led to a general effort to commercialize both agriculture and land itself, through privatization of assets, deregulation of agricultural markets (including land markets) and a roll-back in State involvement in the sector. Nonetheless, varieties of 'tribal', 'communal' or 'traditional' land tenure continue to define large areas of many countries and – while central to the livelihoods of much of the rural population – are often seen by commentators and policy makers as peripheral to, or even incompatible with, the modern economy, leading to numerous long-running (but largely inconclusive) attempts at reform.

The importance attached to land questions, and related questions of the wider agricultural and rural economy, have also fluctuated considerably over the years, both at the level of national governments and within regional institutions such as SADC. In recent years a number of factors have combined to ensure a relatively high level of attention – these include ongoing political instability in Zimbabwe, the food price shock of 2008 and growing international interest in acquiring land in the region for production of both food and biofuels for export.

The importance attached to land – and to the 'land question' – within SADC can be seen in numerous official statements of which the following extract from the official communiqué after the SADC meeting of Ministers Responsible for Land Affairs in Johannesburg in March 2008 is a good example:

> Ministers reaffirmed the centrality of land in the social and economic development of the region and in poverty reduction initiatives and stressed the need to accord prominence to land issues at the regional level. They also noted the complexity and diversity of land issues in the region due to historical differences. The other problems relate to insecurity of tenure, gender imbalances in access to and ownership of land, land utilization and low capacities of land administration institutions. Ministers noted that Member States are at different stages of formulating or implementing reforms to address the problems in line with their national development priorities.
>
> (SADC 2008)

This official emphasis on the importance of land matters is matched by, and at times exceeded, by numerous local struggles over resources that persist despite fluctuations in official policy, but also contribute – through pressure 'from below' – to keeping land issues on the political agenda. This chapter explores the variety of land questions in southern Africa from both a historical and a contemporary perspective. It identifies a number of broad currents that are shaping the land-based economy in the region and driving contemporary political debates and struggles around land and natural resources more generally.

5.2 The legacy of settler-colonialism

A central element of the European colonization of Africa was the alienation of land from the indigenous population. This did not occur to any appreciable extent during the age of mercantilism and the slave trade, but gathered pace in the late nineteenth century as competition between the European powers accelerated the race for control of commodities and territory. Across much of the continent, particularly the French, Belgian, and Portuguese colonies, and the English colonies of West Africa, this meant coercing the indigenous population into production of commodities for the European market, notably cocoa, palm oil and cotton, using both economic and extra-economic means. This was often accompanied by seizure of the best quality lands for establishment of large European plantations. Only in a minority of colonies, however, were European settlers established on a large scale – most notably in Algeria and Kenya and across southern Africa. The introduction of large numbers of European settler-farmers (as opposed to just soldiers or administrators) led to large-scale land dispossession and a range of coercive labour practices, as well as prolonging the struggle for independence in some instances.

Today's SADC region was at the heart of settler-colonialism and, not surprisingly, demands for the return of land to the indigenous population constituted an important element within anti-colonial struggles of the 1950s, 1960s and 1970s. Post-independence, agrarian reform was a widespread priority, but progress in this regard varied greatly.

Immediate post-liberation agrarian reforms took a variety of directions, depending on the prevailing economic conditions and the ideological orientation of the liberation movement and new regimes. In countries where white settlers had caused the greatest dispossession of native people, as in Zambia and Zimbabwe, and further afield in Kenya, redistribution of commercial farmland was a priority. In countries such as Mozambique, where large estates were central to the economy, a policy of continued operation of the estates as state farms or collectives was pursued.

Reform of indigenous, or customary, land tenure, was not as important in southern Africa at this time as it was in the newly independent countries of west and central Africa – a process which had begun in many countries during the colonial period but accelerated following independence. By far the most radical agrarian change in the first decade of independence was what occurred in Tanzania, as all private-property rights in land were extinguished immediately following independence and replaced with occupancy rights, prior to the further wave of collectivization that occurred under the banner of *ujamaa* (Bruce 1993). Nothing on a comparable scale occurred in the south or east of the continent until the overthrow of the Emperor in Ethiopia 1974, when all land was nationalized and distributed amongst peasant associations, and the coming to power of radical Marxist regimes in the former Portuguese colonies of Angola and Mozambique.

Despite this variety of experience, however, there was remarkable continuity between land policies in the colonial and post-colonial periods. Okoth-Ogendo (1993: 262) argues that irrespective of the ideological and other preferences of independence elites, the normative and institutional parameters defined by colonialism did not change: 'Continuity was the rule, rather than the exception'.

Most African countries gained their independence during the 1950s and 1960s, the period that Bernstein (2002) describes as the high point of 'developmentalism', when emphasis was placed on the role of the State as manager of national development (including State-led agriculture and rural development) and the eradication of poverty. The aim was the extension and intensification of commodity production, which was to be achieved by the 'modernization' of agriculture, which often included efforts to redistribute land and wider programmes of rural development.

The downturn in the global economy from 1973 brought an end to this period of State-led development, specifically the economic structural adjustment programmes promoted by the World Bank and the International Monetary Fund which peaked in the 1980s in response to widespread debt and fiscal crises. State expenditure in many countries was dramatically reduced (or at least redirected) in Africa as in the rest of the developing world, markets were liberalized and State agencies responsible for both agricultural production and distribution were either closed down or privatized. In other words, the key pillars of State-led development and regulation were systematically removed, not just in pro-western economies but also in nominally socialist-oriented economies such as Tanzania and Zimbabwe.

Agrarian reform returned to the political agenda internationally, including southern Africa, in the 1990s, but in a new market-oriented form. A number of reasons can be put forward for the renewed interest in agrarian issues: changes in the international economy ('globalization'), changes in the international political climate (most notably, the fall of Soviet communism and the end of the Cold War), and the persistence of extreme poverty and inequality in much of the developing world, particularly in the rural areas. These 'new wave' land reforms, promoted by multilateral institutions such as the World Bank, the Food and Agriculture Organization of the United Nations (FAO) and the International Fund for Agricultural Development (IFAD), have largely replaced the centralized, bureaucratic and confiscatory approaches of the past with a new emphasis on decentralization, negotiation and markets. Critics, particularly on the left, point to the very limited gains made by such policies in Africa, Asia and Latin America, and question the ability of the market to bring about the kind of fundamental restructuring of power and wealth traditionally associated with interventionist States (or popular revolutions).

In line with wider trends in the developing world, the spectrum of land reforms in Africa has narrowed greatly since 1990, with the focus now being largely on tenure reforms (effectively, individualization of communal or traditional lands), some restitution of ancestral lands (largely symbolic at this stage) and very modest redistribution of large-scale commercial farms (via the market) to selected beneficiaries – generally those deemed capable of 'commercial' production, either individually or as part of a group. This is heavily influenced by the recommendations of the World Bank, that continue to emphasize a framework of secure, transparent and enforceable property rights as the critical precondition for investment and economic growth (Quan 2000: 38; Deininger 2003). The exceptions are a small number of countries undergoing market-based redistribution and Zimbabwe, which has rejected the new international orthodoxy.

Nationalization of land and collectivization of agricultural production have virtually disappeared from the agenda, due to their perceived negative political and economic implication. The break up of large estates has also virtually ceased due to perceived difficulties in shifting from large- to small-scale production and from waged to family labour, but also due to growing support for private property rights and political marginalization of peasant movements in many countries. 'Land to the tiller', generally considered to be the most successful model of land reform in the past century, has also dropped off the agenda, due largely to the disappearance of rentier landlords in most parts of the world.

Palmer (2000) outlines some of the key characteristics of land reform in sub-Saharan Africa in the 1990s, and contrasts these with the approaches taken in preceding decades. Of particular importance have been the involvement of a relatively wide range of actors (State and non-State) and popular participation in the reform process, which can be related to the expansion of civil society following the end of the Cold War and the growth of multi-party democracy. Leading examples would be the Uganda Land Alliance and the Mozambican Land Campaign, which each played a key role in bringing about revised land policies in their respective countries (Negrão 1999). In addition, Palmer identifies a greater involvement by agencies from outside the continent, in the form of donors and technical expertise.

Thus, agrarian reform continues to be relevant across much of Africa, but particularly in the former settler colonies of southern Africa. While conditions vary considerably from country to country, a number of broad themes can be identified that provide a common context for the politics of land across the region. First is the shared history of colonialism, and with it the dispossession and impoverishment of rural people, which shapes both patterns of landholding and discourses around the value of different types of land use. Second is the growing impact of neoliberal globalization, in terms of both direct influences on agriculture and rural economies generally and on the policies being promoted by national governments and international agencies. Of particular importance here are the deregulation of markets, the withdrawal of State support to agricultural producers and the reliance on the private sector as the principal agent of development. Third is the ongoing impoverishment of the mass of the rural population and the extreme precariousness of rural livelihoods. High rates of unemployment, poor returns to small-scale agriculture, lack of access to social services such as health and education, recurring drought and a rampant (and largely unaddressed) HIV/AIDS pandemic serve to erode existing livelihood activities and perpetuate relative and absolute poverty in rural areas. Last is the re-emergence of the rural poor as political actors, to varying degrees throughout the region.

Official land reform programmes are, however, just one dimension of ongoing changes in land access and property rights in the SADC region. Developments in local, regional and global economies impose multiple pressures on rural livelihoods, particularly of poorer households, while new opportunities are created for a small minority, both existing farmers and new entrants to the agricultural sector. Staple food crops continue to dominate production, both in terms of self-provisioning by small households and supply to regional markets by larger-scale producers. Producers of a limited range of high-value crops and animal products, some old and some new, exploit niche export markets, with access to lucrative markets in the European Union and elsewhere becoming gradually more liberal for SADC producers.

Such developments continue the long-run process of differentiation among farmers in the region, making it impossible to speak of a 'typical' African farm household. Exodus from the land continues apace across the region, contributing to the major public policy challenges of mushrooming urban slums and informal settlements, pressure on social services such as health and education, and problems of crime and security. Despite various attempts by policy makers to address the property rights of women, ranging from the substantial to the purely rhetorical, women throughout much of southern Africa continue to experience inferior rights to those of men in their communities (Whitehead and Tsikata 2003; Manji 2006).

To the range of staple food crops and older cash crops such as cotton has recently been added a range of crops – jatropha, sugar cane and sweet sorghum – produced specially for manufacture of biofuels. Demand for land for cultivation of biofuel crops has been accompanied by acquisition of massive tracts of land for a new wave of food crop production by international investors, including State agencies, not for the open market but for direct supply to consumer and processors in countries such as China and Saudi Arabia, giving rise to concerns about large-scale 'land grabs'. The following section looks at how these and other processes are shaping the political economy of land in southern Africa today.

5.3 Contemporary land questions

Over the past decade, pressures from within and outside the region have pushed official land policy in SADC countries in a number of directions: most notably various attempts at large-scale redistribution of land from large/white/rich to small/black/poor households, as in Zimbabwe and South Africa; the commercialization/modernization of the agricultural sector through granting of large concessions to commercial operators, and reform of various forms of traditional and communal tenure, for example, in Mozambique in 1997, Tanzania in 1999, South

Africa and Angola in 2004. These and related areas are discussed in more detail below.

5.3.1 Redistribution of land

Given the history of settler colonialism, and the alienation of significant portions of the indigenous population from the land, one might expect the redistribution of land from white to black occupiers (or owners) to be the dominant agrarian policy issue in the southern African region. For extended periods, however, the issue has lain relatively dormant, punctuated by occasional bouts of frenetic activity, along a number of distinct lines.

In the Lusophone colonies of Angola and Mozambique, the violent overthrow of the Portuguese administration was accompanied by the rapid departure of virtually all European landholders and the nationalization of land by the incoming revolutionary Marxist regimes of the FNLA and Frelimo. Large estates and irrigated colonies, typically situated on the best agricultural lands, were converted to State-owned cooperatives or collective farms, with little or no attempt to restore land to the pre-colonial occupiers or, in many cases, the adjoining communities (Bowen 2000; O'Laughlin 1996; Clover 2005).

War in both countries led to widespread displacement of people and communities, as well as major disruptions to the agrarian economy, further weakening the link between many people and the land while creating opportunities for accumulation by powerful elites, including both party loyalists and traditional leaders (chiefs). With the gradual retreat from Marxist economic policies and the liberalization of landholding, beginning in the early 1990s, a range of foreign and domestic 'investors' (typically described as such whether or not they actually have capital to invest) have gained access to substantial tracts of land and other natural resources, noticeably grazing and forestry, in the form of either use rights to specific parcels of land or concessions to extract resources over a wide area, issued by a range of local and national government agencies (Norfolk et al 2002; Foley 2007). Thus, rather than redistribution of resources from rich to poor, both Angola and Mozambique have witnessed ongoing struggles by the rural poor (peasants) to gain access to land and defend their existing resources in the face of pressure from powerful State and private-sector interests (Hanlon 2002). In Angola, this has been particularly concentrated in areas of urban expansion around Luanda; in Mozambique, the greatest contestation has been in deep rural areas such as Zambezia, where the struggle is over access to rich cultivation, grazing and timber resources.

In the former British colonies of Zimbabwe (formerly Southern Rhodesia) and South Africa and, by extension, Namibia (formerly South-West Africa), the revolution in landholding at the time of independence was much less thorough-going and the great majority of European landholders retained their property into the democratic era. Incoming governments in all three countries eschewed outright confiscation or nationalization of land and embarked on a variety of conciliatory approaches to redistribution, with modest targets and compensation for landowners. Zimbabwe in the 1980s, Namibia after 1992 and South Africa from 1994 all followed this model, with mixed results. It was Zimbabwe, somewhat ironically, where the State was most constrained (by the terms of the Lancaster House Agreement[2] that granted strong protections to landholders for a period of ten years) that made the most significant achievements in the immediate post-independence period. Some 52,000 households were resettled on 2.7 million hectares by 1989, rising to 71,000 households on 3.5 million hectares of land by 1996, representing one-fifth of land in the hands of White commercial farmers at independence (Palmer 1990; Moyo 1995; Kinsey 1999).

This early Zimbabwean experience contrasts starkly with the very limited achievements of Namibia and South Africa. Both these countries, unencumbered by externally imposed constraints, voluntarily adopted 'market-based' approaches to redistribution of land which granted generous compensation to landholders and, more importantly, an effective veto on their participation in the programme.[3] In South Africa, the so-called 'willing-seller, willing-buyer' approach has yielded minimal volumes of land for redistribution: by September 2009, just three million hectares (approximately 3.6 per cent) of agricultural land had been transferred to 186,000 beneficiaries (Greenberg 2010: 4). Apart from the slow pace of land transfer, widespread concerns have been raised to the effect that much redistributed land is not being used effectively and the extent to which the rural poor and landless are benefiting under the programme (Lahiff 2007).

A feature of the South African land reform programme – unique in the region – is the policy of restitution, which seeks to return land to its former owners or occupiers, on an individual or communal basis, although limited to land lost since 1913. To date, approximately 2.6 million hectares have been restored to thousands of beneficiaries, with thousands more opting for cash compensation in lieu of land (Greenberg 2010). Due to its rights-based approach, restitution has been far more successful than the market-based redistribution programme in reaching a wide variety of beneficiaries, both poor and better-off, and in acquiring the land that people actually want. Otherwise, it has suffered from many of the same problems that have plagued the redistribution programme, namely land of external support for new landholders, inappropriate land use planning, lack of working capital and dysfunctional relations within very large (community-based) landholder groups (Hall 2007).

The very limited impact of official policy on landholding patterns in both South Africa and Namibia is exacerbated by ongoing displacement of workers and tenants from White-owned farms and a lack of support to smallholders in communal areas, with the result that nearly two decades into the era of independence, landholding patterns, and the livelihood opportunities that flow from them, remain substantially unchanged from the pre-independence period (Werner 2001; Melber 2005).

With the introduction of the 'fast track' approach to land reform in 2000, however, Zimbabwe, and the SADC region, entered a dramatically new phase in the politics of the agrarian question. While the demand for redistribution of the very substantial areas of land that remained in White ownership had not abated, the structural adjustment policies of the late-1980s and early-1990s, and competing political priorities, meant that the successes of the early independence period were not sustained. It took a growing economic crisis, and an accompanying political crisis (as the ruling ZANU-PF party suffered a succession of electoral setbacks between 2000 and 2002) for land reform to be catapulted to the top of the policy agenda (Sachikonye 2002). Mobilization of popular forces, including the powerful war veterans, with strong backing from the State, led to the seizure of White-owned properties, often accompanied by considerable violence, and their occupation by groups that ranged from the rural landless to leading figures in government and the army (Moyo and Yeros 2005).

Over time, a new order was established on the confiscated land, with poorer households allocated modest plots and a share of communal grazing (so-called A1 plots) and better-off and better-connected individuals obtaining more substantial holdings (A2 farms) (Chaumba et al 2003). Unlike the previous White owners, new occupiers did not acquire freehold title to the land, but the lengthy leases issued by the State confer benefits that come close to freehold.

More difficult, however, has been the challenge of continuing, or restarting, agricultural production on redistributed lands. Many of the former commercial farms were stripped of vital equipment during the occupation process, while experienced farm workers were generally marginalized or even expelled in the process (Rutherford 2001: 630). Few new occupiers had the necessary capital to engage in production on a substantial scale, and many lacked the skills necessary for unfamiliar crops and processes. Most significant, however, has been the general economic collapse that paralleled fast track land reform, which not only disrupted input and output markets but was accompanied by a general collapse of State and private support services. Nonetheless, emerging evidence suggests that production has begun on many redistributed farms, and new occupiers are making a living under what continue to be difficult operating conditions (Marongwe 2007). The long-term outlook will, however, depend on the recovery of the wider Zimbabwean economy and the achievement of lasting political stability.

Various lessons can be drawn from these widely divergent experiences of land redistribution in the region, all of which point to the highly political and potentially disruptive nature of land reform. Major changes in landholding have only been achieved during periods of major political, even revolutionary, upheaval, and have tended to be accompanied by considerable violence and economic turmoil. More moderate approaches, whether market-based or State-led, have tended to drag on for lengthy periods, as experience from Namibia, South Africa and Zimbabwe (pre-fast-track) demonstrates, with limited impact on agrarian structure. Large landowners have shown themselves to be adept at managing the reform process to their own advantage while governments for whom land reform is not the central priority have generally been unable or unwilling to take a firmer line with landowners, out of fear of the wider economic and political impacts this would undoubtedly have. A radical approach to land reform inevitably implies conflict with domestic interests (not just landowners but large capital and commercial interests as well) and, as the experience of Zimbabwe since 2000 demonstrates, runs the risk of confrontation with wider international interests – in this case with Western nations led by the UK and the USA and, to a lesser extent, with neighbouring countries such as Botswana.

5.3.2 'Land grabs' for food and biofuels

Outside Zimbabwe, so-called 'land grabs' of various kinds have emerged as probably the most prominent land-related issue in Africa in recent years, raising fundamental questions about national land sovereignty, food security and development policy (Zoomers 2010; Action Aid 2010; Taylor and Bending 2009; Cotula et al 2009; GRAIN 2008). In many ways, these are just the latest in a long-run pattern of Western domination of key resources in Africa, although now joined by actors from the East and Middle-East. Unlike during the colonial era, however, foreign acquisition of land and related resources, such as water, forestry and wildlife, is today driven by a mix of State and private actors, generally by agreement with host governments, and is being actively promoted as part of development strategy by many. Indeed, as a form of foreign direct investment, land acquisition, and the agricultural and agro-processing industries that are expected to flow from it, can be said to be central to current macro-economic policies across the continent. Key recipients of foreign direct investment (FDI) in land-based enterprises in Africa in recent years have included Sudan, Ethiopia, Madagascar and Mozambique, although other SADC countries, such as Tanzania and Zambia, have also featured prominently.

Acquisition of, and investment in, land in the SADC region – as in the rest of Africa and other parts of the developing world – is facilitated by the ongoing globalization of food and other commodity markets and reform of legal, financial and regulatory regimes that make foreign direct investment in the agricultural sector more attractive. This is reflected in a growing number of bilateral and multilateral treaties, and more concerted policies towards investment in Africa by high and middle-income countries such as the Member States of the European Union, China, Japan, South Korea, Syria, Libya, Saudi Arabia and various other Gulf States. It is also reflected in African-driven initiatives such as New Partnership for Africa's Development (NEPAD) and the Comprehensive Africa Agriculture Development Programme (CAADP) which aims to eliminate hunger and reduce poverty through agriculture. To do this, African governments have agreed to increase public investment in agriculture by a minimum of 10 per cent of their national budgets and to raise agricultural productivity by at least 6 per cent. The programme, which was adopted by Assembly of the African Union in Maputo in 2003 as a framework for the restoration of agriculture sector's development, provides the Member States and Regional Economic Communities, in collaboration with their development partners, an opportunity for renewed efforts to reverse decades of stagnating and low agricultural production and declining productivity, food insecurity and increased poverty in the region.[4]

The most controversial example of 'land grabbing' to date has been the attempt by the Korean company Daewoo to acquire a 99-year lease on over a million hectares of land in Madagascar to grow maize and oil palm for export to South Korea, which contributed directly to the overthrow of the government and the cancellation of the deal by the new government (Cotula et al 2009: 37). Other examples of sizeable deals included those by Indian companies, backed by government loans, that have bought or leased hundreds of thousands of hectares across Africa, including Madagascar and Mozambique, to grow rice, sugar cane, maize and lentils for the Indian market.

The Chinese government recently announced a commitment of US$5 billion for Chinese corporations to invest in African agriculture over the next 50 years through the new China–Africa Development Fund, a private equity fund whose shareholder is the China Development Bank. Among the deals identified by a recent study (von Braun and Meinzen-Dick 2009: 5) are investment by ZTE International of China in the Republic of Congo, securing 2.8 million hectares of land for establishment of an oil palm plantation for biofuel; an unknown area of land acquired by investors from Djibouti in Malawi; investment of US$800 million by Chinese companies to expand rice production from 100,000 to 500,000 metric tons; a request from Saudi Arabia for lease of 500,000 hectares in Tanzania; and an expression of interest from China in acquiring 2 million hectares for the cultivation of jatropha in Zambia. There is little doubt that many more smaller and less well-known deals are underway across the region, and the extent of foreign acquisition of land looks set to expand for some time to come.

Only in South Africa does policy appear to be moving in the opposite direction, with suggestions by successive ministers of land affairs and others that restrictions be placed on foreign land ownership (Lahiff 2008). Such restrictions, if implemented, are likely to only impact on outright ownership of land and do not necessarily signal a retreat from South Africa's highly favourable stance on foreign direct investment; indeed, it is likely that it would boost the range of joint ventures between domestic and foreign investors, and thus make a positive contribution to the country's policy of black economic empowerment.

A unique feature of land acquisition in the SADC region is the expansion of white farmers from South Africa and, more recently, from Zimbabwe, into Mozambique, Zambia and Tanzania, albeit on a smaller scale than the large investors from outside the region. Although little is known about this phenomenon, due to the many relatively small transactions involved, it appears that land is generally not being acquired in outright ownership via the open market, but under various forms of lease or concession from national (and local) governments.

In a recent study, Cotula et al (2009) identified some key features of so-called land grabs in Africa: significant and growing levels of activity; significant and growing areas of land being transacted – often above 100,000 (and as high as 452,500 hectares in a single biofuels project in Madagascar); predominance of the foreign private sector, albeit with considerable State involvement; and some involvement of domestic investors. Together, these mark the onset of a major new phase in the political economy of the land question, the consequences of which are likely to be played out over many years to come.

Two main factors – both of them relatively new for the region – are driving this new scramble for land in Africa: concerns about food security (and food prices) in many middle and high-income countries, and a rapidly increasing demand for biofuels as a form of renewable energy. For governments in the region, the attraction – in an echo of the large-scale projects of the 1960s – is macro-economic development, particularly through enhanced export earnings and fiscal receipts, although the limited evidence available suggests that these are likely to be relatively low. While there has been some reference to more local benefits in the form of direct and indirect employment, expansion of agro-industries upstream and downstream, development of transport and power infrastructure, and involvement of small-scale farmers as outgrowers, the dominant picture appears to be one of new large-scale enterprises largely bypassing the domestic agricultural sector.

Across countries and sectors, foreign direct investment and large-scale joint ventures may thus offer little to the development of the domestic agricultural sector, especially the smallholder sector that provides the basis of livelihoods and food security for large proportions of the population in most countries in the region. Indeed, foreign acquisition of land – although predicated on the notion of 'unused land' – may present a direct threat to the livelihoods of smallholders through competition for prime land and resources, the diversion of both State and private support services to cater to the needs of the large-scale export-oriented sector and the widely-reported removal of traditional land users to make way for new enterprises (IWMI 2008: 3; von Braun and Meinzen-Dick 2009: 2).

The sudden introduction of large, well-resourced players, enjoying strong political support, poses a particular threat given the weak protection of traditional land rights in many countries in the region, and the rush to grant strong contractual rights – of as much as 50 or even 90 years – to investors, with minimal consultation with local communities. Case studies reported by Cotula et al (2009) in Mozambique show that consultation with community-based land users is often superficial and overlooks many rights, especially of women. In Tanzania, farmers are being removed from land marked for sugarcane production without any right to compensation as their land is 'general land' as opposed to the more secure 'village land':

> While there is a perception that land is abundant in certain countries, these claims need to be treated with caution. In many cases land is already being used or claimed – yet existing land uses and claims go unrecognized because land users are marginalised from formal land rights and access to the law and institutions.
>
> (Cotula et al 2009: 6)

Particularly prominent in the region is the acquisition of land for biofuels. In Madagascar, GEM Biofuels has reportedly gained exclusive rights for 50 years over 452,500 hectares in the south of the country to plant jatropha for biodiesel production. UK energy company CAMS Group announced in September 2008 that they had acquired a lease over 45,000 hectares of land in Tanzania for investments in sweet sorghum production for biofuels (Cotula et al 2009: 38). China has also been reported to have signed a contract with the Democratic Republic of Congo to grow 2.8 million hectares of palm oil for biofuels, and to have plans for a massive agricultural colony in Mozambique's Zambezi valley (Horta 2008). While fears have been raised by some commentators about speculative acquisition of land for forestry and other projects related to carbon offsets, which may take many years to realize, the available evidence suggests that the focus is predominantly on the cultivation of fast-growing crops such as jatropha and sugarcane as feedstock for large vertically-integrated producers of biodiesel or ethanol. Examples of this trend are to be found in cases of Brazilian sugar companies currently investing in Angola and Mozambique and South African companies in Zambia.

Overall, it is too early to say with certainty how sustainable the current flood of foreign direct investment to the agricultural sector in SADC countries may be, or what the true impact will be on local and national economies or on the livelihoods and land rights of millions of smallholders in the areas directly affected. The available evidence, however, suggests that governments across the region are eager to grant large areas of land to foreign, and some domestic, investors in the hope of a range of direct and indirect benefits, with few safeguards in place to protect established land use patterns and little obvious benefits in terms of domestic food security or stimulation of the smallholder sector (IFAD 2009: 8; Rossi and Lambrou 2009: 3).

5.3.3 Tenure reform

Efforts to transform traditional African systems of land holding – based on community (or tribal) control of lands and allocation of usufruct rights to individuals or households – have been ongoing since colonial times. Western forms of individual property rights – such as freehold – based on survey and registration of land parcels continue to be seen by many as not only more secure but also as a prerequisite for long-term investment and (through the system of collateral) as a means of accessing finance.

Such thinking has been central to most efforts to modernize agriculture in the region, with the notable exception of the Marxist regimes of Mozambique and Angola (at least up to the 1990s) and countries such as Botswana and Swaziland where policy has focused on the strengthening traditional (or quasi-traditional) institutions of local land governance, such as land boards. In recent years, the value attached to formal (surveyed and registered) land rights has been given renewed impetus through the work of the Peruvian economist Hernando de Soto and his Institute for Liberty and Democracy, which has had considerable influence over policy makers in the region, most notably in Tanzania (Nyamu Musembi 2007: 54; Sjaastad and Cousins 2009: 2). Similar positions have been promoted by the World Bank, which has argued that land markets in southern Africa are constrained by traditional restrictions on sales or rentals and require a degree of formalization in order to encourage and protect land transactions (Deininger 2003: 107).

The persistence of traditional forms of African land tenure – albeit often in modified form – can be attributed to a range of factors, of which the relative universality of access to land, minimal cost and unlikelihood of losing land for financial reasons are probably the most significant. However, the power of local interests, including both larger landholders and land administrators – typically chiefs or village councils – has also been important in defending non-market systems of governance based on local custom, often with a considerable degree of colonial or post-colonial regulation. Considerable debate persists around how effective customary systems are in protecting the rights of women in particular, given the inferior legal status of women within many traditional systems and the widespread practice of allocating land to 'heads of households', who tend to be predominantly male (Razavi 2007: 65).

Ongoing efforts have been made in most countries in the region to reform the law governing traditional (or communal) forms of land tenure and land administration, with disappointing results. Manji (2006: 52) has described the last two decades as 'the age of land law reform in Africa' as countries across the region introduced new laws and overhauled systems of land administration, ostensibly to protect traditional land rights but also to facilitate land registration and land transactions. In Mozambique and elsewhere, the demarcation of 'community' lands has also served to identify land which can be made available to outsiders (investors or entrepreneurs), raising fears that communities will lose access to more remote forests and mountain lands that nonetheless contribute to livelihoods in terms of hunting, gathering of wild materials (including medicinal plants and firewood), water sources and grazing, especially in times of ecological stress (Norfolk et al 2002).

The overall impact of such reforms of customary land systems, however, appears to be minimal, as governments across the region fail to invest sufficiently in technical and administrative systems necessary for their implementation; public support for such measures also appears to be lukewarm at best, especially among poorer landholders and the traditional leaders who stand to lose out on their traditional functions. Adams and Palmer (2007) and Kleinbooi (2010) identify countries across the southern African region – including Lesotho, Swaziland, Malawi, Namibia, Tanzania – where reforms of communal land tenure have made little progress or are effectively stalled. In South Africa, for example, the Communal Land Rights Act 2004 was struck down by a South African High Court on the basis of its failure to protect the land rights of smaller or independent communities located within the jurisdictional boundaries of large Traditional Councils (Claassens and Cousins 2008).

Adams and Palmer summarize the slow progress with tenure reform in the region in the following terms:

> Many countries in Eastern and Southern Africa are clearly struggling to implement laws and policies that they have formulated in recent years. There are many reasons for their difficulties, including over-ambition, lack of

> capacity, scarcity of financial resources, and the assumption that customary law can be swept away by the stroke of a pen, or women's land rights protected by another. Social reality at the local level is generally very different from what is imagined in the capital.
>
> Adams and Palmer (2007: 72)

5.4 The politics of land within SADC

With the exception of a narrow focus on the technical aspects of land administration, little attention was paid to land reform or the broader 'agrarian question' within the formal, inter-governmental structures of SADC (and its forerunner the Southern African Development Co-ordination Conference (SADCC)) until the launch of 'fast track' land reform in Zimbabwe in 2000. This lack of attention could be seen as a strategic weakness, given the widely agreed importance of land matters in the region, particularly the unresolved legacy of settler colonialism (frequently referred to in SADC communiqués) and the extensive experience of land reform in the region from the 1960s to the 1980s. Up to 2000, however, land reform was clearly seen as an internal issue for SADC member countries, nearly all of which were engaged in reform to some degree. Moreover, it was not perceived to have significant economic or political risks, particularly at the regional level.

With the more radical position adopted by the government of Zimbabwe from 2000, however, major tensions emerged on the ground in that country (with echoes in South Africa and elsewhere in the region), with the international community (in the form of sanctions and condemnation) and within SADC itself over the position to be taken with regard to the Mugabe government (Lahiff and Cousins 2001). These developments in Zimbabwe, and threats of similar expropriations of White farmers in South Africa and Namibia, brought an unprecedented urgency for SADC to develop a concerted position on land reform. It also, as we will see, led to one of the most controversial showdowns between SADC structures and a Member State, when the SADC Tribunal delivered a ruling highly critical of Zimbabwe's handling of land confiscation.

In August 2001, the SADC Summit recognized that there was urgent need to tackle the land issues given the potential political tensions that could undermine economic growth and food security. Ministers of Lands were directed to develop a regional land reform strategy that would guide national governments in formulating and implementing land reform programmes in line with their national development priorities. In 2003, SADC took the first steps to establish a SADC Land Reform Support Facility integrated in the restructured Food, Agriculture and Natural Resources (FANR) Directorate of SADC. FANR is one of four directorates at the SADC Secretariat, whose main function is the coordination and harmonization of agricultural policies and programmes in the region, as well as to ensure food availability, access, safety and nutritional value; disaster preparedness for food security; equitable and sustainable use of the environment and natural resources; and strengthening institutional framework and capacity building (SADC no date). The process was long drawn out, however, and final approval for the establishment of the Land Reform Support Facility was only given by Ministers responsible for land matters in March 2008.

The official report on the formation of the process set out the need for a land reform facility as follows, while highlighting the various challenges facing the region:

> The Southern African Development Community (SADC) resolved to adopt a regional approach to land reform and to this end establish a SADC Land Reform Support Facility (SLRSF) that would, among other things, support Member States in developing and/or implementing their agrarian and land reform programmes. One of the unique features of the Southern African region is the contrasting colonial land expropriation experience, the nature of the decolonization process, patterns of land distribution and varied land reform experiences. The key land questions facing SADC Member States relate primarily to issues of distribution, utilization, tenure, administration and adjudication. These however vary in each state depending on the history, culture and political consideration.
>
> (SADC 2007: 1)

Further reasons given for establishment of the facility, and for urgent action on land reform, include widespread poverty and malnutrition and the high proportion of people living on under US$1 per day (SADC 2007: 2). Specific challenges facing the region are stated to include both redistribution and tenure, and the new facility includes provision of technical support for reform, land administration, legislative reform and the building of specialized judicial capacity.

The stated objectives of the Land Reform Support Facility are to mobilize technical and financial support for Member States to develop and/or implement pro-poor land and agrarian reform policies and programmes in support of their national development plans. 'In line with the inspirations of the SADC Regional Indicative Strategic Development Plan (RISDP) and the New Partnership for Africa's Development (NEPAD) in particular its Comprehensive African Agricultural Development Programme (CAADP), the Facility will contribute towards achievement of sustainable regional food security, and sustainable environment and land management'.[5]

The new facility was discussed at length at the meeting of SADC Ministers responsible for Land Affairs held in Johannesburg in March 2008,[6] but effectively disappeared from the political landscape as attention among regional leaders shifted to issues such as food security, the ongoing search for a sustainable political solution in Zimbabwe, and the fallout from a divisive judgment by the SADC Tribunal in favour of a group of white landowners dispossessed of their farms in Zimbabwe, which ruled that they should keep their farms because Harare's land reform programme discriminated against them, was contrary to the public good and contravened the SADC treaty by violently seizing the farms. The Tribunal ordered that the government respect those rights and compensate the farmers who had already lost land. After some contradictory messages, including a statement by the President that it would not recognize the ruling, the government of Zimbabwe announced in September 2009 that the country was withdrawing from the Tribunal as it was not properly constituted.

In January 2010, the Zimbabwe High Court, while seemingly recognizing the legitimacy of the Tribunal, held that its ruling was contrary to Zimbabwe law and the public interest and was therefore without effect (*Zimbabwe Telegraph* 2010). The ruling of the Zimbabwe High Court clearly upholds the supremacy of national law over international or regional agreements, and suggests that political will does not yet exist for an effective working of regional structures in areas as politically sensitive as land reform.

Overall, little of substance has come from SADC's collective efforts on land reform to date. Apart from some joint training events for mid-level officials, there is little evidence of sharing of experience between countries or the emergence of consensus as to how best to address pressing land issues in the region. The rejection of the SADC Tribunal's ruling by the Zimbabwe High Court can be seen as the first substantial test of regional cooperation in the area of land reform, with the outcome suggesting that further work is required before such regional institutions can function effectively.

5.5 Conclusion

Land questions remain central to the political economy of southern Africa but, as outlined here, these questions vary considerably between countries and over time. None of the major challenges faced by the region at the end of the colonial era – highly unequal distribution of land, a large but underdeveloped peasant sector and a pressing need to boost the efficiency of the agricultural sector as a contributor to both food security and macro-economic development – can be said to have been resolved, although much progress has been made and rich experience has been accumulated.

White commercial farmers have proved themselves highly resilient and adaptable to changing political and economic environments, and remain a major force within agriculture in the region. Moreover, the dualistic agricultural model that emerged in the zone of settler-colonialism – with relatively few large, well-resourced farms coexisting with many more small, resource-poor holdings – continues to characterize the region, despite some blurring of the old racial boundaries.

The contrasting experience of redistribution in Zimbabwe and South Africa illustrates the difficulties – and risks – associated with a radical restructuring of the agricultural sector. For South Africa, the relatively minor importance of agriculture in the national economy and the desire to appease powerful business interests (foreign and domestic) goes a long way to explain the moderate, market-based approach to reform, and the failure of land issues to emerge – despite some rhetoric to the contrary – as a defining political issue for any of the country's main political parties. Yet, as the experience of its neighbour Zimbabwe clearly demonstrates, such blatant examples of inequality – especially with a strong racial component – are unlikely to disappear of their own accord and are liable to emerge as defining issues at times of radical political and economic upheaval.

The dramatic redistribution of land that occurred under 'fast track' since 2000 was not the cause of the political and economic crisis that gripped that country at the time, but rather an outcome of that crisis. Regardless of the manner in which redistribution was carried out, or the reasons underlying it, the conditions under which it occurred were far from favourable to new farmers and to the creation of a restructured agricultural sector that would contribute significantly to both macro-economic development and to food security and poverty alleviation at the local level. In this sense, the full lessons of Zimbabwe's experience will only be learned over the longer term.

Small-scale farmers across the region, especially the millions living on communal land and poorly integrated into local and regional markets, have been severely neglected in terms of public investment and support, at least since the mid-1980s. The notable exception is Malawi which, in 2005, and in the face of opposition from donors such as the World Bank, introduced subsidies on fertilizers and other inputs for small farmers, specifically targeted at the poorest households (Chinsinga and O'Brien 2008). The success of these measures in terms of boosting production and alleviating hunger in that country holds important lessons for the region – not least in terms of the financial sustainability of such programmes – but would undoubtedly require significant political changes if they were to be repeated in neighbouring countries.

Where smallholders have featured in policy thinking it has been largely in terms of tenure reform. The long drawn-out processes this has involved in most countries, and the few tangible benefits it has brought to date suggests that emphasis on formalization of land rights may be misplaced, and that light-touch recognition of existing (e.g. traditional) rights, allied to support for agricultural production and marketing, may be a more relevant strategy.

In practice, however, the bulk of public and private investment is, for the foreseeable future, likely to be directed towards the large-scale export-oriented agricultural sector. The rapid development of this sector is being driven by foreign direct investment, as discussed above, but is being actively encouraged by governments in the region as a route to development of the macro-economy. Ongoing liberalization of regional and international trade and strategies such as the Comprehensive Africa Agriculture Development Programme are also creating opportunities for domestic entrepreneurs in both agricultural production (including biofuel crops) and in processing and marketing of agricultural commodities. The renewed interest in agriculture by these relatively powerful interests – domestic and foreign – with support from State institutions poses considerable threats to smallholders and the rural poor, particularly in terms of land rights but also in terms of increased competition within domestic markets.

Beneath these headline issues of national (and regional) policy and macro-economic change there continues to be a plethora of local struggles that have the potential to challenge official policy and impact on the political economy of land in the region. These include ongoing struggles by women to protect their land rights and to have their views represented in national and regional policy process. The HIV/AIDS pandemic has hit the region particularly hard and continues to impact severely on the ability of households to sustain agricultural production and other livelihood activities, as well as the ability of social services to cope in the face of exceptional demand. The ongoing struggle against poverty and hunger, both heavily concentrated in the rural areas, poses a great challenge for the region, as do struggles between traditional forms of authority (e.g. tribal chiefs) and those who support alternative (e.g. elected) forms of administration and of land ownership (e.g. individualization). Finally, labour struggles – over wages and union recognition – especially where new forms of commercial agriculture begin employing wage labour on a large scale provide yet another site for struggle, with potentially diverse outcomes.

These local struggles, often hidden from national and international perspectives, will continue to shape political processes in the region and pose challenges both for national governments and the institutions of SADC. In this way, land questions in southern Africa are certain not only to persist but to evolve and throw up new challenges in the years ahead.

Notes

1 Statistics from <http://www.NationMaster.com> (accessed 4 June 2010) (derived from various sources).
2 Signed in 1979, the Lancaster House Agreement provided the basis for transition to democracy and an independent Zimbabwe.
3 A limited 'market-based' redistribution of land – the Community Based Rural Land Distribution Project – has also been underway in Malawi since 2004 (albeit in the absence of white settlers or a widespread formal market in land), with very limited results (see Chinsinga 2008).
4 CAADP homepage at <http://www.nepad-caadp.net/about-caadp.php> (accessed 4 June 2010).
5 *The Establishment of the SADC Land Reform Support Facility* (Gaborone: SADC Secretariat, Food, Agriculture and Natural Resources Directorate), available at <http://www.sadc.int/fanr/environment/landreform/docs/SADC%20Land%20Reform%20Support%20Facility%20brochure%202008.pdf> (accessed 4 June 2010).
6 Speeches and Communiqué from the meeting of SADC Ministers responsible for Land Affairs, Johannesburg, March 2008, available at <http://www.fanrpan.org/documents/d00503/SADC_land_affairs_Mar2008.pdf> (accessed 4 June 2010).

Bibliography

Action Aid (2008) *Food, Farmers and Fuel: Balancing Global Grain and Energy Policies with Sustainable Land Use* (London: Action Aid International).

Action Aid (2010) *Meals Per Gallon: The impact of industrial biofuels on people and global hunger* (London: Action Aid).

Adams, M. and Palmer, R. (eds) (2007) *Independent Review of Land Issues: Eastern And Southern Africa, Volume iii, 2006–2007*, unpublished document, available at <http://www.sarpn.org.za/documents/d0002625/Land_review_SA_Jun2007.pdf> (accessed 4 June 2010).

Benjaminsen, T. A. and Lund, C. (eds) (2003) *Securing Land Rights in Africa* (London and Portland, OR: Frank Cass).

Bernstein, H. (2002) 'Land Reform: Taking a Long(er) View', *Journal of Agrarian Change*, 2(4): 433–63.

Bowen, M. L. (2000) *The State against the Peasantry: Rural Struggles in Colonial and Post-colonial Mozambique* (Charlottesville, VA and London: University Press of Virginia).

Bruce, J. W. (1993) 'The variety of reform: A review of recent experience with land reform and the reform of land tenure, with particular reference to the African experience', International Development Studies Occasional Paper No 9 (Roskilde: International Development Studies).

Bruce J. W. and Mighot-Adholla, S. (eds) (1994) *Searching for Land Tenure Security in Africa* (Washington, DC: World Bank).

Chaumba, J., Scoones, I. and Wolmer, W. (2003) 'New Politics, New Livelihoods: Changes in the Zimbabwean Lowveld Since the Farm Invasions of 2000', *Review of African Political Economy*, 30(98): 585–608.

Chinsinga, B. (2008) 'Exploring the Politics of Land Reforms in Malawi: A Case Study of the Community Based Rural Land Development Programme (CBRLDP)', Discussion Paper Series Number Twenty (Manchester: Institutions and Pro-Poor Growth (IPPG) Project, University of Manchester), available at <http://www.ippg.org.uk/papers/dp20.pdf> (accessed 4 June 2010).

Chinsinga, B. and O'Brien, A. (2008) *Planting Ideas: How agricultural subsidies are working in Malawi* (London: Africa Research Institute).

Claassens, A. and Cousins, B. (eds) (2008) *Land, Power and Custom: Controversies Generated by South Africa's Communal Land Rights Act* (Cape Town and Athens, OH: University of Cape Town Press and Ohio University Press).

Clover, J. (2005) 'Land Reform in Angola: Establishing the Ground Rules', in Chris Huggins and Jenny Clover (eds) *From the Ground Up: Land Rights, Conflict and Peace in Sub-Saharan Africa* (Pretoria: African Centre for Technology Studies and the African Security Analysis Programme of the Institute for Security Studies), pp 347–80.

Cotula, L., Dyer, N. and Vermeulen, S. (2008) *Fuelling Exclusion? The Biofuels Boom and Poor People's Access to Land* (London and Rome: IIED and FAO).

Cotula, L., Vermeulen, S., Leonard, R. and Keeley, J. (2009) *Land Grab or Development Opportunity? Agricultural investment and international land deals in Africa* (London/Rome: IIED/FAO/IFAD).

Deininger, K. (2003) *Land policies for growth and poverty reduction* (Washington, DC and Oxford: World Bank and Oxford University Press).

Foley, C. (2007) *Land rights in Angola: poverty and plenty* (London: Humanitarian Policy Group and Overseas Development Institute).

Genetic Resources Action International (GRAIN) (2008) 'Seized! The 2008 land grab for food and financial security', Briefing (Barcelona: GRAIN), available at <http://www.grain.org/go/landgrab> (accessed 4 June 2010).

Greenberg, S. (2010) *Status report on land and agricultural policy in South Africa, 2010* (Cape Town: Institute for Poverty, Land and Agrarian Studies).

Hall, R. (2007) *The Impact of Land Restitution and Land Reform on Livelihoods* (Cape Town: Programme for Land and Agrarian Studies, University of the Western Cape).

Hanlon, J. (2002) *The land debate in Mozambique: will foreign investors, the urban elite, advanced peasants or family farmers drive rural development?* (Johannesburg: Oxfam).

Horta, L. (2008) *The Zambezi Valley: China's First Agricultural Colony?* (Washington, DC: Centre for Strategic International Studies), 8 June, available at <http://forums.csis.org/africa/?p=120> (accessed 4 June 2010).

International Fund for Agricultural Development (IFAD) (2009) *The growing demand for land: Risks and opportunities for smallholder farmers* (Rome: International Fund for Agricultural Development).

International Water Management Institute (IWMI) (2008) 'Water implications of biofuel crops: understanding tradeoffs and identifying options', Water Policy Brief 30 (Colombo: International Water Management Institute).

Kinsey, B. H. (1999) 'Land Reform Growth and Equity: Emerging Evidence from Zimbabwe's Resettlement Programme', *Journal of Southern African Studies*, 25(2): 173–96.

Kleinbooi, K. (2010) *Review of Land Reforms In Southern Africa* (Cape Town: Institute for Poverty, Land and Agrarian Studies, University of the Western Cape).

Lahiff, E. (2007) '"Willing Buyer, Willing Seller" – South Africa's Failed Experiment in Market-Led Agrarian Reform', *Third World Quarterly*, 28(8): 1577–98.

Lahiff, E. (2008) *Land Reform in South Africa: A Status Report 2008* (Cape Town: Programme for Land and Agrarian Studies, University of the Western Cape).

Lahiff, E. and Cousins, B. (2001) 'The Land Crisis in Zimbabwe Viewed from South of the Limpopo', *Journal of Agrarian Change*, 1(4): 653–66.

Manji, A. (2001) 'Land reform in the shadow of the state: the implementation of new land laws in Sub-Saharan Africa', *Third World Quarterly*, 22(3): 327–42.

Manji, A. (2006) *The politics of land reform in Africa: from communal tenure to free markets* (London: Zed Books).

Marongwe, N. (2007) 'Redistributive Land Reform and Poverty Reduction in Zimbabwe', a working paper for the research project on 'Livelihoods after Land Reform' (Cape Town: Institute for Poverty, Land and Agrarian Studies, University of the Western Cape), available at <http://www.lalr.org.za/zimbabwe/redistributive-land-reform-and-poverty-reduction-in-zimbabwe/> (accessed 4 June 2010).

Melber, H. (2005) 'Land and Politics in Namibia', *Review of African Political Economy*, 103: 135–42.

Moyo, S. (1995) *The Land Question in Zimbabwe* (Harare: SAPES).

Moyo, S. (2000) 'The Political Economy of Land Acquisition and Redistribution in Zimbabwe, 1990–99', *Journal of Southern African Studies*, 26(1): 5–28.

Moyo, S. and Yeros, P. (2005) 'Land Occupations and Land Reform in Zimbabwe: Towards the National Democratic Revolution', in S. Moyo and P. Yeros (eds) *Reclaiming the Land: The Resurgence of Rural Movements in Africa, Asia and Latin America* (London: Zed Books), pp 165–205.

Negrão, J. (1999) 'The Mozambican Land Campaign, 1997–99', paper presented to the Workshop on the Associative Movement, Maputo, 14 December.

Norfolk, S., Nhantumbo, I. and Pereira, J. (2002) '"Só para o Inglese ver" – The Policy and Practice of Tenure Reform in Mozambique', Sustainable Livelihoods in Southern Africa Case Study Paper (Brighton: Institute of Development Studies).

Nyamu Musembi, C. (2007) 'De Soto and Land Relations in Rural Africa: Breathing Life into Dead Theories About Property Rights', *Third World Quarterly*, 28(8): 1457–78.

Okoth-Ogendo, H. W. O. (1993) 'Agrarian reform in sub-Saharan Africa: An assessment of state responses to the African agrarian crisis and their implications for agricultural development', in T. J. Bassett and D. E. Crummey (eds) *Land in African Agrarian Systems* (Madison, WI: University of Wisconsin Press), pp 247–73.

O'Laughlin, B. (1996) 'Through a Divided Glass: Dualism, Class and the Agrarian Question in Mozambique', *Journal of Peasant Studies*, 23(4): 1–39.

Palmer, R. (1990) 'Land Reform in Zimbabwe, 1980–1990', *African Affairs*, 89: 163–81.

Palmer, R. (2000) 'Land Policy in Africa: Lessons from Recent Policy and Implementation Processes', in C. Toulmin and J. Quan (eds) *Evolving land rights, policy and tenure in Africa* (London: IIED/NRI).

Quan, J. (2000) 'Land tenure, economic growth and poverty in sub-Saharan Africa', in C. Toulmin and J. Quan (eds) *Evolving land rights, policy and tenure in Africa* (London:

Department for International Development (DFID)/IIED/University of Greenwich Natural Resources Institute (NRI)), pp 31–49.

Razavi, S. (2007) 'Liberalisation and the Debates on Women's Access to Land', *Third World Quarterly*, 28(8): 1479–500.

Rossi, A. and Lambrou, Y. (2009) *Making Sustainable Biofuels Work For Smallholder Farmers And Rural Households: Issues And Perspectives* (Rome: Food and Agriculture Organization of the United Nations).

Rutherford, B. (2001) 'Commercial Farm Workers and the Politics of (Dis)placement in Zimbabwe: Colonialism, Liberation and Democracy', *Journal of Agrarian Change*, 1(4): 626–51.

Sachikonye, L. M. (2002) 'Whither Zimbabwe? Crisis & Democratisation', *Review of African Political Economy*, 91: 13–20.

Sjaastad, E. and Cousins, B. (2009) 'Formalisation of land rights in the South: An overview', *Land Use Policy*, 26(1): 1–9.

Southern African Development Community (SADC) (no date) 'The Establishment of the SADC Land Reform Support Facility' (SADC Secretariat: Food, Agriculture and Natural Resources Directorate), available at <http://www.sadc.int/fanr/environment/landreform/index.php> (accessed 4 June 2010).

Southern African Development Community (SADC) (2007) *Establishing the SADC Land Reform Support Facility and Inception Activities* (Gaborone: SADC Secretariat, Directorate of Food, Agriculture and Natural Resources).

Southern African Development Community (SADC) (2008) *Communiqué on meeting of Southern African Development Community (SADC) ministers responsible for Land Affairs, Sandton, Johannesburg, South Africa. 27 March 2008.*

Tanner, C. (1996) *The Land Question in Mozambique* (Madison, WI: Land Tenure Centre, University of Wisconsin-Madison).

Taylor, M. and Bending, T. (2009) 'Increasing commercial pressure on land: Building a coordinated response', ILC Discussion Paper (Rome: International Land Coalition).

von Braun, J. and Meinzen-Dick, R. (2009) '"Land Grabbing" by Foreign Investors in Developing Countries: Risks and Opportunities', IFPRI Policy Brief 13 (Washington, DC: International Food Policy Research Institute).

Werner, W. (2001) 'Land Reform and Poverty Alleviation: Experiences from Namibia', NEPRU Working Paper No. 78 (Windhoek: The Namibian Economic Policy Research Unit).

Whitehead, A. and Tsikata, D. (2003) 'Policy Discourses on Women's Land Rights in Sub-Saharan Africa: The Implications of the Return to the Customary', *Journal of Agrarian Change*, 3(1–2): 67–112.

Zimbabwe Telegraph (2010) 'Zimbabwe ignores SADC Tribunal Ruling on Land', 26 January, available at <http://www.zimtelegraph.com/?p=5658> (accessed 4 June 2010).

Zoomers, A. (2010) 'Globalization and the foreignisation of space: seven processes driving the current global land grab', *Journal of Peasant Studies*, 37(2): 429–47.

Part 2

Possibilities and further challenges

6 Farm workers on private agriculture land holdings

A pathway to the common settlement of a Southern African Development Community land issue

Sibo Banda[1]

6.1 Introduction

The Southern African Development Community (SADC) region initiative on land policy, the SADC Land Reform Support Facility (SLRSF),[2] presents an opportunity for addressing the peculiarly southern African agrarian problem that pits land owners against workers, referred to in this chapter as the farm workers' question.[3] A view is taken here that there is a common acknowledgement among public and private institutions within the region of the existence of the farm worker's question and also for action to be undertaken towards the settlement of this question. The contemporary private estate in the SADC region is characterized by tension-filled contradictory claims. On the one hand, private estate owners seek to validate the status quo and particularly the extent to which their legal rights over private estate land have been exercised. On the other hand, an amorphous group representing a variety of interests, including farm workers, advance a variety of 'genuine' counter-claims which challenge the extent private estates owners have exercised their legal rights over private estate land.[4] A common feature in the socio-political history of the SADC region countries is the encounter with western colonial capitalism and associated social, economic and legal disruptions it left in its wake. The process and consequences of the colonial encounter on the social groups of the SADC region including the farm workers class are well documented.[5]

A particularly notable feature that distinguishes the SADC region's social and political history – from, for example, West African European colonialism – is the region's experience of settler colonialism.[6] European migration to the SADC region gave rise to an insatiable demand for land earmarked for private estate agriculture. In response the colonial state built a complex regime of legal instruments which facilitated the dispossession and enclosure of land resulting in the loss of access to land by significant sections of the indigenous population.[7]

As a consequence, this indigenous population's capacity to exercise authority over land, in both the legal and physical senses, became deeply impaired. Furthermore, this indigenous population experienced transformation of their position from communities with independent livelihoods to communities leading livelihoods dependent on the whims of a class that had assumed legal control over land categorized as private land.[8] A poignant illustration of this transformation is provided by the emergence on the private estates of the farm workers class which is defined by the possession of historically determined insecure and non-registrable rights and interests in land characterized as personal and non-proprietary.[9] The legacy of this history on the contemporary production relations on the private estate in the SADC region is an unhappy one and on occasion characterized by violent confrontation. For the most part, the private estates maintain a picture of serenity which masks an undercurrent of despair, discontent and hopelessness among farm workers.

This chapter aims to examine the situation of the farm worker in the SADC region as a legitimate subject of concern to be addressed by the SLRSF. The chapter focuses on the peculiar situation of farm workers as a class that historically possesses insecure and non-registrable rights and interests characterized as personal and non-proprietary. The farm workers are placed in a position that is risk prone and precarious and which has damaging social, economic and developmental effects. These effects are illustrated through a discussion of Malawi's tenant worker. It is an established fact that farm workers lack secure tenure and live under constant threat of summary evictions. At the root of the farm workers' problem is the near universal characterization of their 'rights' and 'interests' as lacking definitive legal recognition and status. An attempt will therefore be made to locate the farm worker's situation within the international human rights framework. Under the International Convention on Civil and Political Rights (ICCPR) and the International Convention on Economic, Social and Cultural Rights (ICESCR), normative standards of good practice relevant to security of tenure have evolved and provide authoritative benchmarks against which state practice is assessed. The SLRSF seeks to provide a forum for the promotion of research on farm workers and land rights as well as on the prospects for SADC land policy norms. It is argued in this chapter that the SLRSF initiative presents a unique opportunity as a conduit through which international human rights norms may be funnelled to national land reform programmes to positively impact on the farm workers' question.

6.2 Overview of conflicting claims on private land holdings and divergent responses to historical inequality

6.2.1 A regional problem

The past two decades have witnessed in the SADC region the growth of a combination of social policy research initiatives[10] and grass roots social movements[11] aimed at researching, highlighting and addressing pressing problems faced by farm workers on private estates. On occasion researchers, activists and grass roots movements have come together in fora aimed at highlighting attention to the abhorrent social conditions of farm workers and influencing change in policy. For instance, in 2001 a communiqué issued by the Southern African Regional Conference on Farm Workers, Human Rights and Security noted that:

> Farm workers constituted a significant proportion (10–20%) of the population of individual SADC countries, but they continue to [sic] marginalized and excluded from mainstream development throughout the region.[12]

The communiqué then recommended that 'National governments should ensure that the living and working conditions and security of farm workers is [sic] acted upon and improved'.[13] The driver of these initiatives is a consensus that farm workers live lives of extreme risk as they lack security of tenure and live under threat of eviction.[14]

In the past 50 years, and with varying levels of commitment and success, the governments of the SADC region have made attempts to institute policy and legal reform aimed at correcting the skewed distribution of land inherited from past colonial regimes. However, the issues pertaining to the problems of farm workers do not appear to feature as a priority in the agendas of most of the national governments.[15] An exception and a positive exemplar in this area is the land policy of the Government of South Africa which has specifically targeted farm workers as beneficiaries of targeted land reform and land law reform initiatives.[16] Despite the lack of uniformity in the attitudes of national governments, the SLRSF provides a unique opportunity for advancing a transnational agenda.[17] The SLRSF can facilitate the galvanizing of efforts towards the development of a concerted approach to what is obviously a clear and present problem of private estate relations and which is a common regional problem of inequitable access to, and distribution of, natural resources.

The SLRSF appears to provide an appropriate vehicle through which a common regional problem can be addressed. In order to attain this it is necessary to recall that the plight of the farm worker is a problem rooted in history and cannot be addressed effectively without a proper appreciation of its social-historical contexts. Therefore this chapter describes comparatively the broad historical impellents and the contemporary responses to the question as it relates to legal relations on the private estates of South Africa and Malawi.

6.2.2 South Africa

The history of the labour tenant's contract in South Africa exemplifies the legal insecurities farm workers in the SADC region face in contemporary times. Under the South African labour tenancy contract a labour tenant occupied and used for his own purpose a parcel of privately owned farm land in exchange for an undertaking by the labour tenant to work for or supply labour to the owner of the land for a specified period of time.[18] The labour tenancy contract therefore provided a mechanism that enabled both land-expropriated blacks and the white landowning class to get around the restrictions on land access by black people – it served a utilitarian purpose.[19] The rights or interests held by the labour tenant were legally insecure. Labour tenancy was a phenomenon that occurred in rural and isolated places and consequently the struggles of the labour tenant enjoyed very poor visibility and very limited legal protection.[20]

6.2.2.1 South Africa's response to historical inequity

Under the post-apartheid democratic dispensation the acquisition and ownership of land was identified as an area that required urgent redress. Measures underpinned by provisions in the South African Constitution were undertaken to address labour tenancy through land tenure reform and land restitution.[21] Land law reform, a component of land reform seeks to make secure forms of tenure which in the past were insecure. The attainment of security of tenure is intended to be achieved through a rights-based approach – as opposed to a permits-based approach.[22] Prior to reform specific to the situation of the labour tenant, the rights of tenure enjoyed by the labour tenant were very limited and depended on the goodwill of the farm owner and the state. South Africa's land law reform, through the adoption of a rights-based approach spells out in detail the relative rights and obligations of the farm owner and the labour tenant. This approach is intended to create certainty by both removing doubts and the possibility for unreasonable and unlawful conduct.[23]

Land tenure and land law reform in South Africa has two aspects potentially relevant to the common regional issue that the farm workers' question is. The first aspect of land tenure reform in South Africa is the 'adjustment of the correlative position between landowner and the holder of lesser rights' in land through the enhancement of security of tenure of the labour tenant.[24] The legislative instrument used for the adjustment of the relative positions of the farm owner and the labour tenant is the Land Reform (Labour Tenants) Act.[25] It provides a framework for the detailed regulation and enhancement of tenure security under the labour tenancy contract. The second relevant aspect of land tenure and land law reform in South Africa is the conversion of the previously personal rights of the labour tenant to proprietary rights. This conversion has been achieved through the Extension of Security of Tenure Act[26] and, arguably through the Labour Tenants Act.

6.2.3 Malawi

Under a tenant worker's contract the private estate owner grants the tenant worker access to a parcel of land on the private estate and also provides material agricultural inputs and services in consideration for an undertaking by the tenant worker to produce and sell the resulting commodities to the private estate owner. In colonial Malawi, the private estate owner could not sustain commodity production on the basis of a wage-earning workforce and therefore, resorted to engaging tenant workers.[27] The post-colonial state has overseen the further intensification of private estate production and the use of tenant workers.[28]

6.2.3.1 Malawi's response to historical inequity

Following the re-introduction of competitive politics in Malawi, the rural population made clear demands for a review of land ownership and access to land. Malawi formulated and adopted what is dubbed a 'comprehensive land policy'.[29] This reform aims to create a long-term framework for the development of land administration, maintenance of various forms of tenure, the regulation of land use and planning as well as the management of the environment.[30] A notable but unfortunate aspect of land policy in this regard is the absence of any mention of the presence of the tenant worker on the private estate.[31] In particular, the land policy document does not recognize the simple and clear fact that tenant workers on the private estates are workers of the land who live on the land and depend on the land for their livelihoods. Nevertheless, the tenant workers do not enjoy any secure tenure and their tenure is dependent on the whims of the private estate owners.

Malawi's land policy does not necessarily and definitively reject private estate commodity production by tenant workers. However, the land policy simply does not make any reference to the tenant worker, to the tenant worker's contract or to the obvious need to undertake corrective action in this regard. This is an indication that land policy will not address the social, economic and legal problems that the tenant workers have, at least not within the context of any land law reform initiative.[32]

6.2.4 Divergent attitudes to a common law problem

This brief review of the responses by the state in South Africa and Malawi to the farm workers' question highlights and suggests the existence of extremely divergent attitudes. In both instances historical events produced a class of farm workers that possessed insecure and non-registrable rights and interests characterized as personal and non-proprietary. Similarly, in both cases the farm worker was effectively treated as a tolerated squatter whose ability to continue to live on the private estate land was dependent on the 'good nature' of the land owning class. In other words, the occupancy of land by the farm worker was never grounded on a firm legal basis. In the following section, the problem of farm workers is defined as a regional issue which is largely about the characterization of farm workers' rights and interests as lacking definitive legal recognition and status. On the basis of relevant international human rights instruments, an alternative perspective is discussed. The international human rights instruments, it is argued, are normative benchmarks for good practice which all SADC region countries ought to comply with.

6.3 Defining the farm workers' question

6.3.1 The farm workers' question as a common law problem

Farm workers across the SADC region invariably can only lay claim legally to insecure and personal non-registrable rights and interests in land. The reason for this is historical and largely shaped by the entrenched ideas society holds about the meaning of property on the one hand and by the brutal factual reality of social and economic privilege that exclusive possession of property delivers on the other hand. It is also an undisputed fact that effective mechanisms for change aimed at making secure forms of tenure which are presently insecure, for the most part, are located at the national constitutional and political levels. However, it is submitted and argued that international human rights instruments equally have an important role to play as normative drivers that provide the impetus for change and as a touchstone that guides reform through good practice as well as standard setting.

As noted, a common aspect of the socio-political history of the SADC countries is their encounter with western colonial capitalism which left in its wake legal artifacts which are an integral part of the contemporary social and economic governance apparatus. In the context of land relations, received law may easily constitute the single most influential artifact and this is a feature that cuts across the expanse of the SADC region. A close inspection of land law in any SADC region country irrespective of its description as a Roman-Dutch or English common law based jurisdiction reveals a common theme – these jurisdictions are legally pluralistic and the dominant law is received law.[33]

Intrinsically, the received law has carried a set of apparently self-evident principles of similar temporal and intellectual origin which create and recognize a complex system of land rights and interests. These range from rights and interests characterized as absolute, superior and proprietary perched at the apex of a hierarchy through to rights and interests described as dependent, inferior and non-proprietary clustered at the base of the hierarchy. For example, in a commentary on the Roman-Dutch common law-based land law of South Africa, Hanri Mostert makes the following observation:

> Rights to immovable property are usually divided into registrable real rights, on the one hand and non-registrable forms of land tenure such as personal rights or statutory grants on the other hand. Real rights in land comprise two broad categories in traditional private law theory in South Africa, namely ownership and limited real rights … Traditionally, ownership is described as the most complete right and the only real right that a person can hold with regard to her own property … The South African system of registration endorses this categorization … Limited real rights are defined as rights to specified uses of property belonging to another which restrict the exercise of the ownership entitlements by the owner thereof. These rights are, in terms of the existing system, the only other kinds of rights capable of being registered … Rights other than ownership are not registrable if they merely place an obligation on a specific person, without burdening the landowner in her capacity as landowner.[34]

Similarly, in a comparative essay on the law of real property in the English common law world, Kevin Grey elucidates the historical and central organizing features of the common law in the following terms:

> Central to the genesis of property ideas in the common law were the twin notions of *tenure* and *estate*. The theory of *tenure* bore a distinctively political aspect and served to identify the ultimate or *radical* title at the back of all relationships in respect of land. By contrast the emerging doctrine of the estate was more closely concerned with the technical quantification of the grades of ownership which might be enjoyed by any particular tenant within a tenurial framework.[35]

The classification of land rights on a sliding scale from ownership to mere personal rights evident in the Roman-Dutch common law-based civil legal systems as well as the quantification of enjoyment of rights of ownership on a temporal continuum in English common law-based legal systems have had a real influence on private estates. In both instances, the idea of marginal claims to enjoyment of insecure and personal rights is a reality that is essentially acknowledged as an incidental, normal and natural feature of the system 'as everybody knows it'. Invariably, this normalization and naturalization condemns the farm workers across the expanse of the SADC region to precarious livelihoods that are dependent on insecure and personal non-registrable rights.

Historically, and in a formal legal sense, the possession of insecure and non-registrable and non-proprietary rights often has two possible implications for the claimants of these limited personal rights and interests. On the one hand, they are cast completely outside any official legal rights-based framework of tenure protection. On the other hand, the claimants are incorporated in a framework of tenure protection that is dependent on official administrative discretion or on contract. As studies of the Malawi tenant worker have shown, for example, the tenant worker hardly ever benefits from the exercise of favourable administrative discretion.[36] Equally, the tenant worker does not have the capacity, on account of a variety of reasons, to negotiate favourable contracts and to enforce breaches of contracts.[37]

A limited number of studies and anecdotal evidence suggest that the farm worker class is the last to benefit from any contemporary initiatives that seek to adjust the correlative common law position of limited personal rights holders and classes with insecure tenure.[38] This may be a consequence of several factors including a non-empathetic attitude that society has of the farm workers as a class perceived to hold a lowly position in society,[39] the effect of official choice of a particular development model,[40] the entrenched ideas that society holds about the meaning of property and the competition for land fuelled by the reality of social and economic privilege that the exclusive possession of property confers.

6.3.2 Locating the farm workers' question in the international human rights law framework

The question of farm workers' possession of insecure, non-proprietary and non-registrable rights and interests is an issue that falls squarely in the realm of land law reform. Inevitably, then, this becomes a political question to be determined largely through national frameworks of political and constitutional governance. Nonetheless, international human rights instruments and their associated obligation producing norms have a particular and important role of setting basic minimum standards which states must conform to in any land law reform process. The following discussion draws from the provisions of the ICCPR and the ICESCR.[41] The countries of the SADC region are signatories to these treaties. International state practice suggests that states which are signatories of these treaties view them as law-making treaties and that they possess exceptional compelling force.

One of the cardinal issues that farm workers raise is that they lack secure tenure and that they live under a constant threat of eviction.[42] This is an issue that has been addressed by international human rights law through the ICCPR and the ICESCR. The provision relevant to the security of tenure under the ICESCR is Article 11 which stipulates in part as follows:

> The States Parties to the present Covenant recognize the right of everyone to an adequate standard of living for himself and his family, including adequate food, clothing and housing, and to the continuous improvement of living conditions.

The relevant provision in the ICCPR is Article 17 which partly states:

> No one shall be subjected to arbitrary or unlawful interference with his privacy, family, home …

The Committee on Economic, Social and Cultural Rights (CESCR) through its General Comment No 4[43] and General Comment No 7[44] and the Human Rights Committee (HRC) through its General Comment No 16[45] have given interpretative accounts which explain the obligations that state parties to the ICESCR and the ICCPR are expected to discharge.[46]

The CESCR through its General Comment No 4 has interpreted the term 'housing' widely to mean 'the right to live somewhere in security, peace and dignity'. The CESCR, in relation to the concept of 'adequacy' in Article 11 as it applies to legal security of tenure, has interpreted it as applicable to a variety of forms of tenure including 'informal settlements' and that:

> Notwithstanding the type of tenure, all persons should possess a degree of security of tenure which guarantees legal protection against forced eviction, harassment and other threats. States parties should consequently take immediate measures aimed at conferring legal security of tenure upon those persons and households currently lacking such protection, in genuine consultation with affected persons and groups.

The CESCR also urges state parties to prioritize the cases of 'social groups living in unfavourable conditions by giving them particular consideration'. The CESCR in its General Comment No 7 has noted in relation to 'forced evictions' that:

> This expression seeks to convey a sense of arbitrariness and of illegality … The term 'forced evictions' as used throughout this general comment is defined as the permanent or temporary removal against their will of individuals, families and/or communities from the homes and/or land which they occupy, without the provision of, and access to, appropriate forms of legal or other protection.

The CESCR also urges state parties to 'refrain from forced evictions' and to enforce the law against agencies of the state and private parties 'who carry out forced evictions'.

Moreover, the CESCR General Comment No 7 urges state parties to develop a system of effective protection built on legislation which among other things includes measures which 'provide the greatest possible security of tenure' and 'are designed to control strictly the circumstances under which evictions may be carried out' and give recourse to mechanism for 'effective legal remedies and procedures' as well as 'legal assistance'. The legislation must be applicable to both agencies of the state and private entities. In circumstances where legislation and policies are in place state parties must review them in order to ensure their compatibility with international human rights law obligations.

The HRC through its General Comment No 16 has observed that state parties to the ICCPR have an obligation to guarantee against 'unlawful interference' emanating from both the agencies of the state as well as from non-state agencies whether natural or otherwise. The HRC has also interpreted Article 17 of the ICCPR as requiring them:

> to adopt legislative and other measures to give effect to the prohibition against such interferences and attacks as well as to the protection of the right.

Furthermore, the expression 'unlawful interference' has been interpreted as encompassing removal which is founded on law and yet is procedurally arbitrary, unreasonable and at variance with the 'aims' and 'objectives' of the ICCPR.

6.3.3 The regional SADC architecture: plotting a course for action

The issuance of the SADC summit directive in 2001 directing SADC ministers responsible for land affairs to develop a strategy for land reform for the SADC region was in principle a progressive act that recognized that land reform encapsulates questions that are regional in character and which require a common approach for them to be addressed effectively. A consequence of the summit directive is the creation of the SLRSF and the SADC secretariat describes the objectives of the SLRSF as intended to:

> Develop or implement a regional land strategy. National Policies remain paramount and the facility will simply provide a resource for

> Members States to call upon when developing or implementing their land and agrarian reforms policies or programmes to address national development priorities.[47]

The activities of the SLRSF will coalesce around areas which SADC member states have identified as requiring priority. The priority areas fall within four programmes of the SLRSF and they are 'policy formulation and implementation; land information and management; capacity building and research'.[48] Particularly interesting in this instance is the identification of 'farm workers and land rights' and the 'prospects for SADC land policy norms' as priority thematic areas on the research programme.

The statement of objectives essentially recognizes that the settlement of land reform and land law reform is ultimately an activity that will be settled through national action through local political and constitutional governance structures. It has been observed that international human rights norms have an important role to play in the land law reform process through the setting of basic minimum standards. The SLRSF provides a potential conduit through which international human rights norms may be channelled to ultimately influence structures, procedures and products of national land law reform programmes. The envisaged SLRSF programmes therefore have the capacity to convey international human rights norms on to the national political and constitutional governance frameworks which are the final arbiters on the land reform question. In the following section, it is shown how the principles of law and the administration of legislation have been employed to reinforce the weak position that the tenant worker has had in relation to private estate land.

6.4 The private estate in Malawi: the legal framework

6.4.1 The tenant worker: a distinct legal class

Malawi law, the Africans on Private Estates Act, 1962 (the Private Estates Act),[49] recognizes a category of persons who reside on the private estate pursuant to land access agreements – referred to under the Act as persons under a 'special agreement'.[50] The tenant worker on the private estates, on complying with required formalities under the Act, falls under the category of a special agreement private estate worker.

6.4.2 The legal regulation of the tenant worker's contract

Functionally, the Malawian special agreement provides a legal framework for the creation of contractual relationships on the private estate whose primary purpose is the production of commodities referred to under the Africans on Private Estates Act as economic crops. The contract must be written and it must provide for access to land. Furthermore, the minister concerned must be satisfied that the terms of the contract guarantee adequate security of tenure and that the contract is fair and equitable.[51] The tenant worker's contract is therefore an example of a contract which potentially may be constituted as a special agreement.

The use of the special agreement as a framework for the constitution of the tenant worker's contract in both the colonial and the post-colonial period has been disappointing. The private estate owning class has always created the impression that on the basis of the principles of law the tenant worker's contract does not confer proprietary rights on the tenant worker – although as an absolute view this position is incorrect both in law and in equity.[52] Inadvertently or otherwise, state practice, the conduct of the private estate owners and the social position of the tenant worker have combined to create a strong and enduring impression that proprietary rights – rights other than personal rights if any – do not extend to the tenant worker by virtue of his contract with the private estate owner. This view of state practice suggests official complicity in the questionable absolutist view that a proprietary jural relationship does not exist between the private estate owner and the tenant worker.

Similarly, the tenant worker has not fared well with regard to the specific question of security of tenure. Although section 25 of the Private Estates Act does attempt to address this question, it may be argued that the question of security of tenure ought to be dealt with independently from the question of whether the tenant worker acquires proprietary rights under a tenant worker's contract. This is mainly because, as the situation of the labour tenant in South Africa shows, these are distinct issues.[53] Moreover, the responsible minister has not adhered to the requirement set by the Private Estates Act that he or she must be satisfied the terms of the contract do guarantee adequate security of tenure.[54] Section 25 is intended to provide a mechanism to prevent or control such practices and to improve the tenant worker's bargaining capacity. However, section 25 is permit-based, as opposed to rights-based;[55] it depends on the initiative of the minister to bring it into operation and the minister has not been successful in that respect.

A consequence of the minister's failure is to place the tenant worker's contract outside the framework of the Private Estates Act and, in turn, this effect undermines efforts to prevent unjust and exploitative tendencies. Section 25 of the Private Estates Act, which is intended to protect a contracted person from economic, social and legal vulnerabilities, potentially enables the tenant worker to attain a dignified existence. Often the contract sets up a patron–client relationship and is susceptible to unjust and exploitative tendencies which include unlawful summary eviction and disregard of contractual provisions that secure the tenant worker's tenure. Tenant workers are often landless intra-territorial migrants compelled by circumstances to work on private estates. They are unable to negotiate for themselves favourable terms or to have them enforced through legal process.[56]

Studies of the tenant worker's contract have shown that the tenant worker's contract retains particular uncertainties over the nature of land access.[57] The framework of the special agreement ideally is intended to provide a mechanism for the resolution of such uncertainties. The placement of the contractual arrangement outside the framework undermines any attempt to minimize the uncertainties. This may manifest itself in the lack of clarity on the terms of access to land or employment protection. Consequently, such terms are assumed to be unreservedly at the discretion of the private estate owner. Inherent in the discretion is an inclination towards understanding the nature of land access as a short-term affair. In other words, the tenant worker has no guarantees of secure tenure whatsoever. Short-term land access or employment are associated with, and have as a symptom, the high turnover rates among tenant workers on the private estates.

From a developmental or a public interest perspective on the one hand and an economic efficiency point of view on the other hand short-term land access has debilitating economic and social costs.[58] Efficient production and investment are basic and crucial conditions if an individual in the tenant worker's circumstances is to raise her living standards. A tenant worker's contract is an economic undertaking. A tenant worker requires as a minimum a contractual relationship that allows him effectively and fairly to negotiate those terms of the contract that impact on financial viability. However, empirical evidence suggests that the tenant worker does not have effective bargaining power in such matters.[59] A case may be made that the lack of long-term access is detrimental to the tenant worker's social development. Consequently, failure to conform to requirements under section 25 frustrates the aim of policy to institute a regime of commodity production on the private estates that is based on social justice and which underlies the Private Estates Act.

6.5 Breach of international human rights obligations

It is an established fact that an important issue farm workers raise is the lack of secure tenure and that they live under a constant threat of eviction. This state of affairs is largely influenced by the nature of claims to the enjoyment of rights and interests in land that tenant workers can make. The claims of farm workers are marginal and are characterized as non-registrable and non-proprietary. In effect, farm workers are cast either completely outside any official rights-based framework of tenure protection or are dependent on administrative discretion or contract. In either case, the tenant worker operates under tenure which is very insecure.

Under the auspices of international human rights law, normative standards of good practice relevant to security of tenure have evolved and are considered 'authoritative' benchmarks against which national practice is measured. The discussion of the Malawi tenant worker illustrates clearly that, in many respects, the regulatory situation of the tenant worker falls short of the standards stipulated by the ICCPR, and the ICESCR and elaborated by the HCR and the CESCR respectively through the relevant general comments.

Immediately relevant to the situation of the tenant worker is the obligation to 'prioritize cases of social groups living in unfavourable conditions' and ensure that, through effective legislative measures, they are provided with 'the greatest possible security of tenure'. The legislative measures must be designed with the aim of controlling 'strictly the circumstances under which evictions' take place. The discussion of the tenant worker further shows that ignorance about the existence of 'effective legal remedies' and 'procedures' as well as lack of access to legal assistance are challenges that require to be addressed. The legislative and common law framework the tenant worker's contract operates in evidently falls short of giving the tenant worker effective legal protection and therefore it requires review. The framework does not satisfy the basic normative standards envisaged by Articles 11 and 17 of the ICESCR and the ICCPR respectively.

6.6 Towards a common settlement: the SLRSF framework as a driver for change

The evident social policy research activity on farm workers, action by grassroots movements of farm workers, and concrete, all be it marginal, social policy initiatives are strong indicators of a common acknowledgment of the existence of the farm workers' question and a cue that urgent action is needed to settle the situation of the farm worker. The establishment of the SLRSF as a regional institutional mechanism dedicated to the SADC region land question is a welcome development as land is a scarce and highly prized resource in the SADC region. An important feature of the SLRSF is its incorporation of the farm workers' question into the SLRSF agenda. This perhaps heralds the dawn of an era in which the question of farm workers will be featured as a priority in the agendas of the national governments of the SADC region.

The SLRSF lists as part of its envisaged programme research on 'farm workers and land rights' and on 'prospects for SADC land policy norms' among priority themes that require policy oriented research. Research activity on 'farm workers and land rights', alongside activity in the other SLRSF programmes, presents an opportunity for informed engagement on a question which until now appears not to have been the focus of robust debate from a concerted state sponsored transnational framework. Similarly, research activity on 'prospects for SADC land policy norms' also provides an opportunity to anchor the land question in general, and the question of farm workers in particular, in the terrain of well established international human rights norms through a regional SADC norm formation and inculcation process.[60]

6.6.1 Research on farm workers and land rights

Research practices are an effective tool for promoting progressive policy initiatives on the farm workers' question. Since policy action on the farm workers' question in the SADC region countries is not uniform, the identification of research on 'farm workers and land rights' as a priority research area presents a rare chance for 'positioning' the farm workers' question at both the national and regional levels. The expression 'positioning' is very significant in two respects. The farm workers must first seek visibility for their cause and, second, must engage in successful marketing of the farm workers' question as a legitimate research question.[61] To begin with Harry Bernstein observes that:

> There is little experience in modern Africa history of popular rural political organization on a broader scale centered on agrarian and land issues, again by contrast with Latin America and Asia with their histories … of rural social movements, and peasant leagues, unions and other forms of organization, and agricultural worker's associations … [62]

The observation by Bernstein suggests that there is very little experience of organized activism among farm workers. Activism entails visibility but effective visibility is not uniformly evident across the SADC region.

Positioning also relates to the capacity of the farm workers to advance a persuasive and sustained argument for research of a particular issue. The term 'positioning' denotes that the SLRSF will effectively create a market for research questions which interest groups will seek to exploit to their advantage. The research theme 'farm workers and land rights' does not necessarily preclude private land owners from using it as a platform in order to advance their own perspective and ultimately to influence policy and law making.[63] A typical example in this respect is given by Deborah James in her review of competition among interest groups in their attempt to influence state land reform policy in South Africa in the mid-1990s to the early years of the millennium. The visions advanced were, on the one hand, a 'populist and egalitarian' approach which favoured land restitution and land redistribution and, on the other hand, an approach a 'developmentalist focus associated with the influence of the World Bank' which promoted the 'primacy of the market' through the 'development of small-through medium to large scale agriculture'.[64]

The market for research then potentially creates space for the advancement of contradictory and competing perspectives and the jockeying for influence through the strategic positioning of ideas. The act of including farm workers' issues as a theme does not necessarily lead to the assumption that research will be sympathetic to the farm worker. It is submitted that there is an important link between visibility and the ability to successfully make a persuasive argument that the farm workers' question is an issue worthy of policy action informed by research. The promotion of the visibility of the farm workers' situation is a basic and a minimum requirement if, from the perspective of the farm worker, the goal is to influence policy makers to be more responsive to the rights and livelihood needs of farm workers.

The intensity (breadth and depth) of research activity on farm workers in the SADC region is not clear. The research that has been generated appears to be from a select number of countries and particularly South Africa and Zimbabwe.[65] For example Edge Kanyongolo writing on the phenomenon of 'illegal' land occupations or 'squatting' in Malawi observes that:

> Land occupations in Malawi have attracted very little academic attention. In the vast literature on the land and agrarian questions in Malawi, land

occupations are generally mentioned in a cursory manner and largely conceptualised as a social pathological phenomenon.[66]

This suggests that there may be countries within the region in which the question of the farm worker needs attention and yet these countries are not normally associated with the question. An implication here is that these countries may also not be addressing the question at the policy, legislative and research levels.[67] The SLRSF programme presents a platform for engaging in comparative research practices which in turn have the potential to draw out common aspects as well as differences from a range of perspectives. The observation made by Moyo and Yeros on the state of the academy's attitude to the agaraian question suggests that the identification of what constitutes relevant and useful 'research' might itself constitute contested terrain.[68]

Moyo and Yeros decry the turn that the discourse on the agrarian question has taken towards 'rarefied debates over identity politics' which they denounce as focusing on irrelevant and non-causative questions. For Moyo and Yeros the reason for this state of affairs lies in the emasculation and 'co-optation of both academia and "oppositional" politics' leading to the abandonment of 'the agrarian question'.[69] The issue which is highlighted by this observation requires to be taken seriously. As a cautionary tale it can equally be applied to the operationalization of the SLRSF research agenda. For example the farm workers' question may, depending on preferences as to the appropriate development model, be considered insignificant. Research activity informed by public choice theory is, for example, likely to argue that regulating the relationship between the farm worker and a land owner imposes costs, results in unintended consequences and ultimately will impede the development goals sought by the SADC region countries.[70]

In some SADC region countries the farm workers' question has suffered not so much from its abandonment as from lack of any meaningful engagement at all. Elsewhere I have suggested, in relation to Malawi, that this lack of engagement is consistent with the development model preferred by the state. Allied to this observation is the nature of the legal paradigm that the farm workers' question labours under. This question is held hostage to hegemonic, entrenched and apparently ineradicable paradigmatic ideas about the legal meaning of property and the incidental exclusivity that this meaning carries with it. The farm workers' situation is one which can only be resolved by transcending these ideas. Consequently, from a legal and policy perspective there will be a need to engage in research activity that seeks to transcend the prevailing orthodoxy. For example comparative research might look into the possibility of replicating the constitutionally inspired statutory and common law changes in South Africa with a view to adjusting the relative positions of the farm worker and the private land owner from the point of view of traditional received Roman-Dutch and English common laws.[71]

6.6.2 Research on prospects for SADC land policy norms

The SLRSF is, as part of its research agenda, also charged with the responsibility for commissioning research aimed at the examination of the 'prospects for SADC land policy norms'. This mandate presents an invaluable window of opportunity in the light of a background of conflict and threats of conflict over land in some of the SADC region countries.[72] In so far as the question of security of tenure on the private estate is concerned, the norms that have evolved at the level of international human rights law provide a starting point in the process of norm formulation and inculcation. In this regard the SLRSF can be viewed as an excellent opportunity for the production of regional transnational norms in an area of immense economic, social and political importance and which until now has been devoid of any common standards.

Farm workers on account of historical reasons across the SADC region have rights and interests in land which are conventionally described as insecure, personal and non-registrable rights. These in effect provide them, formally, with very limited protection. It is also the case that authority for changes in the law aimed at alleviating the precarious situation of the farm workers will emanate from the national constitutional and political frameworks. However, established norms within the international human rights law framework equally have an important role in guiding national reform process through the provision of good standards of practice. The SLRSF land policy norm formation process provides a point of entry through which such international human rights law norms can filter down to national land reform processes.

Scholars of international law and international relations have thrown some light on the norm formation process between states although there is considerable theoretical divergence in their explanations.[73] Exposition by these scholars covers a range of international state interaction contexts. For example Oona Hathaway draws attention to the distinction between international human rights law and commercially oriented international law from a compliance perspective and opines that the impellents for compliance existing in commercial international law are absent in international human rights law. Thus international human rights law neither has 'competitive market forces' nor is it an area where states will engage in retaliatory action on account of perceived compliance related breaches.[74] This chapter limits its focus to international human rights law norm formation and compliance.[75] Consequently, the argument maintained here is that the norm-forming process is especially relevant to farm workers. The ICCPR and the ICESCR are therefore important sources of norms in this regard.

The envisaged land policy norm-formation process, it is submitted, is one that a variety of groups with either a direct or indirect stake in the land reform process will naturally feel they are entitled to engage in.[76] Normativists also recognize the important role that non-governmental activism plays in norm formation and compliance.[77] Although governments are conventionally viewed as the natural protagonists in norm formation at the international interstate level, the picture is much more complicated. The possible participants in this process will certainly not be limited to the SADC governments. This aspect of norm formation is explained from a normativist perspective as follows:

> This process of norm proliferation and socialization is aided by the human rights activism of nongovernmental organizations, which motivate international discourse on human rights, establish international networks of people and institutions to monitor human rights violations, and rally public opinion in support of efforts to convince governments to create human rights regimes and press other states to join them.[78]

This portrait of norm formation indicates that beyond the issue of visibility farm workers groups will, if they are to exert any influence in policy and law making, have to engage with the norm formation process. Ultimately, this process of norm formation is expected to culminate into an overarching and directory structure of standards of good practice against which practices within states and by states are measured.

The issue of participation in turn raises the following question: what are the legitimate sources from which principles of norm formation are to be drawn? In other words, is the assumption that the norms set by the ICCPR and the ICESCR are capable of being viewed as legitimate instruments from which the SADC norm-formation process can draw from a correct one? This question immediately raises a scenario of a complicated and contradictory norm-forming process whose outcome cannot be predicted with certainty. A strand of scholarship on international norm formation emphasizes the importance of 'legitimacy'. This approach is referred to as the 'fairness model'. Legitimacy in this instance is understood as the fairness of the process of norm production as well as the fairness of the practical application of the international normative system or regimes.[79] For example there is indication that the ideals and assumptions underlying the land settlement in Zimbabwe and which apparently inspired the Zimbabwean independence constitutional framework did not enjoy universal legitimacy.[80]

The fairness approach resonates with the peculiar agrarian question in the SADC region. Land reform processes in the region are impelled by a legitimacy deficit in the prevailing land regimes. For example, received law has a peculiar view of 'fairness' which may not be compatible with 'fairness' as understood by those that are on the receiving end of the rough edges of received law. This dissonance permeates the range of the agrarian-based legal, social and economic relations implicated in the land question. An assumption is made here that the 'fairness' view advanced by received law is different from the 'fairness' reflected in the ICCPR and the ICESCR. Consequently, a possible path towards the transcendence of the divide is provided by the international human rights system which has in other contexts managed to attain a measure of respectability and fairness.[81] For example Galit Safarty explains that:

> The language of human rights has become a platform for organizing the international indigenous movement. Its rhetoric has entitled indigenous peoples to claim legitimacy for their campaigns for political, economic and cultural autonomy.[82]

Allied to the legitimacy question is a concern about possible compliance with the dictates of the principles that the SADC states will eventually endorse as the fundamental governing framework for the resolution of the land question. In other words what are the impellents that induce compliance with international norms? Here again, scholars of international law and international relations shed some light though they offer different explanations for state compliance.

Rational actor theorists suggest that states or individuals within decision-making positions in states behave in the same way as '*homo economicus*'; they act as a rational individual would in a market place in order to maximize their self-interest.[83] Consequently, states carry out cost-benefit analyses to determine whether compliance with a particular norm will further the interest of the state.[84] Motivation in this respect can therefore range from a genuine commitment to a particular set of international norms, sheer coincidence between norms and the 'path dictated by self-interest' through to fear of offending a more powerful hegemon who sets great store in a particular set of international norms.[85] For example the controversial land redistribution programme in Zimbabwe is perhaps a consequence of a regime undertaking particular action in order to further its own interest. In other words, the survival of the regime was dependent on demonstrating solidarity with an important constituency in the countryside as opposed to doing the 'optically' right thing as seen from the perspective of the 'international community'.

For normativists, state compliance is brought about purely by 'the persuasive power of legitimate legal obligations'.[86] Normativists argue that compliance comes about either because a treaty articulates legal norms which have an intrinsic authority; whether there is sufficient information and capacity; whether the state is liberal democratic in character; whether the norms are fair and legitimate or whether the state has undergone an iterative interactive process which leads to norm socialization and inculcation. Consequently, the question of compliance is thus dependent on whether there is sufficient information and capacity on the part of the state parties to fulfil the demands of a normative regime; whether the norms are compatible with the states' liberal democratic character; whether the norms are fair and legitimate or whether the state has undergone norm socialization.[87]

Ultimately, it is not clear how the process of land policy norm generation is intended to operate and any comment to that extent will be merely speculative. However, it appears that irrespective of the anticipated overarching normative structure the requirements of the ICCPR and ICESCR are not fundamentally inimical to the existing constitutional and Roman-Dutch and English common law systems of the SADC region countries. In the words of McAuslan what is required is that:

> the law has to be much more specific, detailed and clear. Such aspects as the nature and limits of private rights; how they may be acquired, disposed of, burdened, lost; the whole issue of third party rights; and, where the state is to remain involved, a more exact demarcation of state power and its limits … these all have to be spelt out in detail so that all those who have private rights, or intend to try to obtain private rights in land can predict with reasonable certainty the scope and operation of the law applicable to those rights.[88]

6.7 Conclusion

In 2000, commenting on the situation in Zimbabwe, Ben Chigara observed that the 'issue of inequitable land distribution appears to be the single biggest economic, political and social concern confronting the people'.[89] The uncomfortable truth about this observation is that ten years on it remains a legitimate observation of the current situation in Zimbabwe. This observation is equally applicable to the rest of the SADC region.

A question that looms large in this situation is the identification of groups that ought to be considered as legitimately deserving of equal attention in the land question resolution process. Farm workers in the SADC region have, for over a century, been an important feature of the private estate economy and yet they often tend to be viewed as least deserving. Furthermore, the farm workers' cause has in some countries attained notoriety because the farm workers have been caught between choosing a nuanced approach to resolving the land question and the absolutist view that is implacably hostile to the existence of a private estate economy.[90]

The setting up of the SLRSF by the SADC region countries is a very welcome development as it appears to provide an entry point for the initiation of a region-wide discussion respecting the specific features of the land reform process and the principles which ought to underpin it. In the specific context of the farm workers' question the SLRSF has the capacity to mediate in what is clearly a contemporary problem of regional proportions. For example, it is widely accepted that among the farm workers are nationals of the SADC region countries some of whom have lived in the host countries for decades.[91] Research is therefore a very important aspect to this question.

Obviously, the capacity of farm worker groups to successfully bring about the adjustment of their tenure and proprietary position on the private estate relative to the private estate owner will ultimately be a function of national political and constitutional frameworks. The question is whether the regional states will feel sufficiently persuaded by either self-interest or the inherent legitimacy of the land policy norms in order to accept the ICCPR and the ICESCR inspired normative structure as a useful standard. A possible outcome of the norm-formation process may, in fact, be a bilateral and therefore flexible case-by-case approach as opposed to a multilateral all-encompassing inflexible framework. Irrespective of the approach chosen, there is reason to expect that a normative structure based on the ICCPR and the ICESCR can be successfully introduced at the national level.

Notes

1 PhD, Lecturer, National University of Ireland Maynooth.
2 Available at <http://www.sadc.int/fanr/environment/landreform/index.php> (accessed 16 March 2010).
3 (1997) 'The Southern African Charter on Land, Labour and Food Security', *African Journal of Political Science*, 2(2): 118–31.
4 From a legal perspective, are the cardinal features of the farm workers' question is whether the farm workers have secure tenure and whether their interests are to be

considered proprietary. The private estate land holdings in the SADC region are referred to by a variety of terms including farms, commercial farms, private estates and estates. Similarly, the expression 'farm worker' is intended to capture a range of agriculture workers including employees, sharecroppers, the tenant worker and the labour tenant. This is not an exhaustive list. For comparative discussion of the tenant worker and the labour tenant, see Sibo Banda (2006) 'Land Law Reform: A Comparative Analysis of South Africa's Labour Tenancy Contract and Malawi's Tenant Worker's Contract', *Oxford University Commonwealth Law Journal*, 6(2): 201. For a discussion of commercial farm workers of Zimbabwe, see Blair Rutherford (2001) *Working on the Margins: Black Workers, White Farmers in Zimbabwe* (New York, NY: Zed Books).

5 For Malawi, see J. McCracken (1983) 'Planters, Peasants and the Colonial State: The Impact of the Native Tobacco Board in the Central Province of Malawi', *Journal of Southern African Studies*, 9: 172, and J. McCracken (1985) 'Share-Cropping in Malawi: The Visiting Tenant System in the Central Province c. 1920–1968', in Centre of African Studies, University of Edinburgh, *Seminar Proceedings No 25, Malawi: An Alternative Pattern of Development* (Edinburgh: Centre of African Studies, University of Edinburgh), p 35. For South Africa, see Collin Bundy (1979) *The Rise and Fall of the South African Peasantry* (London: Heinemann), M. Hathorn and D. Hutchison (1990) 'Labour Tenants and the Law', in C. Murray and C. O'Regan (eds) *No Place to Rest: Forced Removals and the Law in South Africa* (Cape Town: Oxford University Press), p 194, and A. Ditlhake (1997) 'Labor Tenancy and the Politics of Land Reform in South Africa', in R. Levin and D. Wiener (eds) *No More Tears: Struggles for Land in Mpumalanga* (Trenton: Africa World Press), p 226.

6 Harry Bernstein (2005) 'Rural Land and Land Conflicts in Sub-Saharan Africa', in Sam Moyo and Paris Yeros (eds) *Reclaiming the land: The Resurgence of Rural Movements in Africa, Asia and Latin America* (London: Zed Books).

7 Ibid, pp 85–86; Ben Chigara (2001) 'From Oral to Recorded Governance: Reconstructing Title to Real Property in 21st Century Zimbabwe', *Common Law World Review*, 30: 36, and Issa Shivji (2000) 'Contradictory Perspectives on Rights and Justice in the Context of Land tenure reform in Tanzania', in Abdullahi A. An-Na'im (ed) *Cultural Transformation and Human Rights in Africa* (New York, NY: Zed Books), pp 192, 195–6.

8 Ibid.

9 The expression 'rights and interests' is here used to describe entitlements other than and distinct from legally recognized rights and interests which are capable of binding third parties and also assigned to third parties. This description as a conceptual legal expression of art is recognized in both the Roman-Dutch (otherwise also referred to as civil law systems) and English common law based legal systems of the SADC region.

10 A good example is a programme run in the University of Western Cape's Institute for Poverty, Land and Agrarian Studies (PLAAS) on farm workers entitled 'Farm workers and farm dwellers in South Africa: tenure, livelihoods and social justice', available at <http://www.plaas.org.za/research/land/farmworkers.> (accessed 16 March 2010). The programme aims to, among other things, 'document and analyse the impact of land reform on farm workers and farm dwellers, as beneficiaries and as non-beneficiaries'.

11 Above, n 3.

12 Above, n 3.

13 Above, n 3.

14 Above, n 3. Andrew Hartnack (2005) 'My life got Lost: Farm workers and displacement in Zimbabwe', *Journal of Contemporary African Studies*, 23(2): 173–92.

15 For example, economically Malawi significantly depends on the tobacco growing and exporting industry and farm workers, who make a very important contribution to the industry, are not mentioned at all in the Malawi Land Policy.

16 D. L. Carey Miller and A. Pope (2000) 'South African Land Reform', *Journal of African Law*, 44: 167, and Ditlhake, above, n 5.

17 Available at http://www.sadc.int/fanr/environment/landreform/index.php (accessed 16 March 2010).
18 Hathorn and Hutchison, above, n 5.
19 Furthermore, the labour tenancy contract did not fall within the ambit of the Natives Land Act 1913 (which restricted ownership of land by blacks) on the basis that it did not constitute an agreement or transaction for the 'purchase, hire or acquisition' of land.
20 N. Haysom (1990) 'Rural Land Struggles: Practising Law Democratically', in C. Murray and C. O'Regan (eds) *No Place to Rest: Forced Removals and the Law in South Africa* (Cape Town: Oxford University Press), p 107. See also Ditlhake, above, n 5, pp 228–30, and Hathorn and Hutchison, above, n 5.
21 Ibid. Carey Miller and Pope, above, n 16, and D. L. Carey Miller (1999) 'The Reform of South African Land Law in its Roman-Dutch Context: New Wine?', in P. Jackson and D. C. Wilde (eds) *Contemporary Property Law* (Aldershot: Ashgate), and for a critque of the measures taken, see Ditlhake, above, n 5.
22 P. McAuslan (1998) 'Making Law Work: Restructuring Land Relations in Africa', *Development and Change*, 29: 525, 528 where it is stated: 'Land reform in South Africa, then, must include land *law* reform because it seeks to change the nature of the legal regime and the legal culture that applies to African-held land. It is to replace, at best, licences or permits held at the mercy of law, with *rights* guaranteed by law' (original emphasis).
23 Although the process has been largely welcomed it nonetheless has had some of its aspects criticised. Ditlhake, above, n 5.
24 Carey Miller and Pope, above, n 16; J. Pienaar, 'Extending Security of Tenure in South Africa: Labour Tenants and Farm Workers', in P. Jackson and D. C. Wilde (eds) *Contemporary Property Law* (Aldershot: Ashgate), p 317; B. Cousins (1998) 'How do Rights Become Real? Formal and Informal Institutions in South Africa's Reform Programme', International Conference on Land Tenure in the Developing World with a Focus on Southern Africa, available at <http://www.geomatics.ucalgary.ca/~barry/Research/Publications/Publications%20Page/PublicationsOnWeb/capetown.PDF> (accessed 27 December 2006).
25 Act 3 of 1996.
26 Act 62 of 1997.
27 Banda, above, n 4.
28 Banda, above, n 4.
29 Republic of Malawi, Ministry of Lands, Housing, Physical Planning and Surveys, Malawi National Land Policy (Lilongwe 2002), available at <http://www.malawi.gov.mw/publications/landpol.htm> (accessed 27 December 2006).
30 Ibid.
31 Ibid.
32 It is noteworthy that corrective legislative action has been envisaged outside the land law reform process, although all efforts in this regard have not yielded positive results to date.
33 See J. P. McAuslan (2003) *Bringing the Law Back In: Essays in Land, Law and Development* (Aldershot: Ashgate), and Ben Chigara (2003) *Land Policy Reform: The Challenge of Human Rights Law* (Aldershot: Ashgate). For a conceptual discussion of legal pluralism, see Gordon Woodman (1998) 'Ideological Combat and Social Observation: Recent Debate about Legal Pluralism', *Legal Pluralism and Unofficial Law*, 42: 21.
34 Hanri Mostert (2003) 'The Diversification of Land Rights and its Implications for a New Land Law in South Africa: An Appraisal Concentrating on the Transformation of the South African System of Title Registration', in E. Cooke (ed) *Modern Studies in Property Law* (Oxford: Hart Publishing), vol II, p 4.
35 Kevin Grey (1996) 'Property in Common Law Systems', in G. E. Van Maanen and A. J. Van der Walt (eds) *Property Law on the Threshold of the 21st Century, Proceedings of the International Colloquium* (Maastricht: Maklu), and Graham Battersby (1998) 'Informally

Created Interests in Land', in S. Bright and J. Dewar (eds) *Land Law: Themes and Perspectives* (Oxford: Oxford University Press), p 487.

36 Banda, above, n 4, and Sibo Banda (2009) 'Constitutional Mimicry and Common Law Reform in a Rights-Based Post-Colonial Setting: The Case of South Africa and Malawi', *Journal of African Law*, 53(1): 142–70.

37 Ibid.

38 Banda, above, n 4.

39 Banda, above, n 4.

40 Banda, above, n 4.

41 <http://www2.ohchr.org/english/law/ccpr.htm> and <http://www2.ohchr.org/english/law/cescr.htm> (accessed 20 February 2010).

42 Jean du Plessis (2005) 'The Growing Problem of Forced Evictions and the Crucial Importance of Community-based, Locally Appropriate Alternatives', *Environment and Urbanisation*, 17(1): 123–34.

43 The right to adequate housing (Art 11.1): 13/12/91, CESCR General Comment 4, available at <http://www.unhchr.ch/tbs/doc.nsf/(Symbol)/469f4d91a9378221c12563ed0053547e?Opendocument> (accessed 20 February 2010).

44 The right to adequate housing (Art 11.1): forced evictions: 20/05/97, CESCR General Comment 7, available at <http://www.unhchr.ch/tbs/doc.nsf/(Symbol)/959f71e476284596802564c3005d8d50?Opendocument> (accessed 20 February 2010).

45 The right to respect privacy, family, home and correspondence, and protection of honour and reputation (Art 17): 08/04/88, CCPR General Comment No 16, available at <http://www.unhchr.ch/tbs/doc.nsf/(Symbol)/23378a8724595410c12563ed004aeecd?Opendocument> (accessed 20 February 2010).

46 The 'role of the General Comment [has] come to take on an almost exclusively "law-making" function … They are widely considered as authoritative interpretative statements, and a device through which treaty bodies articulate their understanding of human rights norms. Far from being merely hortatory, they can in some ways be likened to the advisory opinions of the International Court of Justice'. Conway Blake (2008) 'Normative Instruments in International Human Rights Law: Locating the General Comment', Center for Human Rights and Global Justice, Working Paper No 17, available at <http://www.chrgj.org/publications/docs/wp/blake.pdf> (accessed 20 February 2010).

47 <http://www.sadc.int/fanr/environment/landreform/about.php> (accessed 16 March 2010).

48 Ibid.

49 Banda, above, n 4. The provisions of the Africans on Private Estates Act, 1962 have their origins in the colonial Natives on Private Estates Ordinance, 1962 and the Natives on Private Estates Ordinance, 1928.

50 Ibid.

51 Section 25 of the Private Estates Act provides: '(1) Any owner may enter into a written special agreement with any African [who] … is entitled to reside on the estate of such owner; (2) … an African who enters into such agreement shall be required to work for the owner of the estate for such period during the year as may be agreed upon; Provided that: … (b) no agreement shall be approved by the minister as a special agreement unless he is satisfied that it provides for adequate security of tenure … and is fair and equitable in all circumstances' (emphasis added).

52 Banda, above, n 4. Rutherford, above, n 4.

53 For an informative discussion on this in the context of English law, see Battersby, above, n 35. See also Banda, above, n 4.

54 The task that the minister has is much more complicated than it first appears on its face on account of the requirements of the law (common law and statute law) and equity.

55 Banda, above, n 4.

56 Banda, above, n 4, and Banda, above, n 36.

57 Banda, above, n 4, and Banda, above, n 36.

58 Michael Cardwell, 'Land and Agricultural Production', in S. Bright and J. Dewar (eds) *Land Law: Themes and Perspectives* (Oxford: Oxford University Press), p 406. See also Banda, above, n 4, and Banda, above, n 36.
59 Banda, above, n 4, and Banda, above, n 36.
60 This observation is not a suggestion that there is no research available aimed at influencing policy. Rather research appears to have been done outside any official regional framework such as the SLRSF presents.
61 Positioning relates to the capacity of the farm workers to advance a persuasive and sustained argument for research of a particular issue.
62 Bernstein, above, n 6, p 88.
63 Allison Goebel (2005) 'Is Zimbabwe the Future of South Africa? The Implications for Land Reform in Southern Africa', *Journal of Contemporary African Studies*, 23(3): 345–70.
64 Deborah James (2001) 'Land for the Landless: Conflicting Images or Rural and Urban South Africa's Land Reform Programme', *Journal of Contemporary African Studies*, 19(1): 93, 103.
65 'Farm workers and farm dwellers in South Africa', above, n 10. It is also possible that research may be available but is not published.
66 Fidelis Edge Kanyongolo (2005) 'Land Occupations in Malawi: Challenging the Neoliberal Order', in Sam Moyo and Paris Yeros (eds) *Reclaiming the land: The Resurgence of Rural Movements in Africa, Asia and Latin America* (London: Zed Books), p 118. Farm workers are often labelled illegal land occupiers in order to justify the summary termination of their land tenure. See also Banda, above, n 36, Mfaniseni Fana Sihlongonyane (2005) 'Land Occupations in South Africa', in Sam Moyo and Paris Yeros (eds) *Reclaiming the land: The Resurgence of Rural Movements in Africa, Asia and Latin America* (London: Zed Books), pp 142–43. See also Banda, above, n 4, as regards the combined attitude of farm workers and state in Malawi towards farm workers.
67 Although some research work has been done on the farm worker in Malawi it may be dated. From a policy perspective Malawi has articulated its desire to see the exploitation of children in tenant worker contracts eradicated in an effort to comply with relevant International Labour Organisation standards and particularly the Declaration on Fundamental Principles and Rights at Work in 1998. However, Malawi is an example of a country that has invested very little in comprehensive action at the policy and legislative levels.
68 Sam Moyo and Paris Yeros (2005) 'Land Occupations and Land Reform in Zimbabwe: Towards the National Democratic Revolution', in Sam Moyo and Paris Yeros (eds) *Reclaiming the land: The Resurgence of Rural Movements in Africa, Asia and Latin America* (London: Zed Books), p 165.
69 Ibid, p 166.
70 Bronwen Morgan and Karen Yeung (2007) *An Introduction to Law and Regulation* (Cambridge: Cambridge University Press).
71 For examples of discussion on statutory and judicial limitation or expansion of principles of Roman-Dutch and English common laws see Banda, above, n 36; A. J. Van der Walt (2002) 'Exclusivity of ownership, security of tenure and eviction orders: A critical evaluation of recent case law', *South African Journal on Human Rights*, 18: 372, and A. J. Van der Walt (2002) 'Progressive indirect horizontal application of the Bill of Rights: Towards a co-operative relation between common-law and constitutional jurisprudence', *South African Journal on Human Rights*, 17(3): 341.
72 Moyo and Yeros, above, n 68, p 165. Goebel, above, n 63.
73 Oona Hathaway (2001) 'Do Human Rights Treaties Make a Difference?', *Yale Law Journal*, 111: 1935, 1957. Hathaway in her review of literature on this subject identifies two main theoretical trends and these are approaches influenced by rational choice theory on the one hand and normativist approaches on the other hand.
74 Ibid.
75 Ibid. What motivates states to comply with international human rights law is an area that appears to lack clarity.

76 For example powerful multilateral development oriented organizations and foreign aid and development departments of developed states have been closely associated with the land reform processes happening in the SADC region and their views are often very persuasive.
77 Harold Honhju Koh (1996) 'Transnational Legal Process', *Nebraska Law Review*: 181, 207.
78 Hathaway, above, n 73.
79 Thomas Franck is a major proponent of the 'fairness model'. See Thomas M. Franck (1995) *Fairness in International Law and Institutions* (Oxford: Oxford University Press), and Thomas M. Franck (1998) 'Legitimacy in the International System', *American Journal of International Law*, 82: 705.
80 Chigara, above, n 33, and Goebel, above, n 63, and Moyo and Yeros, above, n 68.
81 For example indigenous groups have appropriated human rights language in order to advance their agenda.
82 Galit A. Sarfaty (2007) 'International Norm Diffusion in the Pimicikamak Cree Nation: A Model of Legal Mediation', *Harvard International Law Journal*, 48(2): 441.
83 Morgan and Yeung, above, n 70.
84 Hathaway, above, n 73.
85 Hathaway, above, n 73; Honhju Koh, above, n 77, and Sarfaty, above, n 82.
86 Hathaway, above, n 73.
87 Hathaway, above, n 73; Honhju Koh, above, n 77, and Sarfaty, above, n 82.
88 McAuslan, above, n 22, pp 525, 528.
89 Chigara, above, n 7.
90 Rutherford, above, n 4.
91 Joyce M. Chadya and Peter Mayavo (2002) '"The Curse of Old Age": Elderly Workers on Zimbabwe's Large Scale Commercial Farms, with Particular Reference to "Foreign" Farm Labourers up to 2000', *Zambezia*, XXIX (i), available at <http://archive.lib.msu.edu/DMC/African%20Journals/pdfs/Journal%20of%20the%20University%20of%20Zimbabwe/ vol29n1/juz029001003.pdf> (accessed 21 March 2010), Blair Rutherford (2002) 'Commercial Farm Workers and the Politics of (Dis)placement in Zimbabwe: Colonialism, Liberation and Democracy', *Journal of Agrarian Change*, 1(4): 626–51, and Blair Rutherford (2008) 'An unsettled belonging: Zimbabwean farm workers in Limpopo Province, South Africa', *Journal of Contemporary African Studies*, 26(4): 401–15.

Bibliography

Banda, Sibo (2006) 'Land Law Reform: A Comparative Analysis of South Africa's Labour Tenancy Contract and Malawi's Tenant Worker's Contract', *Oxford University Commonwealth Law Journal*, 6: 201.

Banda, Sibo (2009) 'Constitutional Mimicry and Common Law Reform in a Rights-Based Post-Colonial Setting: The Case of South Africa and Malawi', *Journal of African Law*, 53: 142.

Battersby, Graham (1998) 'Informally Created Interests in Land', in S. Bright and J. Dewar (eds) *Land Law: Themes and Perspectives* (Oxford: Oxford University Press).

Bernstein, Harry (2005) 'Rural Land and Land Conflicts in Sub-Saharan Africa', in Sam Moyo and Paris Yeros (eds) *Reclaiming the land: The Resurgence of Rural Movements in Africa, Asia and Latin America* (London: Zed Books).

Blake, Conway (2008) 'Normative Instruments in International Human Rights Law: Locating the General Comment', Center for Human Rights and Global Justice, Working Paper No 17, available at <http://www.chrgj.org/publications/docs/wp/blake.pdf> (accessed 20 February 2010).

Bundy, Collin (1979) *The Rise and Fall of the South African Peasantry* (London: Heinemann).

Cardwell, Michael (1998) 'Land and Agricultural Production', in S. Bright and J. Dewar (eds) *Land Law: Themes and Perspectives* (Oxford: Oxford University Press).

Carey Miller, D. L. (1999) 'The Reform of South African Land Law in its Roman-Dutch Context: New Wine?', in P. Jackson and D. C. Wilde (eds), *Contemporary Property Law* (Aldershot: Ashgate).

Carey Miller, D. L. and Pope, A. (2000) 'South African Land Reform', *Journal of African Law*, 44: 167.

Chadya, Joyce M. and Mayavo, Peter (2002) '"The Curse of Old Age": Elderly Workers on Zimbabwe's Large Scale Commercial Farms, with Particular Reference to "Foreign" Farm Labourers up to 2000', *Zambezia*, XXIX (i), available at <http://archive.lib.msu.edu/DMC/African%20Journals/pdfs/Journal%20of%20the%20University%20of%20Zimbabwe/vol29n1/juz029001003.pdf> (accessed 21 March 2010).

Chigara, Ben (2001) 'From Oral to Recorded Governance: Reconstructing Title to Real Property in 21st Century Zimbabwe', *Common Law World Review*, 30: 36.

Chigara, Ben (2003) *Land Policy Reform: The Challenge of Human Rights Law* (Aldershot: Ashgate).

Cousins, Ben (1998) 'How do Rights Become Real? Formal and Informal Institutions in South Africa's Reform Programme', International Conference on Land Tenure in the Developing World with a Focus on Southern Africa, available at <http://www.geomatics.ucalgary.ca/~barry/Research/Publications/Publications%20Page/PublicationsOnWeb/capetown.PDF> (accessed 27 December 2006).

Ditlhake, Albie (1997) 'Labor Tenancy and the Politics of Land Reform in South Africa', in R. Levin and D. Wiener (eds) *No More Tears: Struggles for Land in Mpumalanga* (Trenton: Africa World Press).

du Plessis, Jean (2005) 'The Growing Problem of Forced Evictions and the Crucial Importance of Community-based, Locally Appropriate Alternatives', *Environment and Urbanisation*, 17: 123.

Franck, Thomas M. (1988) 'Legitimacy in the International System', *American Journal of International Law*, 82: 705.

Franck, Thomas M. (1995) *Fairness in International Law and Institutions* (Oxford: Oxford University Press).

Goebel, Allison (2005) 'Is Zimbabwe the Future of South Africa? The Implications for Land Reform in Southern Africa', *Journal of Contemporary African Studies*, 23(2): 173.

Grey, Kevin (1996) 'Property in Common Law Systems', in G. E. Van Maanen and A. J. Van der Walt (eds) *Property Law on the Threshold of the 21st Century, Proceedings of the International Colloquium* (Maastricht: Maklu).

Hartnack, Andrew (2005) 'My life got Lost: Farm workers and Displacement in Zimbabwe', *Journal of Contemporary African Studies*, 23(2): 173.

Hathaway, Oona (2001) 'Do Human Rights Treaties Make a Difference?', *Yale Law Journal*, 2: 1935.

Hathorn, M. and Hutchison, D. (1990) 'Labour Tenants and the Law', in C. Murray and C. O'Regan (eds) *No Place to Rest: Forced Removals and the Law in South Africa* (Cape Town: Oxford University Press).

Haysom, N. (1990) 'Rural Land Struggles: Practising Law Democratically', in C. Murray and C. O'Regan (eds) *No Place to Rest: Forced Removals and the Law in South Africa* (Cape Town: Oxford University Press).

James, Deborah (2001) 'Land for the Landless: Conflicting Images or Rural and Urban South Africa's Land Reform Programme', *Journal of Contemporary African Studies*, 19(1): 93.

Kanyongolo, F. Edge (2005) 'Land Occupations in Malawi: Challenging the Neoliberal Order', in Sam Moyo and Paris Yeros (eds) *Reclaiming the land: The Resurgence of Rural Movements in Africa, Asia and Latin America* (London: Zed Books).

Koh, Harold Honhju (1996) 'Transnational Legal Process', *Nebraska Law Review*: 181.

McAuslan, J. P. (1998) 'Making Law Work: Restructuring Land Relations in Africa', *Development and Change*, 29: 525.

McAuslan, J. P. (2003) *Bringing the Law Back In: Essays in Land, Law and Development* (Aldershot: Ashgate).

McCracken, J. (1983) 'Planters, Peasants and the Colonial State: The Impact of the Native Tobacco Board in the Central Province of Malawi', *Journal of Southern African Studies*, 9: 172.

McCracken, J. (1985) 'Share-Cropping in Malawi: The Visiting Tenant System in the Central Province c. 1920–68', in Centre of African Studies, University of Edinburgh, *Seminar Proceedings No 25, Malawi: An Alternative Pattern of Development* (Edinburgh: Centre of African Studies University of Edinburgh).

Morgan, Bronwen and Yeung, Karen (2007) *An Introduction to Law and Regulation* (Cambridge: Cambridge University Press).

Mostert, Hanri (2003) 'The Diversification of Land Rights and its Implications for a New Land Law in South Africa: An Appraisal Concentrating on the Transformation of the South African System of Title Registration', in E. Cooke (ed) *Modern Studies in Property Law* (Oxford: Hart Publishing).

Moyo, Sam and Yeros, Paris (2005) 'Land Occupations and Land Reform in Zimbabwe: Towards the National Democratic Revolution', in Sam Moyo and Paris Yeros (eds) *Reclaiming the land: The Resurgence of Rural Movements in Africa, Asia and Latin America* (London: Zed Books).

Pienaar, J. (1999) 'Extending Security of Tenure in South Africa: Labour Tenants and Farm Workers', in P. Jackson and D. C. Wilde (eds) *Contemporary Property Law* (Aldershot: Ashgate).

Rutherford, Blair (2001) *Working on the Margins: Black Workers White Farmers in Zimbabwe* (New York, NY: Zed Books).

Rutherford, Blair (2002) 'Commercial Farm Workers and the Politics of (Dis)placement in Zimbabwe: Colonialism, Liberation and Democracy', *Journal of Agrarian Change*, 1: 626.

Rutherford, Blair (2008) 'An unsettled belonging: Zimbabwean farm workers in Limpopo Province, South Africa', *Journal of Contemporary African Studies*, 26(4): 401.

Sarfaty, Galit A. (2007) 'International Norm Diffusion in the Pimicikamak Cree Nation: A Model of Legal Mediation', *Harvard International Law Journal*, 48: 441.

Shivji, Issa (2000) 'Contradictory Perspectives on Rights and Justice in the Context of Land Tenure Reform in Tanzania', in Abdullahi A. An-Na'im (ed) *Cultural Transformation and Human Rights in Africa* (New York, NY: Zed Books).

Sihlongonyane, Mfaniseni Fana (1997) 'The Southern African Charter on Land, Labour and Food Security', *African Journal of Political Science*, 2(2): 118.

Sihlongonyane, Mfaniseni Fana (2005) 'Land Occupations in South Africa', in Sam Moyo and Paris Yeros (eds) *Reclaiming the land: The Resurgence of Rural Movements in Africa, Asia and Latin America* (London: Zed Books).

Woodman, Gordon (1998) 'Ideological Combat and Social Observation: Recent Debate about Legal Pluralism', *Journal of Legal Pluralism*, 42: 21.

Other sources

Institute for Poverty, Land and Agrarian Studies (PLAAS) Farm workers and farm dwellers in South Africa: tenure, livelihoods and social justice, available at <http://www.plaas.org.za/research/land/farmworkers.> (accessed 16 March 2010).

International Covenant on Civil and Political Rights, available at <http://www2.ohchr.org/english/law/ccpr.htm> (accessed 20 February 2010).

International Covenant on Economic, Social and Cultural Rights, available at <http://www2.ohchr.org/english/law/cescr.htm> (accessed 20 February 2010).

Republic of Malawi, Ministry of Lands, Housing, Physical Planning and Surveys, Malawi National Land Policy (Lilongwe 2002), available at <http://www.malawi.gov.mw/publications/landpol.htm> (accessed 27 December 2006).

The right to adequate housing (Art 11.1): 13/12/91, CESCR General Comment 4, available at <http://www.unhchr.ch/tbs/doc.nsf/(Symbol)/469f4d91a9378221c12563ed0053547e?Opendocument> (accessed 20 February 2010).

The right to adequate housing (Art 11.1): forced evictions: 20/05/1997, CESCR General Comment 7, available at <http://www.unhchr.ch/tbs/doc.nsf/(Symbol)/959f71e476284596802564c3005d8d50?Opendocument> (accessed 20 February 2010).

The right to respect of privacy, family, home and correspondence, and protection of honour and reputation (Art 17): 08/04/1988, CCPR General Comment No 16, available at <http://www.unhchr.ch/tbs/doc.nsf/(Symbol)/23378a8724595410c12563ed004aeecd> (accessed 20 February 2010).

The SADC Land Reform Support Facility (SLRSF), available at <http://www.sadc.int/fanr/environment/landreform/index.php> (accessed 16 March 2010).

7 Property guarantees in old and new southern African Constitutions

Clement Ng'ong'ola

7.1 Introduction

Several countries in southern Africa have plural or multi-layered land tenure systems under which land is classified as private or freehold land, customary or tribal land and state land or public land. Private land and public land were appropriated from customary land almost at the onset of colonial rule. Private land was land appropriated from the customary pool for occupation and use by settlers of European descent, under forms of tenure then unknown to indigenous communities, such as leases, freehold rights or rights of ownership. In countries with larger settler communities, most of the land suitable for commercial agriculture fell into this category. State or public land is land originally appropriated for government use by colonial authorities, and passed on to succeeding governments at independence. State land in some of the countries is also the residual land category, encompassing all land that may not be classified as private or customary land. In yet other countries in sub-Saharan Africa, radical title to customary land may be vested in the state, thus blurring the distinction between these two categories.

In southern African countries with a significant settler presence, one of the most difficult and intractable land tenure problems has for long been reclamation of some private or freehold land from settler control, so that commercial agricultural production may be indigenized. In some political and other circles, the problem is accentuated by constitutional constraints passed on at independence, particularly those requiring payment of adequate or fair compensation for expropriation of land required for public purposes. This work attempts a textual description and analysis of property guarantees in the Constitutions of several southern African countries, namely: Botswana, Namibia, South Africa and Malawi. Botswana is one country in the region that has not seen fit to overhaul the Constitution under which political independence was negotiated and attained in 1966. Are the property guarantees in Botswana's Constitution quintessential examples of the problem alluded to above? As some clamour for accelerated land reclamation and redistribution in southern Africa, unimpeded by obstructive legal and constitutional devices, others contend, perhaps not so loudly, that land problems must be addressed in a manner consistent with the rule of law. Namibia (1990), South Africa (1993 and 1996), and Malawi (1994 and 1995), are the southern

African countries with newer Constitutions,[1] imbued with strong or religious adherence to the rule of law, constitutionalism, and respect for human rights.[2] What can we glean from the property guarantees in these Constitutions, in contrast to what is in the Botswana Constitution? The issue to be broached or determined at the end of these case studies is whether popular political and academic vilification of property guarantee clauses in discourses on land tenure in southern Africa is in order, or whether the proverbial finger of blame for lack of success must point elsewhere.

7.2 Core elements of property guarantee clauses

Property guarantees in most Constitutions, including those studied in this work, employ obscure legal concepts that often give rise to complicated legal disputes, and copious academic commentaries that many outside specialist legal circles find inaccessible.[3] The mysteries and legal obfuscations, however, may be clarified, or avoided, by teasing out and explaining in this preliminary section the functions and underlying values generally served by such clauses, and the core concepts employed.

7.2.1 Functions and underlying values

Property guarantee clauses generally appear to have three main functions.[4] First, they may affirm the right to have or hold property as a 'fundamental' right of the same stature as the so-called first-generation civil and political rights, such as the rights to life and liberty, or freedoms of expression, conscience, religious belief, assembly or association. They may in this respect echo Article 17 of the Universal Declaration of Human Rights, which in part states that 'everyone has the right to own property, alone as well as in association with others'. Second, property guarantee clauses will almost invariably attempt to regulate loss of property rights at the behest of government, even if there is no affirmation of the right to hold or have property. In most Constitutions, restriction of the possibilities and circumstances of loss is the main form of protection or guarantee of property. Third, for those who have no property to lose, a Constitution may attempt to provide an assurance that it shall be provided. This type of assurance may also be incorporated in constitutional clauses on second-generation socio-economic rights such as rights to health, education, water, a safe and healthy environment and housing.

Two sets of competing values or theories underlie and influence the structuring of property guarantee clauses. The dominant set of values would appear to be libertarian in outlook. According to Allen, 'Liberal theorists regard the constitution's purpose as the preservation of an area of individual choice in the face of governmental coercion. Property is part of this protected area of individual choice'.[5] The description of the right to property in terms of rights of the individual in Constitutions is a reflection of the influence of liberal theory. The countering set of values and theory are communitarian in outlook. The contention is that the wider interests of the community may justify attenuation of the rights and liberty of an individual.[6] It may be in the interests of justice, or for purposes of maintaining social order, that a person should not be allowed to retain even the fruits of his or her own labour. Some communitarian theories also regard rights to property as twinned with obligations, to serve the wider interests of the society or community in which individual rights are enjoyed.

In some political and academic circles, the mere inclusion in a Constitution of a property guarantee clause, or the part of the clause that affirms the right to property, are regarded as affirmation of the pre-eminence of libertarian values, and as obstructive of social projects requiring attenuation of property rights in the public interest. On the other side, libertarians have been known to be sceptical, hostile even, to the inclusion of guarantees of socio-economic rights in Constitutions, including assurances of land or housing for the landless. Whether a Constitution tilts the scale in favour of one or the other of these competing values, however, may depend on the articulation of key defining terms in the part of the clause that deals with loss of property. The key defining terms or concepts are property, deprivation of property, expropriation or compulsory acquisition, public purposes and compensation. An analysis of the interpretation and application of these concepts in landmark cases might indicate whether the courts in a particular country are keen to lean in favour of or against a libertarian or a communitarian approach.

7.2.2 The concept of property

This is a rarely defined concept in property guarantee clauses. It is also the most technical of the key defining terms. In ordinary everyday language it probably is understood as referring to the 'ownership' of an object or a 'thing' that has physical shape. This could be something that can be moved about and kept with the person claiming it, or it could be an immovable object such as land. The legal understanding goes beyond the reference to the object, and focuses on the rights that can be claimed in reference to the object. The law of property can broadly be described as the law regulating competing claims of persons over or in reference to objects. In the system of legal thought prevailing in southern Africa,[7] the focus in the law of property is on the so-called 'real rights'. These are rights that if necessary can be enforced over the object of the claims. Claims enforceable against a person, and not related to an object, are personal rights, and regarded as more appropriate in the law of obligations.

The complications of this understanding of property are, first, that other real rights less than ownership, such as tenancy rights, are equally deserving of protection in a Constitution. The right of ownership itself can also be unbundled into a number of incidences or entitlements of the owner, such as the rights to possess, use, consume, or dispose of the object. Complications for constitutional protection of property arise where only one of these incidences, such as the right to dispose of the object, is taken away or restricted. For some, a Constitution that protects all types of real rights and incidences of ownership may be overly protective of property interests. But, as was appreciated, or feared, during the making of the interim South African Constitution, a clause that only guarantees property, understood as referring to 'ownership', may be perceived as ignoring other important property claims.[8] It may be regarded as not sufficiently communitarian.

The second problem is that legal concepts do not consider only real rights in corporeal objects as worthy of protection. There is not much disagreement over the treatment of incorporeal 'objects', such as shares or intellectual property rights, as property worthy of protection under a property guarantee clause. The difficulty is with the extension of protection to some purely personal rights, such as the right to receive compensation, a pension, or some social welfare benefit. Some of these could be rights of economic value, and worthy of protection by this yardstick. But there is no agreement in law as to how to apply such a test and where to draw the line. Admitting all such rights as property could also impose unbearable financial responsibilities on governments and other expropriating authorities. Legal devices employed in some jurisdictions to limit the potential liability of expropriating authorities include exclusion of some of these rights from the concept of property, which may be unjust in some cases, or restricting in a property guarantee clause the types of losses for which compensation is payable.[9]

7.2.3 Deprivation or expropriation of property

Some property guarantee clauses distinguish between deprivation and expropriation or compulsory acquisition property. The purpose of this distinction is to empower the state or other expropriating authorities to interfere with and regulate property without facing compensation claims.[10] Some property clauses provide for the payment of compensation only for interferences resulting in the transfer of the property to the state or expropriating authority. In such instances, the word deprivation does not carry its full connotation in ordinary parlance of denying a person the use of his or her property, even by taking it away. Expropriation or compulsory acquisition is the taking away of property without the agreement of the owner or affected person. This partially artificial distinction between deprivation and expropriation may be regarded as supportive of communitarian interests. Deprivations in some instances may, however, cause as much loss or harm as acquisitions or takings. Some property guarantee clauses may therefore provide for payment of compensation even for deprivations. Constitutions that permit recovery of compensation for deprivations may be regarded as more sympathetic to libertarian interests.

7.2.4 Public purposes

Property guarantee clauses often require that deprivations and or acquisitions should not be arbitrary; they should be effected under some law, and for a public interest or purpose. Some clauses provide an indication of the public purposes or interests that should be served. The delineation can be effusive, covering a wide range of interests, needs or purposes. The interpretation and application of the public purposes requirement by the courts can also be generous. It has been held in some jurisdictions in the British Commonwealth that the requirement would be satisfied if 'the general interest of the community' were likely to be served.[11] The requirement has been met even in cases where the expropriated property was destined for private use or commercial exploitation.[12] As will be confirmed in one of our case studies below, courts may also be unwilling to interrogate assessment by public officers of the suitability of a targeted property for a perceived public purpose. It is therefore not likely that expropriation of private land for redistribution to land hungry indigenous communities would in most countries in southern Africa not be regarded as a justifiable public purpose. This is one element of a property guarantee clause on which communitarian interests are probably too generously served.

7.2.5 Compensation

The requirement for payment of compensation for compulsory acquisitions (and for deprivations in some cases) is the most controversial of all the core elements of a property guarantee clause. The requirement is for payment of compensation or what may be described as 'full, adequate, just, fair, equitable or appropriate' compensation. Where the measure or method of computing compensation is not indicated or suggested, the traditional legal assumption is that the deprived or dispossessed person must be indemnified for the loss suffered, and the market value of the property is the fairest way of measuring the loss. This is widely regarded as one element that most reflects the dominance of libertarian interests in some property guarantee clauses. The employment of market value can lead to generous awards for property owners. In land cases this may involve taking into consideration speculative and subjective factors and values bearing little resemblance to what would have been invested in the land.[13]

There is, however, no sacrosanct principle of constitutional law requiring that loss of property must invariably be indemnified in reference to its market value. Under the European Convention on Human Rights, for example, it is acknowledged that it would be legitimate in appropriate cases to attempt to strike a fair balance between the general interests of the community and the requirement for the protection of individual fundamental rights.[14] This might entail a departure from a full market value assessment. The challenge for southern African and other countries is to construct property guarantee clauses that allow departures from market value assessment in appropriate cases, while adhering to respect for the rule of law and protection of individual human rights.

7.3 Property guarantees in Botswana's Constitution

Property guarantees can be located in sections 3, 8 and 14 in Chapter II of the Botswana Constitution. Chapter II is entitled as affording 'Protection of fundamental rights and freedoms of the individual', but unofficially identified as a Bill of Rights. Bills of Rights and the property guarantees in them were fairly standard in Constitutions negotiated for the independence of several African countries.

The Bill in the Botswana Constitution was mostly a reproduction of the Bill in the Uganda Independence Constitution of 1962.[15] The templates were the European Convention on Human Rights of 1950 and the Bill of Rights derived from it for the Nigerian Constitution.[16]

A necessary footnote to add here is that the crafting of Botswana's Bill of Rights was hardly influenced by its trajectory towards political independence. Botswana, unlike some of its neighbours in southern Africa, had a relatively trouble-free transition from colonial rule to independence, culminating in what the chairperson of the working sessions at the constitutional conference described as 'one of the briefest and most peaceful constitutional conferences for some time'.[17] There was no war of independence, no civil disobedience, or the type of agitation or campaigning that would have compelled colonial authorities to restrain or incarcerate nationalist leaders.[18] Further, land issues did not feature much in the clamours for independence. The settler population was relatively small, and not much African land had been commandeered for settler use.[19] The 'independence struggle', therefore, was not a struggle for land. This notwithstanding, it was felt necessary to include fairly strong property guarantees in the Constitution, for the purpose of providing assurance that there might be economic and political stability in the new nation.[20]

7.3.1 Section 3 and protection of property from deprivation

Paragraph (c) of section 3, the opening clause or *chapeau* of the Bill of Rights, can be read as offering every person 'protection for the privacy of his or her home and other property and from deprivation of property without compensation', just as every person is guaranteed the first generation civil and political rights enumerated in paragraphs (a) and (b) of the section. This is one reading and interpretation of the section. The other is that the section is merely preambular and an introduction to the fundamental rights more elaborately described in other sections in the Bill of Rights. Under this reading and interpretation, the protection from deprivation of property without compensation in paragraph (c) is essentially the same fundamental right more elaborately described in section 8, which can also be read as protection of property from compulsory acquisition (or expropriation) without compensation. This reading and interpretation of section 3 was preferred by a minority of the Court of Appeal in the leading case of *Attorney General v Dow*.[21] The majority of a full bench of the Court regarded section 3 as the 'key or umbrella provision in Chapter II under which all rights and freedoms protected under that Chapter must be subsumed'. The Court suggested that the other clauses in Chapter II, elaborating on the fundamental rights or freedoms guaranteed, should not be interpreted in a manner that restricts a right covered by the section. Thus, section 15, elaborating on protection from discrimination, could not be interpreted in a manner that restricts interpretation of section 3, so that discrimination on the basis of gender could be regarded as permissible.[22]

If we take, as we should, a majority decision of the Court of Appeal as settling the law, we can conclude that Botswana has what may be termed a double or combined property guarantee clause in its Constitution.[23] Section 3(c) protects property from deprivations in the sense described in section 7.2.3 (above). Section 8, the second property guarantee offers protection from compulsory acquisition of property. As suggested above, it is commonplace to impose a requirement for payment of adequate compensation for all compulsory acquisitions. In some jurisdictions, however, compensation is not required for deprivations that do not involve taking over of the property. Payment of compensation for deprivations is a fundamental right in Botswana. What the measure of compensation should be is not clear from section 3. If it must be adequate, and to be paid in the same manner as required for compulsory acquisitions, then Botswana would appear to have an extremely pro-libertarian property guarantee in section 3(c). Whether excessive and untenable demands for compensation can be countered by reference to the limitations added to section 3 is a moot point yet to be tested in the courts. Section 3 concludes with an indication that all the fundamental rights and freedoms secured may be abridged by 'limitations designed to ensure that the enjoyment of the said rights and freedoms by any individual does not prejudice the rights and freedoms of others or the public interest'.

7.3.2 Section 8 and protection of property from compulsory acquisition

Section 8, the second property guarantee clause in the Botswana Constitution, also appears to espouse more libertarian than communitarian values. In subsection (1), protection from compulsory acquisition is extended to 'property of any description', whether in law it is conceived of as a thing or as an object, movable or immovable, or whether it is conceived of as a right or interest in an object. Property is protected mainly through the stiff conditions set for any compulsory acquisition or taking to be regarded as legitimate under the Constitution. The first condition in section 8(1)(a) is that the taking must be 'expedient or necessary' for certain specified public purposes and interests. The second condition in section 8(1)(b) is that it must be effected in terms of a law that provides for 'prompt payment of adequate compensation' and for reference to the High Court, directly or on appeal, for resolution of disputes pertaining to the legality of the acquisition and the adequacy or promptness of the payment of compensation. The third condition in section 8(2) is that the person entitled to compensation should not be prevented from remitting the whole amount (free of deductions), within a reasonable period, to any country of his or her choice outside Botswana.

The description of the public purposes and interests by which compulsory acquisition must be justified, in section 8(1)(a) of the Constitution, and in the law providing for prompt payment of adequate compensation, is quite expansive and not at all likely to restrain government or any expropriating authority.[24] For example, it is legitimate to expropriate in the interests of defence, public safety, public order, public morality and public health. It is also legitimate to expropriate for town and country planning and land settlement purposes; for purposes of securing the development or utilization of the mineral resources of Botswana; and for purposes of securing the development or utilization of any property for a purpose beneficial to the community.

On top of the wide and accommodating description of public purposes, the Court of Appeal has confirmed that courts should not hasten to interrogate identification by the President, the expropriating authority under the Acquisition of Property Act, of the public interest or purpose by which expropriation is reportedly justified.[25] The Court rejected a contention, accepted in the High Court,[26] that government officers had acted in bad faith and with an ulterior motive when a notice for the compulsory acquisition of the Molopo Ranch, a 121,613 hectare freehold farm, was hurriedly published in 1996. It was alleged by government in court papers that the ranch and the cattle on it were required for the purpose of restocking in Ngamiland, an administrative district in which all cattle had earlier been exterminated on government orders for the purpose of controlling and containing a cattle lung disease. The respondents contended, on the other hand, that government officers acted with great haste merely to pre-empt conclusion of an agreement under which control of the ranch would have passed to them, probably because they were citizens of Botswana of Afrikaner or Boer extraction. The Chief Justice agreed with the respondents in the High Court, but the Court of Appeal held that the purpose alleged by government was on the face of it legitimate, and allegations of bad faith or ulterior motive accepted in the *court a quo* were unproven.[27] As it turned out, the ranch was subsequently put to commercial use and never utilized for the purpose for which it was acquired.

As regards the requirements in section 8(1)(b), the law under which compulsory acquisition must be attempted, and compensation computed and paid, was in Botswana enacted during the colonial era and merely adjusted and aligned to the new legal and constitutional order after independence.[28] This revision and adjustment of the law, however, overlooked one key aspect. The colonial law was devised for compulsory acquisition of 'real property', defined as real rights in immovable property outside Tribal Territories. This scope was retained after independence, implying that Botswana at independence had no law authorizing compulsory acquisition of personal or real rights in movable property, or of immovable property in the tribal territories. The *lacunae* as regards compulsory acquisition of rights in tribal land was subsequently addressed in Part V of the Tribal Land Act, Chapter 32:01, passed in 1968. But, as the Court of Appeal appreciated and held in the *Molopo Ranch* case, there still is no law in Botswana providing for compulsory acquisition of movable property.[29] An attempt by government to acquire both the ranch and the cattle was unconstitutional and unsustainable as regards the cattle. There is, therefore, absolute protection of personal or real rights in movable property in Botswana, by default rather than by design.

The Acquisition of Property Act, as revised after independence, prescribes the market value of the property on the date of the expropriation as the principal measure of adequate compensation, discounting such factors as the reason for the acquisition and the reluctance of the affected person to part with the property or his rights.[30] It also prescribes that compensation must be paid upon registration of title in the name of the state, or within two months of the settlement of a contested award.[31] In the only case, so far, to reach the High Court on the adequacy of compensation,[32] the market value of the property was interpreted as referring to 'market price' or the price that the property would have realized if sold in an open market by a willing seller to a willing buyer. The Court further held that the assessment should take into account potential uses to which the property could be put, for this is what a willing seller would take into account. The Court suggested that market price or market value would otherwise not amount to 'adequate compensation' as required by the Constitution. The result in this case was a high award that was slightly more than 100 per cent of what government had offered, on the basis of prices of comparable land.

I have argued elsewhere that the High Court was arguably wrong in its interpretation of the concepts of adequate compensation and market value and in its computation of an adequate award.[33] If it is my review and appreciation of the case that is wrong, we have in this case a good illustration of what makes compulsory acquisition expensive and unviable as a strategy for reclaiming and indigenization of settler agricultural land in southern Africa, even in a country like Botswana which was fairly solvent after discovery and exploitation of its diamond resources. The requirement in section 8(2) of the Constitution that government must permit remission of compensation to any country chosen by the person entitled to it exacerbates the problem, and is now probably time worn. It may be time worn because property now is more likely to be expropriated from citizens, and Botswana has long liberalized its exchange control regime for citizens and non-citizens alike.

The difficulties and expense of compulsory acquisition of freehold land may have been a factor in the evolution of another strategy for reclamation and indigenization freehold agricultural land in Botswana. This is in the Land Control Act, passed and enacted in 1975.[34] This Act attempts to create, for citizens of Botswana, an opportunity to intervene in a proposed transfer of an interest in agricultural land to a non-citizen. It imposes a requirement for prior ministerial approval of every 'controlled transaction'. This includes the sale, transfer, lease capable of running for a period of five years or more, exchange, partition or other disposal or dealing with agricultural land in the freehold sector, where the party acquiring the interest is not a citizen. It also covers the disposal of shares in a private company owning any agricultural land to a non-citizen. The citizenship of a company is for these purposes determined by reference to incorporation in Botswana as well as the nationality of individuals beneficially holding the majority of all classes of shares in the company. Before ministerial consent is sought, the proposed transaction must be advertised in a prescribed manner, to give citizens interested in the property sufficient time to intercede. It is suggested that citizens who express an interest in the transaction must be given priority, but the minister's decision to grant or refuse consent is also final and may not be challenged in any court.

The Land Control Act was carefully and cleverly structured to avoid infringing the property guarantees in the Constitution. There is no compulsory acquisition of the property by the President; and the interposition of a citizen purchaser willing to acquire the property at the advertised transaction price would not amount to deprivation of property in terms of section 3. The Act does not regulate the price and other terms upon which the property may be transferred to an interested citizen. This may also be its main weakness. The land can be priced out of the range of most potential citizen purchasers. Anecdotal evidence suggests that this weakness, and difficulties of policing and monitoring transfers of shares in companies owning agricultural land from citizens to non-citizens, are factors that may have rendered the Act not so effective in the 25 years that it has been in operation.

Although the property guarantee in section 8 of the Constitution is exceedingly pro-libertarian and problematic, it has features other than the expansive description of the public purposes that would have assisted government in the pursuit of some of its communitarian agendas. We have already noted, for example, that it is legitimate and constitutional to expropriate for the purpose of 'securing the development or utilization of the mineral resources of Botswana'. In a similar vein, section 8(3) indicates that the requirement for prompt payment of adequate compensation shall be deemed satisfied if mineral rights are expropriated under a law that provides for payment of adequate royalties at reasonable intervals.

Other notable derogations from protection of property in section 8 are in subsections (4), (5) and (6). Subsection (4) permits attachment of compensation or the imposition of reasonable restrictions on its externalization, if so authorized by an order of a competent court. Subsection (5) excludes the application of section 8 to takings or acquisitions authorized by laws relating, *inter alia*, to the following: enforcement of payment of taxes, rates or other taxes that may be due; enforcement of judgments, penalties or orders issued in civil or criminal proceedings; prescription or limitation of actions; or the taking over of property of enemies, insolvents, deceased persons, and other persons that are by law disabled from administering their own affairs. Subsection (6) precludes the application of the property guarantee to acquisition in the public interest of any property, interest or right held by 'a body corporate established by law for public purposes in which no moneys have been invested other than moneys provided by Parliament'. It should be recalled that the bulk of the land in Botswana falls within the category of tribal land. Authorizing compulsory acquisition of tribal land for public purposes was only an incidental purpose of the Tribal Land Act of 1968. Its main purpose was to provide for transfer of title to tribal land from tribal communities to land boards, and to vest in the land boards powers relating to land administration previously vested in chiefs and other tribal authorities. Land boards are bodies corporate established for public purposes sustained entirely by moneys provided by Parliament. No compensation is therefore payable to a land board for tribal land acquired for public purposes. Compensation is payable only to other persons whose rights or interests are thereby affected.[35] Assessment of adequate compensation is compounded and compromised by the widespread notion that land is or was not a marketable commodity under customary law. In this way, the Botswana government has not been severely constrained by its pro-libertarian Constitution in acquiring land for public purposes from what today is the main source of such land.

7.3.3 Section 14 and preservation of aboriginal title in the Central Kgalagadi Game Reserve

The third property guarantee in the Botswana Constitution is embedded in one of the derogations to freedom of movement in section 14(3). It is declared in section 14(1) that 'no person shall be deprived of his or her freedom of movement' which, for these purposes, 'means the right to move freely throughout Botswana, the right to reside in any part of Botswana, the right to enter Botswana and immunity from expulsion from Botswana'. Section 14(3) provides at least three derogations relevant to the property dimensions of freedom of movement. First, it is acknowledged in paragraph (a) that it may be necessary to impose restrictions on freedom of movement that are reasonably required 'in the interests of defence, public safety, public order, public morality or public health'. It is also acknowledged that restrictions may be imposed 'on the acquisition or use by any person of land or other property in Botswana', but such restrictions may be contested if 'shown not to be reasonably justifiable in a democratic society'. Second, paragraph (b) indicates that freedom of movement shall not be violated by an act done under a law that provides for the imposition of restrictions on movement of any person who is not a citizen of Botswana, but it is not suggested that such restrictions may be contested if shown not to be reasonably justifiable in a democratic society. This suggests that government will be less constrained in restricting the right of non-citizens to enter or move freely within Botswana, as well as to acquire property for the purpose of residing in any part of the country. Third, paragraph (c) acknowledges that freedom of movement shall not be violated by a law providing 'for the imposition of restrictions on entry into or residence within defined areas of Botswana of persons who are not Bushmen to the extent that such restrictions are reasonably required for the protection of the well-being of Bushmen'.

Paragraph (c) was successfully invoked in *Sesana and Others v The Attorney-General*[36] by several Bushmen communities resisting attempts by government to forcibly relocate them from their tribal territories in the Central Kgalagadi Game Reserve (CKGR). It emerged from the evidence adduced in the case that the CKGR was proclaimed in 1961,[37] on lands appropriated for the Crown as *terra nullius* or *terra incognita*, but which were also known to contain traditional territories or ranges of several Bushmen communities. The original plan was that the CKGR should be a sanctuary for game, as well as for 'several thousand Bushmen' desirous of maintaining their traditional hunting and gathering modes of existence, unmolested by other people or communities.[38] Prior to the insertion of section 14(3)(c) in the independence Constitution, laws and regulations on access to or hunting in the CKGR always preserved rights of Bushmen indigenous to the area to enter the reserve without a permit and to hunt game, albeit with restrictions requiring licences, and regulating what could be hunted, and with what weapons.[39] With this background, the High Court held, by a majority of two to one, that the Bushmen applicants in the case were indigenous to the Reserve. They had been in possession of their lands in the CKGR from time immemorial. Their rights survived the appropriation of the land for the Crown, the proclamation of the CKGR, and the conversion of Crown lands into state land at independence. Attempts to forcibly relocate them from the reserve, for example by terminating the supply of certain essential services was unlawful despoliation of their land rights and unconstitutional.

Section 14(3)(c) thus anchored a finding by the High Court that the Bushmen applicants in the case had aboriginal title to their lands in the CKGR, which could be abrogated only in a manner permitted by the Constitution.[40] Although the Court did not explicitly so state, we can surmise that such abrogation would require compliance with the property guarantees and other fundamental rights enshrined in the Bill of Rights. The salutary lesson from this case is that pro-libertarian property guarantees crafted for protection of settler land rights can, so many years after independence, serve other nobler causes. It is not always advisable to hurriedly abrogate these guarantees after independence.

7.4 Property guarantees in the Constitution of Namibia

The Namibian Constitution was the first 'internally constructed' independence Constitution in southern Africa. It has one property guarantee clause, Article 16, which must be read and interpreted in the light of Article 22, on limitations applicable to all fundamental rights enshrined in Chapter 3, the Bill of Rights chapter of the Constitution.

Article 16 apparently resembles the First Protocol of the European Convention on Human Rights in its brevity, and it was constructed in the positive manner of German law.[41] It offers rights instead of protecting against violations of rights. Article 22 also borrows from German law in providing limitations for all the fundamental rights and freedoms. Although brief, spanning only two paragraphs, all but one of the core elements of property guarantee clauses identified above can be located in the two paragraphs and in Article 22. Paragraph (1) of Article 16 is an assurance or affirmation of the right to property in Namibia. It provides a positive assurance that 'all persons shall' be entitled to hold property in Namibia, but legislation may curtail the right of non-citizens to do so.

The conception of property in paragraph (1) is the typical 'thing-ownership' approach of Roman-Dutch common law. The assurance is for rights 'to acquire, own, dispose of and bequeath' all forms of 'movable or immovable provable property'. This is, first, a specification of a limited range of real rights. Rights to dispose of or bequeath property are also only a few of the incidences of ownership. As such, it may not have been necessary to specify them alongside the right to own. The concept of ownership is also jurisprudentially troublesome, and probably should have been avoided. The specification of the right of ownership in this clause might have been reassuring to libertarian interests seeking constitutional guarantees over freehold land in constitutional negotiations, but the danger is that other more personal rights could have been written out of the property guarantee. The moot point is whether the Namibian clause recognizes as property new types of wealth, which cannot be readily understood in terms of movable and immovable things, such as the right to performance under a contract, or to a pension or a welfare benefit. It is also notable that property rights are assured for both individuals and associations. This was strictly an unnecessary detail. If the intention here was to recognize group rights or communal property rights under customary law, the description of property in terms of rights of ownership would have compounded the understanding and protection of such rights.

Paragraph (2) of Article 16 is, again, a positively constructed expropriation clause. The state, or a competent organ of it, is authorized to expropriate, upon compliance with specified conditions. In the British colonial style of drafting, as noted in the Botswana case study, property is protected from compulsory acquisition, except in specified situations. The requirements for the exercise of power are similar. Expropriation must be effected under a law, in the public interest, and coupled with payment of 'just compensation'. There is no elaboration of what may be in the public interest, but this is unlikely to lead to a less expansive treatment of the concept in the courts. The clause concludes in a manner suggesting that Parliament could and should legislate on how just compensation should be computed, if need be, in a manner that would deviate from the market value basis of assessment. If this has not been done, courts are not likely to interpret 'just compensation' differently from 'adequate', 'equitable', 'fair', or just plain 'compensation'.

There is no paragraph in the Namibian clause referring to deprivation as opposed to expropriation of property. Since the clause is constructed in a positive manner, courts are not likely to interpret it as authorizing expropriations as well as deprivations. What is not stated may be deemed as purposely excluded. This could seriously handicap the Namibian government in its efforts to regulate land affairs and generally exercise 'police powers' over property. The omission of a deprivation paragraph or clause was probably in deference to libertarian values and interests in the negotiation of the Constitution.

Article 22, lastly, requires that any law abridging any of the fundamental rights guaranteed by the Constitution shall be of general application, shall not target a particular individual, shall not negate the essential content of the right, and shall be more specifically drawn.[42] One moot point arising from this in reference to Article 16(1) is whether the law regulating property rights of aliens in Namibia can abolish their 'right to own land' without negating the essential content of the guaranteed right.

The tentative conclusion to be drawn from this purely textual analysis of the Namibian clause is that it leans towards over protection of libertarian values and property interests. If the intention was to provide a property clause that would assist in the transformation of land ownership in Namibia, perhaps a brief clause was not what was required, and different language should have been employed in the conception of property. A clause such as this one leaves critical issues for interpretation by the judiciary, which in the early years of decolonization may be dominated by those more sympathetic to libertarian interests.

7.5 Property guarantees in the South African Constitution

Three clauses in the Bill of Rights (Chapter 2) of the South African Constitution can be considered as offering some form of protection of property. These are section 25, covering deprivation as well as expropriation of property; section 26 on rights to housing; and section 36 which, like Article 22 in the Namibian Constitution, provides for the limitation of all rights in the Bill.

The South African Constitution employs a more general conception of property in the property guarantees. Section 25, in contrast to Article 16 of the Namibian Constitution, does not guarantee specified rights or incidences in property. It has been suggested that this leads to protection of a wider range of rights and interests, which may include performance rights or claims, if they are a source of wealth, and are vested and not merely contingent.[43] If this is indeed the case, it probably was not necessary to specify in section 25(4)(b) that property is not limited to land for the purposes of the section.

Section 25(1) protects property from deprivation in a negative manner. It prohibits deprivations that are not authorized by a law of general application, and laws that permit arbitrary deprivation of property. There is no reference to payment of compensation for unjustifiable deprivations. This gives the South African government considerable latitude in regulating property matters without imposing liability on the fiscus.

Section 25(2), on protection of property from expropriation, is more positively couched. It reads as if authorizing expropriation, but only if attempted in terms of a law of general application, for a public purpose or in the public interest, and subject to payment of compensation, which may be agreed upon or determined by a court. As if there would have been any doubt, Section 25(4)(a) confirms that public interest for these purposes includes the nation's commitment to land reform, and reforms proposed for redressing the iniquities of apartheid. One may venture to suggest that anywhere in the region, regardless of the structuring of the property guarantee, land reform, equitable land re-distribution, land restitution, and the types of transformations envisaged in subsections (5) to (8) would readily qualify as public interests justifying deprivation or expropriation of property. As elsewhere in southern Africa, the issue more likely to be contested is compensation for the loss of property.

The first notable innovation in the South African property guarantees is the manner in which section 25(3) attempts to guide the assessment of compensation, to balance property rights and public interest or libertarian and communitarian goals and values. It requires that the 'amount of the compensation and the time and manner of payment must be just and equitable, reflecting an equitable balance between the public interest and the interests of those affected'. It further states that the balancing of interests must take into account all relevant factors including current use, history of acquisition and use of the property, market value, state investment and subsidies in the acquisition or improvement of the property, and the purpose of the expropriation.

South African courts have now had time to work with these guidelines. In one of the notable cases, the Land Claims Court (LCC) decided that striking a balance between property rights and public interest involved establishing the market value of the property first and thereafter subtracting from or adding to the amount as the facts of the case may require. Compensation awarded under section 25(3) may thus be lower or higher than the market value of the property.[44] In line with international standards and comparative law, which South African courts are enjoined to take into consideration when interpreting the Constitution, the LCC suggested that just and equitable compensation is likely to be more objectively assessed in reference to the market value of the property which, in turn, must also be assessed in reference prices in comparable transactions.

As acknowledged in some of the cases, assessment of market value is not an exact science. There is much conjecture, and the amount of the award often turns on impressions left on the Court by particular valuers. The result may be over-generous awards, contrary to the communitarian spirit behind section 25(3). Generous awards, paradoxically, would not be amiss in some of the situations indicated in section 25 as calling for payment of compensation. It probably would be in order, for example, to over-compensate a community in lieu of restitution under section 25(7), but probably not when property is required for purposes of making land available to the landless, as suggested in subsections (5) and (8). The challenge for the courts and other entities tasked with observance of these requirements is to act consistently in complex and varying situations.

The other notable innovation in the South African Bill of Rights is that the property guarantees address typical or standard existing property claims, as well as atypical or weaker claims of those without property, who seek to be assured that it shall be provided. Section 25(5), for example, assures citizens that they shall have access to land on an equitable basis. Section 26, on the right to housing, also provides an assurance of access to housing, as well as protection for those already housed. Section 26(1) is probably too ambitious and unrealistic, as it provides that 'everyone' has a right to have access to 'adequate housing'. The obligations of the state in this regard are delineated in section 26(2). It must take 'reasonable legislative and other measures, within its available resources, to achieve the progressive realization of this right'. Protection of the right to housing is offered in section 26(3), which is structured like section 25(1), the protection from deprivation clause. It prohibits eviction from, or demolition of, a home without an order of a court made after considering all the relevant circumstances. It also outlaws legislation that permits arbitrary evictions. Section 26(3) appears to be aimed at protecting unlawful occupiers of residential properties, otherwise commonly referred to as squatters, from quick and speedy evictions under the common law, or under some of the statutes fashioned under apartheid to deal with the problem of urban squatting.[45] The Constitution in this respect offers temporary protection to the landless, at the expense of those for whom property guarantees are traditionally conceived.

It should be underlined that the right to housing, in the first two subsections of section 26 is addressed to the state. In other jurisdictions, whether a socio-economic right of this nature, addressed to the state, is enforceable is a matter for academic debate. Some prefer to regard such rights as merely directional, to guide the shaping of government policy. In South Africa, the Constitutional Court held in the *Certification* case that such rights are justiciable, notwithstanding the financial burden this could impose on the government.[46] In the *Grootboom* case[47] the Court attempted an assessment of government performance in reference to ensuring access to housing under section 26 and shelter for children under section 28. Mrs Grootboom was one of 390 adults and 510 children forcibly evicted from a piece of land on which they were squatting. They relocated in desperation to a sports field and a nearby community hall where they were living in appalling conditions. The Provincial High Court ordered the authorities to provide them with amenities as part of the entitlement for children to shelter in terms of section 28. On appeal the Constitutional Court held that although section 26 did not provide every person with the right to demand access to housing, government programmes could be assessed for compliance with duties expected of it under sections 26 and 28. The Court concluded that government performance in this case failed to comply with these provisions because no provision was made for the temporary relief of those in desperate need, such as the respondents. The Court perhaps demanded more from the responsible authorities in this case than was generally feasible in the light of the acknowledged scale of the squatting problem in the area and in the country. But the salutary aspect of the case, from which other countries in southern Africa could learn, is in the eagerness of the Court to subject government policy to critical legal assessment.

As regards section 36, the limitation of rights clause, it may be noted that it too permits limitation of all the fundamental rights, but only in terms of a law of general application. However, unlike Article 22 of the Namibian Constitution, section 36 does not explicitly state that the limitation 'shall not negate the essential content' of the right and 'shall not be aimed at a particular individual'. Section 36 instead requires that limitations must be assessed as 'reasonable and justified in an open democratic society based on human dignity, equality and freedom, taking into account all relevant factors', including: the nature of the right; the purpose of the limitation; the nature and extent of the limitation, the relation between the limitation and its purpose; and whether the purpose may be achieved through less restrictive means. The moot point that arises here is whether section 36 could at all be a useful barometer in assessing a law that attempts to attenuate the property guarantees in section 25. A law that provides for deprivations or expropriations in the manner suggested by section 25 is not likely to be regarded as out of consonance with section 36.

7.6 Property guarantees in the new Malawi Constitution

In 46 years of existence as an independent state, Malawi has had three Constitutions, each with differing approaches to the protection of property. The Bill of Rights and property guarantees in the Independence Constitution of 1964 were substantially the same as in the 1966 Botswana Independence Constitution. On 6 July 1966, Malawi became a republic under a Constitution which replaced an elaborate Bill of Rights with a brief 'Statement of Fundamental Principles'.

Article 2(1)(iv) of the Statement stated that 'No person shall be deprived of his property without payment of fair compensation, and only where the public interest so requires'. But Article 2(2) of the Statement also stated that nothing done 'under the authority of any law shall be held to be inconsistent with or in contravention of the [fundamental principles] to the extent that the law in question is reasonably required in the interests of defence, public safety, public order or the national economy'.

This provided underlying constitutional support for Draconian legislation violating property as well as civil and political rights during the long period of single-party rule under Life President Kamuzu Banda, from 1966 to 1994. One of the notorious pieces of legislation passed during this period was the Forfeiture Act of 1966, which provided for seizure without compensation of property of perceived political foes of the regime.[48] The other, more measured, property-related legislation was the Land Acquisition Act of 1970.[49] This provided for compulsory acquisition of land whenever it was deemed 'desirable or expedient in the public interest', and subject to payment of 'fair compensation'. It also provided for calculation of compensation in reference to the price paid by the person expropriated, or the price for comparable land, the value of unexhausted improvements effected by the expropriatee and, in appropriate cases, the appreciation in value of the land. The Act emphasized that under no circumstances should compensation exceed the current market value of the land. The Act empowered the minister to determine the amount of compensation to be awarded and, in keeping legislative trends at that time, provided that the minister's award shall be final and shall not be subject to appeal or review in the courts.

Given this background, one would have expected property guarantees as strong as guarantees of the other civil and political rights in the Constitution for the Second Republic finalized in 1995. However, sections 28 and 44, the property guarantees in Chapter IV of the Bill of Rights, suggest that not much attention or thought was given to this subject.

Section 28 is the main property protection clause, and section 44 is the limitations clause. Section 28 is too brief. The first subsection positively asserts that every person shall be able to acquire property, alone or in association with others. The second subsection tersely provides that no person shall be arbitrarily deprived of property. The obvious shortcomings of the clause include the fact that only the 'right to acquire' property is assured. As noted above, even the equally brief Article 17 of the Namibian Constitution is better constructed, as it refers to rights to acquire, own, dispose of and bequeath all forms of movable and immovable property. The Namibian clause also immediately qualifies the guarantee for persons who are not citizens of Namibia. Ownership of particularly freehold land is a concern in Malawi as it is elsewhere in southern Africa. A land policy developed not long after the Constitution was adopted proposes prohibiting non-citizens from acquiring freehold land, or converting freehold titles held by non-citizens into leasehold titles.[50] This was not and should have been anticipated in the drafting of section 28.

The other shortcoming in section 28 is the prohibition of arbitrary deprivations. It is not clear whether deprivation is used in the same manner as the concept of expropriation used in section 44, or whether, as in the South African guarantees, it refers to interferences that do not involve taking of property, and do not attract payment compensation. The courts unfortunately failed to clarify this ambiguity in the only case so far in which the property guarantees were invoked. In November 1995, the Minister of Finance moved a motion in the National Assembly to suspend a Standing Order so that the Press Trust Reconstruction Bill could be debated as a matter of urgency before it had been published for a period of not less than 21 days. The Bill sought to restructure the management of the trust, ostensibly to maximize attainment and realization of its objectives. The Trust was established by Dr Banda in 1982, with the broad objective of promoting and advancing the well-being and welfare of the Malawi nation. The Bill sought to replace as trustees some members of the Malawi Congress Party (MCP), Dr Banda's party, which was in opposition, with the Minister of Finance and other persons appointed by the party then in government. This was obviously going to affect levels of funding the MCP was receiving from the trust. MCP members of Parliament walked out of the National Assembly when the motion to suspend the relevant standing order was presented. The motion was carried, and the Bill was read and passed while they were still out. Parliament was in consequence not quorate when this was done. One of several constitutional issues taken up in the courts afterwards was whether the resulting Act infringed sections 28(2) and 44(4) of the Constitution. The High Court held that there was arbitrary deprivation of property, as relevant stakeholders such as Dr Banda and the MCP were not consulted and given sufficient time to debate the measures in the Act.[51] The Supreme Court of Appeal disagreed.[52] It held that 'to act arbitrarily is to act without reasonable cause'. There was reasonable cause for the Act. Its sole purpose was to ensure that the trust was properly managed, in the interest of the beneficiaries of the trust, the people of Malawi. The Court added that if the Act effected an expropriation, it would have been for a 'public utility' and valid in terms of the other requirements of section 44(4). The Court further suggested that the trustees likely to be affected by the reconstruction of the management of the trust did not have the type of property rights protected under sections 28 and 44(4) the Constitution.

The confusion in the courts as to whether the Press Trust Reconstruction Act effected a deprivation or an expropriation of property emerges from the use of the concept of expropriation in the limitation clause, and not in section 28, the substantive property guarantee. Section 44, the limitations clause in the Malawi Constitution, is structured differently from the comparable provisions in the Namibian and South African Constitutions. First, it provides an indication in subsection (1) of all fundamental rights and freedoms in respect of which there 'shall be no derogation, restrictions or limitations'. These are the so-called 'non-derogable rights' in the emerging constitutional law jargon of Malawi. All other rights not listed in the subsection are by implication derogable. They can be restricted under laws of general application, that 'do not negate the essential content of the right or freedom in question',[53] and if the restrictions can be said to be 'reasonable, recognized by international human rights standards, and necessary in an open and democratic society'.[54] Section 44(4) then mentions that expropriation shall be permissible, if several conditions are satisfied. These are when it is done for 'a public utility', and for payment of 'appropriate compensation'. There must also be 'adequate notification' and a 'right of appeal to a court of law'.

If section 44(4) is a separate and distinct property guarantee, the question that arises is whether qualifiers like 'public utility' and 'appropriate compensation' were deliberately and purposely employed. The reference to 'public utility' could conceivably have been a deliberate attempt to restrict the powers of the state and accord greater protection of property than was hitherto the case under the single party regime. This moot point was not raised in the Press Trust Reconstruction Case, and pronouncements of the Court of Appeal suggested that it regarded the phrase as similar to 'public interest' or 'public purpose'. A similar question is whether the reference to 'appropriate compensation' was also a deliberate attempt to continue with frugal, pro-communitarian approach developed during the harsh dictatorial rule of Dr Banda. If account is taken of the requirement that limitations of fundamental rights must be 'reasonable, recognized by international human rights standards, and necessary in an open and democratic society', it is not likely that there would be much difference between what a court guided by these precepts would regard as appropriate or adequate consideration.

7.7 Concluding observations

One obvious observation from the foregoing review is that the property guarantees in the new Constitutions in southern Africa are brief, perhaps too brief to the point of obfuscation of some core elements in the cases of Malawi and Namibia. The clauses are brief partly due to borrowing from German constitutional practice the technique of providing in one clause principles and conditions by which all the fundamental rights in the Constitution may be restricted. This obviates the need to attach claw-back clauses to each right in a Bill of Rights. It is not necessary in the new Constitutions to elongate property guarantees with claw-back clauses such as those in subsections (4) to (6) of section 8 the Botswana Constitution.

Although brief, almost all the core elements of property guarantee clauses identified at the beginning of this chapter appear to be covered in our case studies. There is a direct or an indirect assurance of the right to have or to own property. Property is conceived in wide terms as embracing movable and immovable objects or certain rights or interests therein. In the South African and Malawi Bills, protection of property is attempted through regulation or restriction of both deprivation and expropriation. Compensation is not listed as a requirement for deprivation, but it is one of the requirements for expropriation. The other requirements are that expropriation must be effected under some law and for some public purpose, interest or utility. In Constitutions imbued with adherence to the rule of law and respect for human rights, it may not be necessary to spell out, as in section 8(2) of the Botswana Constitution, examples of such public interests or purposes. Government conduct and action in these matters will always be subject to interrogation in the courts.

As regards the first few core elements of property guarantees, therefore, the conclusion appears inescapable that guarantees in the new Constitutions are as libertarian as the guarantees in Botswana's old Bill of Rights. The fundamental difference, however, is as regards the requirement for compensation. As noted above, there is no mention of compensation for deprivations in the South African and Malawi guarantees. In all the new Constitutions, furthermore, compensation for expropriations is qualified by descriptors other than adequate. References to payment of just, just and equitable or appropriate compensation insinuate that the measure, taking into account other considerations, could be less than what the market would establish as adequate. The South African Constitution probably has the most explicit guidelines in any Constitution on the need to balance property rights and public interests in the assessment of compensation for expropriations. This is one feature of that Constitution that can be recommended to other countries in the sub-region. The other is the accommodation in the guarantees of land and other socio-economic rights for landless and under-privileged citizens.

On the face of it, therefore, it is possible to address in home-grown constitutional instruments the problem of over-compensating owners for land required for genuine public purposes. The challenge, however, may be in the interpretation and application of such provisions by courts enjoined by the same Constitution to adhere to the rule of law and to have strong regard for individual human rights. These are core libertarian values likely to override communitarian concerns. The stark choice in southern Africa would appear to be to have strong constitutional guarantees of individual human rights, which also entail fairly strong protection of property, or to forego strong regard for fundamental human rights so that old land scores can be settled relatively cheaply. If a society or community is inclined to the latter choice, it must be remembered that after old scores have been settled, it is everyone's property rights that became vulnerable. One lesson from Botswana's retention of colonial property guarantees is that long after settlers have left the scene, some of the most marginalized in the community are set to benefit from the same.

Appendix 1: Property guarantees in the Constitution of Botswana

Section 3: Fundamental rights and freedoms of the individual

Whereas every person in Botswana is entitled to the fundamental rights and freedoms of the individual, that is to say, the right, whatever his or her race, place of origin, political opinions, colour, creed or sex, but subject to respect for the rights and freedoms of others and for the public interest to each and all of the following, namely –

(a) life, liberty, security of the person and the protection of the law;
(b) freedom of conscience, of expression and of assembly and association; and

(c) protection for the privacy of his or her home and other property and from deprivation of property without compensation,

the provisions of this Chapter shall have effect for the purpose of affording protection to those rights and freedoms subject to such limitations of that protection as are contained in those provisions, being limitations designed to ensure that the enjoyment of the said rights and freedoms by any individual does not prejudice the rights and freedoms of others or the public interest.

Section 8: Protection from deprivation of property

(1) No property of any description shall be compulsorily taken possession of, and no interest in or right over property of any description shall be compulsorily acquired, except where the following conditions are satisfied, that is to say

(a) the taking of possession or acquisition is necessary or expedient –

(i) in the interests of defence, public safety, public order, public morality, public health, town and country planning or land settlement;
(ii) in order to secure the development or utilization of that, or other, property for a purpose beneficial to the community; or
(iii) in order to secure the development or utilization of the mineral resources of Botswana; and

(b) provision is made by a law applicable to that taking of possession or acquisition

(i) for the prompt payment of adequate compensation; and
(ii) securing to any person having an interest in or right over the property a right of access to the High Court, either direct or on appeal from any other authority, for the determination of his interest or right, the legality of the taking of possession or acquisition of the property, interest or right, and the amount of any compensation to which he is entitled, and for the purpose of obtaining prompt payment of that compensation.

(2) No person who is entitled to compensation under this section shall be prevented from remitting, within a reasonable time after he has received any amount of that compensation, the whole of that amount (free from any deduction, charge or tax made or levied in respect of its remission) to any country of his choice outside Botswana.
(3) Subsection (1) (b) (i) of this section shall be deemed to be satisfied in relation to any law applicable to the taking of possession of minerals or the acquisition of rights to minerals if that law makes provision for the payment at reasonable intervals of adequate royalties.

(4) Nothing contained in or done under the authority of any law shall be held to be inconsistent with or in contravention of subsection (2) of this section to the extent that the law in question authorizes –

(a) the attachment, by order of a court, of any amount of compensation to which a person is entitled in satisfaction of the judgment of a court or pending the determination of civil proceedings to which he is a party; or
(b) the imposition of reasonable restrictions on the manner in which any amount of compensation is to be remitted.

(5) Nothing contained in or done under the authority of any law shall be held to be inconsistent with or in contravention of subsection (1) of this section –

(a) to the extent that the law in question makes provision for the taking of possession or acquisition of any property –

(i) in satisfaction of any tax, rate or due;
(ii) by way of penalty for breach of the law whether under civil process or after conviction of a criminal offence under the law in force in Botswana;
(iii) as an incident of a lease, tenancy, mortgage, charge, bill of sale, pledge or contract;
(iv) in the execution of judgments or orders of a court in proceedings for the determination of civil rights or obligations;
(v) in circumstances where it is reasonably necessary so to do because the property is in a dangerous state or injurious to the health of human beings, animals or plants;
(vi) in consequence of any law with respect to the limitation of actions; or
(vii) for so long only as may be necessary for the purposes of any examination, investigation, trial or inquiry or, in the case of land, for the purposes of the carrying out thereon of work of soil conservation or the conservation of other natural resources or work relating to agricultural development or improvement (being work relating to such development or improvement that the owner or occupier of the land has been required, and has without reasonable excuse refused or failed, to carry out),

and except so far as that provision or, as the case may be, the thing done under the authority thereof is shown not to be reasonably justifiable in a democratic society; or

(b) to the extent that the law in question makes provision for the taking of possession or acquisition of –

(i) enemy property;
(ii) property of a deceased person, a person of unsound mind, a person who has not attained the age of twenty one years, a prodigal, or a person who is absent from Botswana, for the purpose of its

administration for the benefit of the persons entitled to the beneficial interest therein;

(iii) property of a person declared to be insolvent or a body corporate in liquidation, for the purpose of its administration for the benefit of the creditors of the insolvent or body corporate and, subject thereto, for the benefit of other persons entitled to the beneficial interest in the property; or

(iv) property subject to a trust, for the purpose of vesting the property in persons appointed as trustees under the instrument creating the trust or by a court, or by order of a court, for the purpose of giving effect to the trust.

(6) Nothing contained in or done under the authority of any law shall be held to be inconsistent with or in contravention of subsection (1) of this section to the extent that the law in question makes provision for the compulsory taking of possession in the public interest of any property, or the compulsory acquisition in the public interest in or right over property, where that property, interest or right is held by a body corporate established by law for public purposes in which no moneys have been invested other than moneys provided by Parliament.

Section 14: Protection of freedom of movement

(1) No person shall be deprived of his or her freedom of movement, and for the purposes of this section the said freedom means the right to move freely throughout Botswana, the right to reside in any part of Botswana, the right to enter Botswana and immunity from expulsion from Botswana.

(2) Any restriction on a person's freedom of movement that is involved in his or her lawful detention shall not be held to be inconsistent with or in contravention of this section.

(3) Nothing contained in or done under the authority of any law shall be held to be inconsistent with or in contravention of this section to the extent that the law in question makes provision –

(a) for the imposition of restrictions that are reasonably required in the interests of defence, public safety, public order, public morality or public health or the imposition of restrictions on the acquisition or use by any person of land or other property in Botswana and except so far as that provision or, as the case may be, the thing done under the authority thereof, is shown not to be reasonably justifiable in a democratic society;

(b) for the imposition of restrictions on the freedom of movement of any person who is not a citizen of Botswana;

(c) for the imposition of restrictions on the entry into or residence within defined areas of Botswana of persons who are not Bushmen to the extent that such restrictions are reasonably required for the protection or well-being of Bushmen;

(d) for the imposition of restrictions upon the movement or residence within Botswana of public officers; or

(e) …

(4) If any person whose freedom of movement has been restricted by order under such a provision as is referred to in subsection (3)(a) of this section (other than a restriction which is applicable to persons generally or to general classes of persons) so requests at any time during the period of that restriction not earlier than six months after the order was made or six months after he or she last made such request, as the case may be, his or her case shall be reviewed by an independent and impartial tribunal presided over by a person, qualified to be enrolled as an advocate in Botswana, appointed by the Chief Justice.

(5) On any review by a tribunal in pursuance of this section of the case of a person whose freedom of movement has been restricted, the tribunal may make recommendations, concerning the necessity or expediency of continuing the restriction to the authority by which it was ordered but, unless it is otherwise provided by law, that authority shall not be obliged to act in accordance with any such recommendations.

Appendix 2: Property guarantees in the Namibian Constitution

Article 16: Property

(1) All persons shall have the right in any part of Namibia to acquire, own and dispose of all forms of immovable and movable property individually or in association with others and to bequeath their property to their heirs or legatees: provided that Parliament may by legislation prohibit or regulate as it deems expedient the right to acquire property by persons who are not Namibian citizens.

(2) The State or a competent body or organ authorised by law may expropriate property in the public interest subject to the payment of just compensation, in accordance with requirements and procedures to be determined by Act of Parliament.

Article 22: Limitation upon fundamental rights and freedoms

Whenever or wherever in terms of this Constitution the limitation of any fundamental rights or freedoms contemplated by this chapter is authorised, any law providing for such limitation shall:

a) be of general application, shall not negate the essential content, and shall not be aimed at a particular individual;

b) specify the ascertainable extent of such limitation and identify the article or articles on which authority to enact such limitation is claimed to rest.

Appendix 3: Property guarantees in Constitution of the Republic of South Africa, 1996

Section 25: Property

(1) No one may be deprived of property except in terms of law of general application, and no law may permit arbitrary deprivation of property.

(2) Property may be expropriated only in terms of law of general application–

(a) for a public purpose or in the public interest; and

(b) subject to compensation, the amount of which and the time and manner of payment of which have either been agreed to by those affected or decided or approved by a court.

(3) The amount of the compensation and the time and manner of payment must be just and equitable, reflecting an equitable balance between the public interest and the interests of those affected, having regard to all relevant circumstances, including –

(a) the current use of the property;

(b) the history of the acquisition and use of the property;

(c) the market value of the property;

(d) the extent of direct state investment and subsidy in the acquisition and beneficial capital improvement of the property; and

(e) the purpose of the expropriation.

(4) For the purposes of this section –

(a) the public interest includes the nation's commitment to land reform, and to reforms to bring about equitable access to all South Africa's natural resources; and

(b) property is not limited to land.

(5) The state must take reasonable legislative and other measures, within its available resources, to foster conditions which enable citizens to gain access to land on an equitable basis.

(6) A person or community whose tenure of land is legally insecure as a result of past racially discriminatory laws or practices is entitled, to the extent provided by an Act of Parliament, either to tenure which is legally secure or to comparable redress.

(7) A person or community dispossessed of property after 19 June 1913 as a result of past racially discriminatory laws or practices is entitled, to the extent provided by an Act of Parliament, either to restitution of that property or to equitable redress.

(8) No provision of this section may impede the state from taking legislative and other measures to achieve land, water and related reform, in order to redress the results of past racial discrimination, provided that any departure from the provisions of this section is in accordance with the provisions of section 36(1).

(9) Parliament must enact the legislation referred to in subsection (6).

Section 26: Housing

(1) Everyone has the right to have access to adequate housing.
(2) The state must take reasonable legislative and other measures, within its available resources, to achieve the progressive realisation of this right.
(3) No one may be evicted from their home, or have their home demolished, without an order of court made after considering all the relevant circumstances. No legislation may permit arbitrary evictions.

Section 36: Limitation of rights

(1) The rights in the Bill of Rights may be limited only in terms of law of general application to the extent that the limitation is reasonable and justifiable in an open and democratic society based on human dignity, equality and freedom, taking into account all relevant factors, including –

  (a) the nature of the right;
  (b) the importance of the purpose of the limitation;
  (c) the nature and extent of the limitation;
  (d) the relation between the limitation and its purpose; and
  (e) less restrictive means to achieve the purpose.

(2) Except as provided in subsection (1) or in any other provision of the Constitution, no law may limit any right entrenched in the Bill of Rights.

Appendix 4: Property guarantees in the Constitution of the Republic of Malawi

Section 28: Property

(1) Every person shall be able to acquire property alone or in association with others.
(2) No person shall be arbitrarily deprived of property.

Section 44: Limitations on rights

(1) There shall be no derogation, restrictions or limitation with regard to—

  (a) the right to life;
  (b) the prohibition of torture and cruel, inhuman or degrading treatment or punishment;
  (c) the prohibition of genocide;
  (d) the prohibition of slavery, the slave trade and slave-like practices;
  (e) the prohibition of imprisonment for failure to meet contractual obligations;
  (f) the prohibition on retrospective criminalization and the retrospective imposition of greater penalties for criminal acts;
  (g) the right to equality and recognition before the law;

(h) the right to freedom of conscience, belief, thought and religion and to academic freedom; or
(i) the right to habeas corpus.

(2) Without prejudice to subsection (1), no restrictions or limitations may be placed on the exercise of any rights and freedoms provided for in this Constitution other than those prescribed by law, which are reasonable, recognized by international human rights standards and necessary in an open and democratic society.
(3) Laws prescribing restrictions or limitations shall not negate the essential content of the right or freedom in question, shall be of general application.
(4) Expropriation of property shall be permissible only when done for public utility and only when there has been adequate notification and appropriate compensation, provided that there shall always be a right to appeal to a court of law.
(5) Wherever it is stated in this Constitution that a person has the right to the services of a legal practitioner or medical practitioner of his or her own choice, that right shall be without limitation, save where the State is obliged to provide such services of a legal practitioner or medical practitioner, in which case an Act of Parliament may prescribe that the choice of the legal practitioner or medical practitioner should be limited to those in Government service or employment.

Notes

1 Zambia (1991), and Lesotho (1992) are other southern African countries with revised constitutional arrangements, but they have not been included as case studies because they revived or retained from old order human rights chapters of the type in the Botswana Constitution.
2 See J. de Waal, I. Currie and G. Erasmus (2001) *The Bill of Rights Handbook* (4th edn, Juta & Co. Ltd), 9–10 for an indication of what these constitutional values entail. Essentially, government should derive its powers from and be guided and restrained in its conduct by the Constitution, and protect and promote individual rights encoded in the Constitution.
3 For excellent surveys on this subject, see A. J. Van der Walt (1999) *Constitutional Property Clauses* (Cape Town: Juta & Co.), and T. Allen (2000) *The Right to Property in Commonwealth Constitutions* (Cambridge: Cambridge University Press).
4 de Waal, Currie and Erasmus, above, n 2, p 411.
5 Allen, above, n 3, p 143.
6 For an accessible discussion of theories underlying the property debate see A. J. Van der Walt (1995) 'Property rights, land rights, and environmental rights', in D. van Wyk, J. Dugard, B. de Villiers and D. Davis, *Rights and Constitutionalism, The New South African Legal Order* (Cape Town: Oxford University Press and Juta & Co), pp 445–501, especially pp 455–61.
7 Botswana, Lesotho, Namibia, South Africa, Swaziland and Zimbabwe apply the body of law called Roman-Dutch common law.
8 Van der Walt, above, n 6, pp 478–88.
9 The leading case in the region on this is the Zimbabwean case of *Hewlett v Minister of Finance and Another*, 1982 (1) SA 490 which concerned the cancellation by the Zimbabwe

Government of compensation paid to 'victims of terrorism' under an old Rhodesian law. The Supreme Court held that the award of compensation was property, but it refused to award compensation on the ground that the cancellation of the award was not a taking of the property. It was a deprivation for which compensation was not payable under the Constitution of Zimbabwe at that time. For a critical assessment of the case, see T. Roux (1996) 'Constitutional property rights review in Southern Africa: the record of the Zimbabwe Supreme Court', *African Journal of International and Comparative Law*, 8: 755.

10 Allen, above, n 3, ch 6, pp 162–200.

11 Allen, above, n 3, pp 205–12.

12 One such case from Botswana is *President of the Republic of Botswana and Others v Bruwer and Another* [1998] BLR 86 (Court of Appeal), partly discussed below.

13 See C. Ng'ong'ola (1989) 'Compulsory Acquisition of private land in Botswana: the Bonnington Farm case', *Comparative and International Law Journal of Southern Africa*, 22: 298–319

14 Allen, above, n 3, pp 242–43, referring to the interpretation of Article 1 of the First Protocol of the Convention in *Sporrong and Lonnoroth v Sweden*, A52 (1982) 5 EHRR 35, para 69.

15 P. Fawcus and A. Tilbury (2002) *Botswana: The Road to Independence* (Gaborone: Pula Press and The Botswana Society), p 134.

16 Allen, above, n 3, pp 54–69.

17 N. Parsons, W. Henderson and T. Tlou (1995) *Seretse Khama, 1921–1980* (Bramfontein: Macmillan Boleswa), p 243.

18 Sir Ketumire Masire (2002) 'Foreword', in P. Fawcus and A. Tilbury, *Botswana: The Road to Independence* (Gaborone: Pula Press and The Botswana Society), p ix.

19 At independence on 30 September 1966, freehold or private land mostly under occupation and use by settlers amounted to 6 per cent of the total land area of the country. Tribal land was 48 per cent, and State land 47 per cent. See B. Machacha (1986) 'Botswana's land tenure: institutional reform and policy formulation', in J. W. Arntzen, L. D. Ngcongco and S. D. Turner (eds), *Land Policy and Agriculture in Eastern and Southern Africa* (Tokyo: United Nations University), p 39. Tribal land now stands at over 70 per cent of the total land area. State land is 25 per cent, and freehold land is about 5 per cent. See Republic of Botswana (2002) *National Development Plan 9, 2003 – 2009* (Gaborone: Ministry of Finance and Development Planning, Gaborone), para 17.1, p 332.

20 Allen, above, n 3, pp 58–59 observes that there was no illusion in Britain that a Bill of Rights would deter a determined nationalist government from proceeding against settler proprietary interests, but strong property guarantees had an important psychological value. They provided the assurance to settlers that there might be economic and political stability in the new nations.

21 [1992] BLR 119. Schreiner JA at p 187 regarded section 3 as only 'declaratory, in general terms, of the goal which it is sought to be reached by the provisions of the chapter as a whole … '. Section 3, in his view, did not create specific rights and freedoms which do not fall specifically within the more detailed provisions of section 4 to 15.

22 [1992] BLR 119, pp 133–34.

23 For a discussion of such clauses and some of the problems they may engender, see A. J. Van der Walt (1998) 'Double property guarantees: a structural and comparative analysis', *South African Journal on Human Rights*, 14: 560–586.

24 Compare with section 3(1) of the Acquisition of Property Act, Chapter 32:10, Laws of Botswana. The only example of a public interest in section 8(1)(a) of the Constitution not included in section 3(1) of the Acquisition of Property Act is an acquisition for purposes of securing the development or utilization of the mineral resources of Botswana.

25 Above, n 12.

26 *Bruwer and Another v President of the Republic of Botswana and Others* [1997] BLR 477.

27 In so holding, the Court of Appeal adopted an approach similar to that in *Tati Company Ltd v The High Commissioner for the Bechuanaland* (1959) HCTLR 32–53 when a colonial High Court not surprisingly held that it would not review a decision to expropriate land on the basis that it was wrong in fact, inequitable and taken in ignorance of a relevant fact. What is surprising is that a Court of Appeal called upon to intervene in terms of the Independence Constitution would be equally reticent.
28 This was the Bechuanaland Protectorate Acquisition of Property Proclamation No 80 of 1954. It became the Acquisition of Property Act, Chapter 32:10 after independence.
29 Above, n 12.
30 Section 16.
31 Section 21(b).
32 *Attorney General v Western Trust (Pty) Ltd*, Civil Appeal No 12 of 1981 (High Court), belatedly reported in [2006] 2 BLR 1.
33 See Ng'ong'ola, above, n 13, pp 298–319.
34 Act No 23 of 1975, Chapter 32:11, Laws of Botswana.
35 Section 33 of the Tribal Land Act.
36 [2006] 2 BLR 633.
37 The CKGR was proclaimed under High Commissioner's Notice No 33 included in section 5 of the First Schedule of the Fauna Conservation Proclamation No 22 of 1961. At about 52,800 square kilometres, it was at the time one of the largest game reserves in Africa.
38 G. Silberbauer (1965) *Report to the Government of Bechuanaland on the Bushman Survey* (Gaborone: Government Press), p 132.
39 Clive Spinage (1991) *History and Evolution of Fauna Conservation Laws of Botswana* (Gaborone: Botswana Society), p 31; Fauna Conservation Proclamation, 22 of 1961, especially sections 4, 7, 34 and 57; and section 2 of the Central Kalahari Game Reserve (Control of Entry) Regulations, GN 38 of 1963.
40 For an extensive review and discussion of the case, see C. Ng'ong'ola (2007) 'Sneaking aboriginal title into Botswana's legal system through a side door', *University of Botswana Law Journal*, 6: 107–30.
41 Allen, above, n 3, pp 71–73.
42 In British Colonial style of drafting, comparable provisions would be the curious statements splattered in various clauses, including section 8(5)(a) of the Botswana Constitution, suggesting that derogations from specified rights shall be 'reasonably justifiable in a democratic society'.
43 de Waal, Currie and Erasmus, above, n 2, pp 415–16.
44 *Former Highlands Residents, In Re Ash v Department of Land Affairs* [2002] 2 All SA 26, LCC Case No 116/198, at pp 12–21. Another authority is *M. J. Khumalo and Others v H.W. Potgieter and Others*, LCC Case No 34/99, 17 December 1999 (unreported).
45 P. J. Badenhorst, J. Pienaar and H. Mostert (eds) (2003) *Silberberg and Schoeman's Law of Property* (4th edn, Durban: LexisNexis, Butterworths), pp 229–33.
46 *Ex parte Chairperson of the Constitutional Assembly: In Re Certification of the Constitution of the Republic of South Africa*, 1996, [1996] 4 SA 744.
47 *Government of the Republic of South Africa and Others v Grootboom and Others*, Case CCT 11/00, 4 October 2000, Constitutional Court.
48 Act No 1 of 1966. See S. Roberts (1966) 'The Malawi Forfeiture Act – A surfeit of discretion', *Journal of African Law*, 10: 131.
49 Act No 21 of 1970. See C. Ng'ong'ola (1992) 'The post-colonial era in relation to land expropriation laws in Botswana, Malawi, Zambia and Zimbabwe', *The International and Comparative Law Quarterly*, 41: 117–36, especially pp 127–32.
50 Government of the Republic of Malawi (2001) *Malawi National Land Policy* (Ministry of Lands and Housing, 7 September), para 4.12, p 30.
51 *Malawi Congress Party and Others v Attorney-General and Others*, High Court, Civil Cause No 2074 of 1995.

52 *Attorney-General and Others v Malawi Congress Party and Others*, MSCA, Civil Appeal No 22 of 1996.
53 Section 44(3). This is comparable to Article 22(a) of the Namibian Constitution.
54 Section 44(2). This is in part comparable to section 36(1) of the South African Constitution.

8 Southern African Development Community within the region

The African Union approach to land issues

*Rachel Murray**

8.1 Introduction

As well as being subject to Southern African Development Community (SADC) instruments, SADC states also operate within the broader regional system, as provided for under the Constitutive Act of the African Union (AU) and the various human rights mechanisms and instruments available. The principal instrument for the region is the African Charter on Human and Peoples' Rights (ACHPR) and its African Commission.[1] An African Court on Human and Peoples' Rights has also recently started deciding cases and eventually it will be replaced by the African Court of Justice and Human Rights.[2] The various AU organs and its predecessor the Organisation of African Unity (OAU) have dealt with land issues in a variety of different contexts, from independence and self-determination in the early days of the OAU, to unconstitutional changes of government, indigenous peoples and other land disputes in more recent years.

This chapter examines how the concept of land has been interpreted by the AU organs and the African Commission on Human and Peoples' Rights in particular. It argues that the approach of the AU organs has been conservative and has upheld state sovereignty, in contrast to the more rights-based approach of the African Commission on Human and Peoples' Rights and its special mechanism. There is evidence of a shift, however, by the AU to a more holistic stance to land issues which incorporates human and peoples' rights.

8.2 Self-determination

In line with Africa's historical colonial past, the AU and its predecessor, the OAU, have upheld the territorial integrity and sovereignty of African states post-independence.[3] Initially, the OAU focused on the concept of self-determination in its external form, stressing state independence as Africans gained statehood from the 1950s onwards. Once this was no longer an issue the OAU shifted its attention to internal aspects. Declarations and resolutions on unconstitutional changes of government,[4] for example, and democratic elections, culminating in the adoption of the African Charter on Democracy, Elections and Governance in 2007,[5] underlined that self-determination was now viewed as an internal issue and one which could not challenge existing state boundaries. The principle of *uti possidetis*, despite the unequal manner in which the boundaries were drawn in the first place by colonial rulers, and despite some early calls to the contrary,[6] has thus been continually upheld by the OAU and the AU.[7]

The African Commission has similarly upheld this concept, noting that self-determination, as set out in Article 20(1) of the ACHPR,[8] 'is exercised within the standards and according to the modalities which are compatible with the territorial integrity of the Nation States'.[9] In contrast to the right of self-determination in a decolonisation context, current claims for self-determination can therefore be defined, in a number of ways.[10] These include as 'the management of [a people's] "internal and local affairs" and to their participation as citizens in national affairs on an equal footing with their fellow citizens'.[11] Therefore, in relation to indigenous peoples, for example, the African Commission has held that self-determination can be seen as 'a series of rights relative to the full participation in national affairs, the right to local self-government, the right to recognition so as to be consulted in the drafting of laws and programs concerning them, to a recognition of their structures and traditional ways of living as well as the freedom to preserve and promote their culture'.[12]

8.3 Indigenous peoples and land

One area where the OAU and AU have been challenged with respect to land is with claims by indigenous peoples. Here, the African Commission on Human and Peoples' Rights on the one hand diverged from the rest of the AU on the other, in its approach to the issue. The former has taken a human rights-based approach, stressing that there is no conflict between the rights of indigenous peoples and the principles of state sovereignty and territorial integrity. The AU organs on the other hand have had more difficulties and have seen recognition of indigenous peoples' rights, particularly how they relate to land, as a potential threat to African states.

As a result of the sustained commitment of the International Work Group for Indigenous Affairs (IWGIA) and other individuals, the African Commission began to look at the issue of indigenous peoples formally on its agenda in May 1999.[13] With the particular support of a number of Commissioners, the non-governmental organisations (NGOs) attempted to convince the rest of the Commission and those participating in the sessions that they should move beyond the barrier of considering the phrase 'indigenous people' to be a derogatory colonial term, to a proper examination of the discrimination and violations suffered by various groups within the African continent. As evidence of the success of their lobbying, the Commission adopted a resolution in November 2000 establishing a Working Group of Experts of Indigenous Populations/Communities in Africa to further examine the issues and produce recommendations in this regard.[14] The outcome of their deliberations was a progressive report adopted in 2003 by the African Commission in which it recognised the variety of individual and peoples' rights that had been violated by indigenous peoples and their members and which, although refusing to define the concept of 'indigenous peoples' was willing to set out 'characteristics' to help identify them. These included:

- 'their cultures and ways of life differ considerably from the dominant society';
- 'their cultures are under threat in some cases to the extent of extinction';
- 'a key characteristic for most of them is that the survival of their particular way of life depends on access and rights to their traditional land and the natural resources thereon';
- 'they suffer from discrimination as they are being regarded as less developed and less advanced than other more dominant sectors of society';
- 'they often live in inaccessible regions, often geographically isolated and suffer from various forms of marginalization, both politically and socially';
- 'they are subject to domination and exploitation within national political and economic structures that are commonly designed to reflect the interests and activities of the national majority'.[15]

Whilst this report received some praise and attention from among those working on indigenous peoples, it was not noticed by the AU organs in Addis Ababa. Therefore, the African Commission had adopted this report and continued to work on this issue since then, yet African states involved in discussions at the United Nations (UN) on the Declaration on the Rights of Indigenous Peoples took an entirely different approach.

The divergence of opinion centred around the content of the UN Draft Declaration on the Rights of Indigenous Peoples. The Draft Declaration was adopted by the Human Rights Council in June 2006,[16] but its progress was halted at the level of the General Assembly due in the main to the concerns of the African states and a proposal by Namibia for a resolution to defer adoption of the Declaration until it had been considered further. In November 2006 the Africa Group adopted an Aide-Memoire in which it referred to the preamble of the UN Declaration which stated 'the control by indigenous peoples over developments affecting them and their lands, territories and resources will enable them to maintain and strengthen their institutions, cultures and traditions and to promote their development according to their aspirations and needs'.[17] The Africa Group considered this to be 'impracticable within the context of the countries concerned. In accordance with the constitutional provisions of these countries, the control of land and natural resources is the obligation of the State'.[18] The AU Summit in January 2007 then followed this up with a Decision on the UN Declaration which called for further consideration of a number of issues including:

- 'The definition of indigenous peoples;
- Self-determination;
- Ownership of land and natural resources;
- Establishment of distinct political and economic institutions; and
- National and territorial integrity'.[19]

This concern with indigenous peoples' rights was despite the forthright stance taken by its human rights body, the African Commission on Human and Peoples' Rights and its Working Group. The African Commission in a specific response to the Africa Group's position, adopted an Advisory Opinion in 2007. It noted in relation to indigenous peoples, that 'a special attachment to and use of their traditional land whereby their ancestral land and territory have a fundamental importance for their collective physical and cultural survival as peoples'.[20] The Commission also drew attention to Article 21(1) of the ACHPR and the right to freely dispose of natural resources.[21]

In an attempt to allay the fears of the African states, it pointed out that concerns with rights of indigenous peoples seemed to be based on what was happening in the Americas,[22] but that in the African context it had interpreted indigenous peoples' rights '*within the context of a strict respect for the inviolability of borders and of the obligation to preserve the territorial integrity of State Parties,* in conformity with the principles and values enshrined in the Constitutive Act of the AU, the African Charter on Human and Peoples' Rights (the African Charter) and the UN Charter'.[23] After some intense negotiations and delegations from the African Commission and members of its Working Group to African states delegations, the UN Declaration was eventually adopted in September 2007 by the General Assembly.[24]

Subsequent to these discussions the African Commission has continued to take a strong stance towards the protection of indigenous peoples' rights and their ability to access and to enjoy their land. For example, in its concluding observations on the state report from Uganda, it noted:

> … the exploitation, the discrimination and the marginalization of indigenous populations, in particular the BATWA people of Uganda, who are deprived of their ancestral lands and live without any land titles.[25]

It therefore recommended that the state adopt measures for the effective protection of the Batwa people by establishing laws that protect land rights and natural resources of indigenous populations.[26] In this context, as will be noted further below, land covers houses and shelter, and Article 14 of the ACHPR protects against the expropriation or destruction of such.[27] The African Commission recognises, however, that indigenous peoples continue to be affected by logging, mining and the creation of national parks which has had an impact on their ability to remain on their ancestral lands.[28] In this sense, the rights of indigenous peoples and their culture, religion and way of life are 'intimately intertwined with their ancestral lands … and without access to their ancestral land, the Endorois are unable to fully exercise their cultural and religious rights, and feel disconnected from their land and ancestors'.[29]

Land is therefore crucial in an understanding of the right to religion of indigenous peoples and their ability to practice that religion.[30] Denying them access to ancestral land, therefore, restricts their 'freedom to practice their religion and was not justified in the public interest, nor for any economic or ecological protection', neither would permitting them to use the land 'detract from the goal of conservation or developing the area for economic reasons'.[31] In this case, relating to the rights of the Endorois people in Kenya, the African Commission found a violation of Article 8 of the Charter.[32]

8.4 The Zimbabwe situation

The other issue which has caused concern for both the African Commission and the AU organs, and one on which they have taken a similar stance, is that of Zimbabwe and land redistribution by the Zimbabwean government. As this became a global political hot potato, both the AU and African Commission have been forced to examine the issue. Both have dealt with this as a colonial issue. In 2000 the OAU's Assembly of Heads of State and Government adopted a Declaration on the Resolution of the Land Question in Zimbabwe in which it 'reiterated its demand for Britain to honour its colonial obligation to fund the land resettlement programme in Zimbabwe in accordance with the Lancaster House Agreement' and referred to the 'colonial legacy' of the land question.[33] In contrast to its proactive stance on indigenous peoples, the African Commission has similarly stressed the colonial element of the Zimbabwe situation, rather than a more rights-based approach and shied away from a detailed consideration of the issue.

In part, this can be explained by the fact that at one stage one of its Commissioners, Andrew Chigovera, was also the current Attorney-General of Zimbabwe. Add to the very politically sensitive nature of the situation, and in line with similar attitudes when faced with such issues, the African Commission, principally a reactive body, did not display a progressive stance. Although it sent a mission to the state in 2002, the findings were couched in very cautious language:

> There is no doubt that from the perspective of the fact-finding team, the land question is critical and that Zimbabweans, sooner or later, needed to address it. The team has consistently maintained that from a human rights perspective, land reform has to be the prerogative of the government of Zimbabwe. The Mission noted that Article 14 of the African Charter states "The right to property shall be guaranteed. *It may only be encroached upon in the interest of public need or in the general interest of the community and in accordance with the provisions of appropriate laws*". It appears to the Mission that the Government of Zimbabwe has managed to bring this policy matter under the legal and constitutional system of the country. It now means that land reform and land distribution can now take place in a lawful and orderly fashion.[34]

For its part, the Zimbabwean government strenuously contended that 'the land question is central to the problems bedevilling the country'.[35] In a subsequent communication against the state in 2002, *Zimbabwe NGO Human Rights Forum v Zimbabwe*, Communication 245/2002,[36] the African Commission found violations of Articles 1 and 7 of the ACHPR, although not on other rights in part because of the finding that many of the violations were alleged to have been carried out by non-state actors.

8.5 The concept of land under the ACHPR

The ACHPR makes no reference to land, although its African Commission has referred to this under a number of Articles. First, it is clear that land is property,[37] as provided for under Article 14 of the Charter and an ancestral home, for example, can be property for the purposes of inheritance.[38] The African Commission has spent little time examining Article 14 of the ACHPR and in the few cases in which it has done so, they have related to land. It has laid down some broader principles. First:

> the right to property is a traditional fundamental right in democratic and liberal societies. … The role of the state is to respect and to protect this right against any form of encroachment, and to regulate the exercise of this right in order for it to be accessible to everyone, taking public interest into due consideration.[39]

This right includes 'ownership and peaceful enjoyment',[40] access, as well as the right not to have the property encroached upon,[41] and use and control as the owner deems fit.[42] The obligations of the state include positive duties 'to establish conditions, as well as provide the means, to ensure the protection of both life and property, during peace time and in times of disturbances and armed conflicts. The Respondent State also has the responsibility to ensure that persons who are in harms way … are resettled in safety and with dignity in another part of the country'.[43] However, the right to property is broader than this and property encompasses 'the rights, interests and benefits of such communities in their traditional lands'.[44] The state therefore has obligations to respect and protect the right.[45]

The right also does not depend on legal title. Therefore, in a case relating to, among other things, the displacement of indigenous Black African tribes in the Darfur region of Sudan including Fur, Marsalit and Zaghawa tribes, the African Commission held:

> It does not matter whether they had legal title to the land, the fact that the victims cannot derive their livelihood from what they possessed for generations means they have been deprived of the use of their property under conditions which are not permitted by Article 14.[46]

Similarly, where the Endorois people were not given title to the land the African Commission has simply recognised that 'the trust land system has proved inadequate to protect their rights'.[47] As a result of this, the African Commission concluded 'traditional possession of land by indigenous people has the equivalent effect as that of a state-granted full property title'[48] and furthermore, that this 'traditional possession entitles indigenous people to demand official recognition and registration of property title'.[49] If, however, the lands were transferred lawfully to third parties in good faith, then although the indigenous people could not claim them back they should be able to claim 'restitution thereof or to obtain other lands of equal extension and quality'.[50]

The right to property can then only be deprived of in certain circumstances, namely for the purposes of 'to control the use of property in accordance with the public or general interest, by enforcing such laws as they deem necessary for the purpose'.[51] The African Commission has held that this public interest test is higher where the land in question is indigenous land and the ancestral land of indigenous peoples. It also introduced the test of proportionality in this context and that the eviction of the Endorois from their lands is not proportionate and could have been pursued by alternative means.[52]

In such instances the Commission held that three elements should be applied: 'effective participation' of the people, 'reasonable benefit enjoyed by the community' and 'a prior environment and social impact assessment' carried out.[53]

Destruction of property or forcible evictions from 'normal places of residence' by the state or armed groups believed to be supported by the state will violate the right to property under Article 14.[54] These actions may also violate Article 18 of the Charter which prohibits 'arbitrary or unlawful interference with the family'. States should 'refrain from any action that will affect the family unit, including arbitrary separation of family members and involuntary displacement of families'.[55] Forcible eviction of individuals from their homes, among other things:

> threatens the very foundation of the family and renders the enjoyment of the right to family life difficult. By not ensuring protection to the victims, thus allowing its forces or third parties to infringe the rights of the victims, the Respondent state is held to have violated Article 18(1) of the African Charter.[56]

Denial of access to ancestral land of indigenous peoples may also violate cultural rights in Article 17(2) and (3) of the Charter and rights of access to natural resources and development in Articles 21 and 22.

Forced evictions and destruction of housing will also violate Article 5 of the Charter and the right to be free from cruel, inhuman and degrading treatment or punishment, even if carried out by non-state actors and 'the state fails to protect the victims from such a violation of their human rights'.[57] The Commission links this specifically with human dignity and that the forced eviction of a civilian population from their homes and villages by militia groups was a failure by the state to protect the victims against the same violations: 'in the opinion of the Commission, this kind of treatment was cruel and inhuman and threatened the very essence of human dignity'.[58] Neither would it permit Article 27(2) of the ACHPR[59] to be used as a defence for the evictions:

> for such reasons to be justifiable, the Darfurian population should have benefited from the collective security envisage (sic) under Article 27(2). To the contrary, the complaint has demonstrated that after eviction, the security of the IDP camps was not guaranteed. The deployment of peacekeeping forces from outside the country is proof that the Respondent State failed in its obligation to guarantee security to the IDPs and the civilian population in Darfur.[60]

In the context of displacement, the Commission has linked freedom of movement and residence as being 'two sides of the same coin'.[61] Displacement 'by force, and without legitimate or legal basis' will therefore violate the latter rights.[62]

A failure by the state to prevent forced evictions will also violate Article 12(1) and states should take 'urgent steps to ensure displaced persons return to their homes'.[63]

On several occasions the African Commission has also interpreted the rights in the ACHPR as including the right to access water[64] and in the context of land has stated that evictions from land which thereby prevent a people from accessing water may violate Article 4 of the ACHPR and the right to life. Thus, on 10 August 2010 the African Commission issued a press release in which it expressed concern over the situation of the Bushmen of the Central Kalahari Game Reserve in Botswana.[65] In this it set out that, contrary to a ruling by the High Court in the country which held that they were not entitled to use a well to access water:

> the right and access to water are essential to the full enjoyment of the right to life and all the rights contained in the African Charter. A denial of such right is a denial of the basic right and the denial of the right to life as enshrined in the article 4 of the African Charter. ... refusal to allow the Bushmen to use their existing borehole at Mothomelo can only be interpreted as a clear sign that the government of Botswana is determined to continue what is perceived as a policy of keeping the Bushmen from returning home.[66]

8.6 Conclusion: the concept of land under the AU: a shift to a rights-based approach?

At the level of the AU, outside of the indigenous peoples and Zimbabwe issues there is evidence that in recent years it has taken a more holistic and proactive stance to land as a concept. Indeed, in contrast to the rhetoric surrounding the discussion of the UN Declaration on Indigenous Peoples, the AU displayed a rights-based approach to land over a decade ago.[67] For example, the New Partnership for Africa's Development (NEPAD) process recognised the fundamental role that land played on the continent.[68] In a Declaration on Land Issues and Challenges in Africa, the Assembly of Heads of State of the AU noted 'the centrality of land to sustainable socio-economic growth, development and the security of the social, economic and cultural livelihoods of our people', noting in particular the 'diversity and complexity of the systems under which land and related resources are held, managed and used'.[69] It then went on to note 'the need for strong systems of land governance rooted in principles of sustainability in an effort to ensure preservation, protection and renewability of Africa's land and related resources'.[70]

In 2009 the Assembly of Heads of State of the AU approved the Framework and Guidelines on Land Policy in Africa[71] which was the result of a process to consider land policy on the continent. In part this was the result of the broader consideration of development issues and agriculture and natural resources. The Framework and Guidelines recognises various aspects to the land issue on the continent, including the 'social and cultural context', noting in particular 'the system of patriarchy' and 'discrimination against women', and 'other forms of marginalization' including 'certain categories of indigenous people', noting that 'land reform policies must also address these concerns'.[72] The Framework and Guidelines approach the issue from a more proactive rights-focused stance recognising such marginalised groups need to be considered, including the impact of traditional structures on discrimination against women and the 'legitimacy of indigenous land rights'.[73] As a result it recommends that there is a need to recognise 'indigenous structures, institutions and land rights regimes and to provide a necessary interface between them and state-led systems of land management and administrations'.[74] This can be achieved through continued consultation with the public and 'deep' engagement with civil society organisations, among other things.[75]

Furthermore, 'better and more productive use of land requires that the land rights of women be strengthened through a variety of mechanisms … To ensure full enjoyment of land rights, these measures must be part of an ideology which removes issues regarding the land rights of women from the private sphere of marriage and family, and places them in the public domain of human rights'.[76]

The Framework and Guidelines acknowledge that the issue of land in the African context is one that touches upon a wide range of issues, from agriculture, to inheritance, but these are often dealt with as separate, distinct issues. As has been noted above, the African Commission on Human and Peoples' Rights' has displayed what has been seen as a progressive approach to protection of land through its decisions on indigenous peoples and the conclusions of Working Group. Although there was a discrepancy in the attitude adopted by the other AU organs to land and indigenous peoples, the recent AU Framework and Guidelines suggest that there may now be a shift to a more rights-based approach to the issue of land. This gives some hope towards a more holistic consideration but what is still needed is greater coordination between the African Commission and AU organs to ensure that a common stance and policies are taken to these issues.

Notes

* Professor of International Human Rights Law, University of Bristol.

1 Article 30 of the ACHPR.

2 See Protocol on the Statute of the African Court of Justice and Human Rights, adopted July 2008.

3 E.g. Decision on Somalia, AHG/Dec 146 (XXXVI); Decision on the Comoros, AHG/Dec 149 (XXXVI).

4 See Decision on Unconstitutional Changes of Government in Africa, AHG/Dec 150 (XXXVI), Thirty Third Ordinary Session in Harare, Zimbabwe, June 1997; Declaration on the Framework for an OAU Response to Unconstitutional Changes of Government, AHG/Decl 5 (XXXVI).

5 Adopted at the Eighth Ordinary Session of the Assembly of Heads of State and Government of the AU, Addis Ababa, 30 January 2007.

6 'It is hereby resolved by the All African Peoples' Conference that the Conference (a) denounces artificial frontiers drawn by imperialist powers to divide the peoples of Africa, particularly those which cut across ethnic groups and divide people of the same

stock; (b) calls for the abolition or adjustment of such frontiers at an early date to this problem founded upon the true wishes of the people; (c) calls upon the Independent States of Africa to support a permanent solution', First All African Peoples' Conference, Accra, 5–13 December 1958, Makonnen, *International Law*, at pp 458–59. In addition, the Resolution on Somaliland had same principle, Second All African Peoples' Conference, Tunis, 25–30 January 1960. See also K. Nkrumah (1963) 'United we Stand', address, Proceedings of the Summit Conference of Independent African States, Addis Ababa, Vol 1, Section 2, Summit CIAS/GEN/INF/36, May, at p 7.

7 'Solemnly declares that all Member States pledge themselves to respect the frontiers existing on their achievement of national independence', Resolution on the Intangibility of Frontiers, AHG/Res 16(I), July 1964.

8 Article 20 reads: '1. All peoples shall have the right to existence. They shall have the unquestionable and inalienable right to self-determination. They shall freely determine their political status and shall pursue their economic and social development according to the policy they have freely chosen. 2. Colonized or oppressed peoples shall have the right to free themselves from the bonds of domination by resorting to any means recognized by the international community. 3. All peoples shall have the right to the assistance of the State Parties to the present Charter in their liberation struggle against foreign domination, be it political, economic or cultural'.

9 Advisory Opinion of the African Commission on Human and Peoples' Rights on the UN Declaration on the Rights of Indigenous Peoples, adopted 41st session, Accra, Ghana, May 2007 (hereinafter 'Advisory Opinion of the African Commission'), paras 22–23.

10 *Katangese People Congress v Zaire*, Communication No 75/92, 8th Annual Activity Report of the African Commission on Human and Peoples' Rights.

11 Advisory Opinion of the African Commission, paras 26–27.

12 Ibid, paras 26–27.

13 Agenda of the 25th Ordinary Session of the African Commission, 26th April – 5th May 1999, Twelfth Activity Report of the African Commission on Human and Peoples' Rights, 1998–99, AHG/215 (XXXV), item 8(j).

14 Resolution on the Rights of Indigenous Populations/Communities in Africa, November 2000, ACHPR/Res 51 (XXVI)/130.

15 African Commission on Human and Peoples' Rights, Report of the African Commission's Working Group of Experts on Indigenous Populations/Communities Submitted in accordance with the Resolution on the Rights of Indigenous Populations/Communities in Africa, adopted at 35th session of the African Commission, p 63.

16 Report to the General Assembly on the First Session of the Human Rights Council, A/HRC/1/L 10, 30 June 2006.

17 Draft Aide Memoire, African Group (2006) United Nations Declaration on the Rights of Indigenous People, 9 November, New York, available at <http://www.iwgiaipacc.org.za/uploads/docs/Africanaidememoire.pdf> (accessed 14 March 2011).

18 Ibid.

19 Assembly/AU/Dec 141 (VIII), para 6.

20 Advisory Opinion of the African Commission, p 4.

21 Article 21 reads: '1. All peoples shall freely dispose of their wealth and natural resources. This right shall be exercised in the exclusive interest of the people. In no case shall a people be deprived of it. 2. In case of spoilation, the dispossessed people shall have the right to the lawful recovery of its property as well as to an adequate compensation. 3. The free disposal of wealth and natural resources shall be exercised without prejudice to the obligation of promoting international economic cooperation based on mutual respect, equitable exchange and the principles of international law. 4. State Parties to the present Charter shall individually and collectively exercise the right to free disposal of their wealth and natural resources with a view to strengthening African Unity and solidarity. 5. State Parties to the present Charter shall undertake to eliminate all forms of foreign exploitation particularly that practised by international

monopolies so as to enable their peoples to fully benefit from the advantages derived from their national resources'.

22 Advisory Opinion of the African Commission, para 38.

23 Ibid, para 6 (original emphasis).

24 A/RES/61/295. See R. Murray (2011) 'The UN Declaration on the Rights of Indigenous Peoples in Africa. The Approach of the Regional Organisations to Indigenous Peoples', in S. Allen and A. Xanthaki, *Reflections on the United Nations Declaration on the Rights of Indigenous Peoples and International Law* (Oxford: Hart Publishing).

25 Concluding Observations of the African Commission on the 3rd Periodic Report of the Republic of Uganda, May 2009, available at <http://www.achpr.org/english/other/Con_Oberservations/uganda_3rd_rpt.pdf> (accessed 14 March 2011), para 39.

26 Ibid, para V.i.

27 *Malawi African Association, Amnesty International, Ms. Sarr Diop, Union Interafricaine des Droits de l'Homme and RADDHO, Collectif des Veuves et Ayants-droit, Association Mauritanienne des Droits de l'Homme v Mauritania*, Communication Nos 54/91, 61/91, 98/93, 164/97–196/97, 210/98, para 128.

28 Progress Report of the ACHPR's Working Group on Indigenous Populations/Communities, Inter-session period between 43rd and 44th ordinary sessions of the ACHPR, available at <http://www.achpr.org/english/Commissioner%27s%20Activity/44th%20OS/Special%20Rapporteurs/WGIP.pdf> (accessed 14 March 2011), para 17.

29 *Centre for Minority Rights Development (Kenya) and Minority Rights Group International on behalf of Endorois Welfare Council v Kenya*, Communication No 276/2003, 27th Activity Report of the African Commission on Human and Peoples' Rights, 2010, Annex V, para 156.

30 Ibid, para 167.

31 Ibid, para 173.

32 Article 8 reads: 'Freedom of conscience, the profession and free practice of religion shall be guaranteed. No one may, subject to law and order, be submitted to measures restricting the exercise of these freedoms'.

33 AHG/Decl 2 (XXXVII).

34 African Commission on Human and Peoples' Rights, Executive Summary of the Report of the Fact Finding Mission to Zimbabwe, 24th–28th June 2002, Seventeenth Annual Activity Report of the African Commission on Human and Peoples' Rights, Annex II, p 14.

35 Ibid, p 24.

36 21st Activity Report of the African Commission on Human and Peoples' Rights, EX. CL/322 (X), Annex III.

37 *Malawi African Association and Others v Mauritania*, Communication Nos 54/91, 61/91, 98/93, 164/97, 196/97 and 210/98 (2000), para 128.

38 *Bah Ould Rabah v Mauritania*, Communication No 197/97, Seventeenth Annual Activity Report of the African Commission on Human and Peoples' Rights, 2003–4, Annex VII, para 30.

39 *Interights, Institute for Human Rights and Development in Africa, and Association Mauritanienne des Droits de l'Homme v Islamic Republic of Mauritania*, Communication No 373/2009 (formerly 242/2001), 28th Activity Report of the African Commission on Human and Peoples' Rights, EX CL/600 (XVII), Annex II, para 43.

40 Ibid, para 44. Although in this case it was not shown by the state that the property was taken in the public interest or 'in accordance with any established law' and as a result 'was arbitrary'.

41 *The Social and Economic Rights Action Center and the Center for Economic and Social Rights v Nigeria*, Communication No 155/96, 15th Annual Activity Report of the African Commission on Human and Peoples' Rights, 2001–2, para 54.

42 *Hurilaws v Nigeria*, Communication No 225/98, 14th Activity Report of the African Commission on Human and Peoples' Rights, para 52. Search without warrant and seizure of property was held to be in violation of Article 14.

43 *Sudan Human Rights Organisation and the Sudan Center on Housing Rights and Evictions v Sudan*, Communication Nos 279/03 and 296/05, 28th Activity Report of the African Commission on Human and Peoples' Rights, EX CL/600 (XVII), Annex V, para 201.
44 *Centre for Minority Rights Development (Kenya) and Minority Rights Group International on behalf of Endorois Welfare Council v Kenya*, Communication No 276/2003, para 187. Referring to *Dogan and others v Turkey*, 2004, European Court of Human Rights, para 138–39.
45 Communication No 276/2003, ibid, para 191.
46 Communication Nos 279/03 and 296/05, above, n 43, para 205.
47 Communication No 276/2003, above, n 44, para 199.
48 Communication No 276/2003, above, n 44, para 209.
49 Communication No 276/2003, above, n 44.
50 Communication No 276/2003, above, n 44.
51 Communication No 373/2009 (formerly 242/2001), above, n 39, para 44. Although in this case it was not shown by the state that the property was taken in the public interest or 'in accordance with any established law' and as a result 'was arbitrary'.
52 Communication No 276/2003, above, n 44, para 214–15.
53 Communication No 276/2003, above, n 44, para 228.
54 Communication Nos 279/03 and 296/05, above, n 43, paras 194 and 201.
55 Communication Nos 279/03 and 296/05, above, n 43, para 213.
56 Communication Nos 279/03 and 296/05, above, n 43, para 215. See also *Union Inter Africaine des Droits de l'Homme, Federation Internationale des Ligues des Droits de l'Homme, Rencontre Africaine des Droits de l'Homme, Organisation Nationale des Droits de l'Homme au Sénégal and Association Malienne des Droits de l'Homme au Angola v Angola*, Communication No 159/1996, Eleventh Annual Activity Report of the African Commission on Human and Peoples' Rights, 1997–98, para 17.
57 Communication Nos 279/03 and 296/05, above, n 43, para 159, in line with other treaty body decisions, as referred to in the Commission's findings: *Hijrizi v Yugoslavia*, Communication No 161/2000, UN Doc CAT/C/29/D/161/2000, 2 December 2000; and *Selçuk and Asker v Turkey*, European Court of Human Rights, Judgment of 24 April 1998, Reports 1998-II, 900.
58 Communication Nos 279/03 and 296/05, above, n 43, para 164.
59 This reads: 'The rights and freedoms of each individual shall be exercised with due regard to the rights of others, collective security, morality and common interest'.
60 Communication Nos 279/03 and 296/05, above, n 43, para 166.
61 Communication Nos 279/03 and 296/05, above, n 43, para 188.
62 Communication Nos 279/03 and 296/05, above, n 43, para 189.
63 Communication Nos 279/03 and 296/05, above, n 43, para 190.
64 See e.g. Communication No 155/96, above, n 41.
65 Press Release on the Situation facing the Bushmen of the Central Kalahari Game Reserve in Botswana, 10 August 2010, available at <http://www.achpr.org> (accessed 14 March 2011).
66 Ibid.
67 See CSSDCA Solemn Declaration, 'Respect for the sovereignty and the territorial integrity of all Member States ... upholding respect for human and peoples' rights', CSSDCA Solemn Declaration, AHG/Decl 4 (XXXVI). Prior to the establishment of the African Union, the Conference on Security, Stability Development and Cooperation in Africa (CSSDCA) was a policy development process under the OAU and AU intended to deal with a wide range of issues.
68 Its African Peer Review Mechanism (APRM) focuses on a number of areas, including democracy and good political governance which adopts a human rights-based approach, Declaration on Democracy, Political, Economic and Corporate Governance, AHG/235 (XXXVIII), Annex I.
69 Assembly/AU/Decl 1 (XIII) Rev 1.

70 Ibid.
71 AU, ECA, ADF, Framework and Guidelines on Land Policy in Africa, Revised Version, March 2009.
72 Ibid, pp 22–23.
73 Ibid, pp 30–31.
74 Ibid, para 4.5.2.
75 Ibid, paras 4.5.3, 4.5.4 and 5.3.5.
76 Ibid, p 31.

Bibliography

(2008) Protocol on the Statute of the African Court of Justice and Human Rights, adopted July 2008.

African Commission on Human and Peoples' Rights (2000a) Report of the African Commission's Working Group of Experts on Indigenous Populations/Communities Submitted in accordance with the Resolution on the Rights of Indigenous Populations/Communities in Africa, adopted at 35th session of the African Commission.

African Commission on Human and Peoples' Rights (2000b) Resolution on the Rights of Indigenous Populations/Communities in Africa, November, ACHPR/Res.51 (XXVI)/130.

African Commission on Human and Peoples' Rights (2002) Executive Summary of the Report of the Fact Finding Mission to Zimbabwe, 24th–28th June, Seventeenth Annual Activity Report of the African Commission on Human and Peoples' Rights, Annex II.

African Commission on Human and Peoples' Rights (2007a) Advisory Opinion of the African Commission on Human and Peoples' Rights on the UN Declaration on the Rights of Indigenous Peoples, adopted at 41st session, Accra, Ghana, May.

African Commission on Human and Peoples' Rights (2007b) 21st Activity Report of the African Commission on Human and Peoples' Rights, EX.CL/322 (X).

African Commission on Human and Peoples' Rights (2008) Progress Report of the ACHPR's Working Group on Indigenous Populations/Communities, Inter-session period between 43rd and 44th ordinary sessions of the ACHPR, available at <http://www.achpr.org/english/Commissioner%27s%20Activity/44th%20OS/Special%20Rapporteurs/WGIP.pdf> (accessed 14 March 2011).

African Commission on Human and Peoples' Rights (2009) Concluding Observations of the African Commission on the 3rd Periodic Report of the Republic of Uganda, May, available at <http://www.achpr.org/english/other/Con_Oberservations/uganda_3rd_rpt.pdf> (accessed 14 March 2011).

African Commission on Human and Peoples' Rights (2010) 'Press Release on the Situation facing the Bushmen of the Central Kalahari Game Reserve in Botswana', 10 August, available at <http://www.achpr.org/english/Press%20Release/press%20release_bushman_botswana.htm> (accessed 14 March 2011).

African Union (AU), Economic Commission for Africa (ECA), African Development Forum (ADF) (2009) Framework and Guidelines on Land Policy in Africa, Revised Version, March.

Assembly of Heads of State and Government (AHG) (1964) Resolution on the Intangibility of Frontiers, AHG/Res 16(I), July.

Assembly of Heads of State and Government (AHG) (1997) Decision on Unconstitutional Changes of Government in Africa, AHG/Dec.150 (XXXVI), Thirty Third Ordinary Session in Harare, Zimbabwe, June.

Assembly of Heads of State and Government (AHG) (2000a) Decision on Somalia, AHG/Dec 146 (XXXVI).

Assembly of Heads of State and Government (AHG) (2000b) Decision on the Comoros, AHG/Dec 149 (XXXVI).

Assembly of Heads of State and Government (AHG) (2000c) Declaration on the Framework for an OAU Response to Unconstitutional Changes of Government, AHG/Decl 5 (XXXVI).

Assembly of Heads of State and Government (AHG) (2002) Declaration on Democracy, Political, Economic and Corporate Governance, AHG/235 (XXXVIII).

Bah Ould Rabah v Mauritania, Communication 197/97 (2003–4), Seventeenth Annual Activity Report of the African Commission on Human and Peoples' Rights, Annex VII.

Centre for Minority Rights Development (Kenya) and Minority Rights Group International on behalf of Endorois Welfare Council v Kenya, Communication 276/2003 (2010), 27th Activity Report of the African Commission on Human and Peoples' Rights, Annex V.

Conference on Security, Stability Development and Cooperation in Africa (CSSDCA) (2000) Solemn Declaration, AHG/Decl 4 (XXXVI).

Draft Aide Memoire, African Group (2006) United Nations Declaration on the Rights of Indigenous People, 9 November, New York, available at <http://www.ipacc.org.za/uploads/docs/Africanaidememoire.pdf> (accessed 14 March 2011).

Hurilaws v Nigeria, Communication 225/98, 14th Activity Report of the African Commission on Human and Peoples' Rights.

Interights, Institute for Human Rights and Development in Africa, and Association Mauritanienne des Droits de l'Homme v Islamic Republic of Mauritania, Communication 373/2009 (formerly 242/2001), 28th Activity Report of the African Commission on Human and Peoples' Rights, EX CL/600 (XVII), Annex II.

Katangese People Congress v Zaire, Communication 75/92, 8th Annual Activity Report of the African Commission on Human and Peoples' Rights.

Malawi African Association, Amnesty International, Ms. Sarr Diop, Union Interafricaine des Droits de l'Homme and RADDHO, Collectif des Veuves et Ayants-droit, Association Mauritanienne des Droits de l'Homme v Mauritania, Communications 54/91, 61/91, 98/93, 164/97–196/97, 210/98.

Murray, R. (2011) 'The UN Declaration on the Rights of Indigenous Peoples in Africa. The Approach of the Regional Organisations to Indigenous Peoples', in S. Allen and A. Xanthaki, *Reflections on the United Nations Declaration on the Rights of Indigenous Peoples and International Law* (Oxford: Hart Publishing).

Nkrumah, K. (1963) 'United we Stand', address, Proceedings of the Summit Conference of Independent African States, Addis Ababa, Vol 1, Section 2, Summit CIAS/GEN/INF/36, May.

Sudan Human Rights Organisation and the Sudan Center on Housing Rights and Evictions v Sudan, Communications 279/03 and 296/05, 28th Activity Report of the African Commission on Human and Peoples' Rights, EX CL/600 (XVII), Annex V.

The Social and Economic Rights Action Center and the Center for Economic and Social Rights, Communication 155/96 (2001–2), 15th Annual Activity Report of the African Commission on Human and Peoples' Rights.

Union Inter Africaine des Droits de l'Homme, Federation Internationale des Ligues des Droits de l'Homme, Rencontre Africaine des Droits de l'Homme, Organisation Nationale des Droits de l'Homme au Sénégal and Association Malienne des Droits de l'Homme au Angola v Angola, Communication 159/1996 (1997–98), Eleventh Annual Activity Report of the African Commission on Human and Peoples' Rights.

9 Deconstructing Southern African Development Community[1] land relations challenges

Towards a new, sustainable land relations policy?

Ben Chigara

9.1 Introduction

This book analyses and evaluates the resilience of Southern African Development Community (SADC) land issues from a variety of perspectives. It shows that certain commonalities distinguish South Africa, Namibia and Zimbabwe from other SADC States to make them the worst affected in the sub-region with regards to unequal land distribution that is directly linked to apartheid-rule. Although the other SADC States parties had achieved political freedom from their European colonial masters under the United Nations (UN) decolonization programme[2] in the early 1960s, South Africa had had to wait until 1994; Namibia until 1990; and Zimbabwe until 1980. This makes these three States the longest apartheid-governed African colonies ever. Consequently, they face more serious challenges in relation to land use/allocation in the African sub-region also because farming is a dominant sector of SADC economies.

Although the former Portuguese colonies of Angola and Mozambique had also gained their independence rather late in comparison – November 1975 and June 1975 respectively, the white settlers had chosen to retreat at independence rather than stay and insist on the legal protection of the economic and social legacy of *assimilado* and other dehumanising colonial practices they had benefited from. This is in stark contrast to Zimbabwe, South Africa and Namibia where significant proportions of the beneficiaries of apartheid-rule appear determined to use legal means to frustrate their respective majority-rule governments' efforts to correct the salient economic and social legacy of apartheid-rule.

Briefly, *assimilado* was the status granted to native Africans considered by the colonial authorities to have met certain formal standards indicating that they had successfully absorbed the Portuguese language and culture. It was supposed to grant them many of the race and class privileges of Europeans[3] and release them from forced labour and paying of hut taxes. They could travel without seeking prior authorization. They could register the births of their children and obtain a Portuguese identity card. However, the process of attaining *assimilado* itself was a long and degrading affair, and the status itself remained under threat of revocation. Isaacman writes that in 1948 the Mozambique Central Office for Native Affairs had revoked that status against *assimilados* that had been adjudged to have either backslidden to their native ways, or could no longer satisfy the new and more stringent requirements.[4]

This chapter examines SADC land reform challenges with a view to recommending a possible new, sustainable land relations policy. It shows that there is a nexus between the invisible legacy of apartheid-rule, namely, psychological distortions of the significance of human worth according to skin-colour; and the visible legacy of apartheid-rule, namely, unequal land use/allocation along racial lines. SADC governments' neglect of this nexus has impeded several of their land reform policies. The chapter argues that to succeed in their social reconstruction effort, SADC States must be mindful of this nexus and target both the invisible and visible legacies of apartheid-rule and not the visible only. That distorted psychology of human worth on which the visible legacy of apartheid had been premised had been taught also in the family, the church, schools, employment relations forums, social relations, and handed down from generation to generation. Therefore, SADC governments could not simply wish it away. Without correcting it first, they face uphill struggles to implement and ensure their social reconstruction agendas.

9.2 The apartheid system

Although racial segregation had been championed by Europeans who had settled in southern Africa right from the very beginning, apartheid ideology is traceable to the efforts of the Afrikaner Brotherhood (*Broederbond*) – an extremist organization founded in Johannesburg at the end of the First World War in 1918.[5] 'The Afrikaner drive for self-preservation provided the primary impetus for the formulation of the apartheid ideology'.[6] Their doctrine found political favour of South Africa's Afrikaner National Party which had elevated it to the status of a Christian ideal to be pursued and served by all of God's children.[7] The prevalence of the view that apartheid was God's rather than man's idea was endemic.[8]

Dr J. Verkuyl[9] writes that the *Broederbond* had two basic ideas, namely the 'Christian motif' and the 'Guardianship motif'. The Christian national motif prioritized and targeted the creation of a separate Afrikaans nation identifiable by Western Christian standards of civilization and 'appointed by God to play a dominant role in South Africa until the end of time'.[10] The guardianship motif was premised on the creation of a racial caste system for the perpetuation of white monopoly on power. This white power monopoly, in turn, formed ' … the basis upon which and the pre-supposition whereby all other groups are assigned a subordinate place at all levels of society'.[11] Consequently, from the cradle to the grave apartheid would determine the dreams that one could dream, or not dream, according to one's skin-colour. It would determine also one's friends, career opportunities, marriage possibilities, etc on the basis of one's skin-colour. South Africa's National Party had won the 1948 election on a mandate to formalize with appropriate laws and to enforce the ideals of the Afrikaner Brotherhood (*Broederbond*).

The society that had resulted from that social experiment developed a psychology so offensive to human dignity and so inhumane that both the oppressor and the oppressed were forced into semi-authentic existences. Non-whites were compelled to accept subjugation, oppression and exploitation as a matter of course. Whites were compelled to hold non-whites with such contempt that many rebelled in protest by joining black-led organizations that had committed themselves to the overthrow of apartheid-rule and to replace it with a more humane system of governance.

The liberation movements of Zimbabwe – ZANLA and ZIPRA; South Africa – Umkhonto we Sizwe; Namibia – SWAPO; Mozambique – FRELIMO; and Angola – MPLA, all had whites amongst their ranks. They fought and sacrificed their lives alongside their black comrades for the overthrow of apartheid-rule. They include Joe Slovo – a founding member of Umkhonto we Sizwe; Albie Sachs – later appointed by President Nelson Mandela to the Constitutional Court of South Africa in 1994; Garfield Todd who devoted his later years assisting Zimbabwe's freedom fighters in their war against Ian Smith's Rhodesia Front government; and Anton Luboski of SWAPO, Namibia. Others like Alan Paton,[12] Athol Fugard[13] and Donald Woods[14] used their writings to expose and oppose the indignities of apartheid-rule.

The enforcement of apartheid laws and accompanying administrative procedures had evolved and developed a distorted psychology that premised human worth according to one's skin-colour. The human damage to SADC communities from this social experiment remains immeasurable. What is curious though is that majority-rule governments of the SADC appear to have failed to characterize it appropriately as the debilitating and invisible legacy of apartheid rule, and made it the foremost concern of their social reconstruction programmes. Nonetheless, it comprises the single biggest threat to all governmental efforts to ensure social reconstruction.

Apartheid laws had established a culture of superiority and subjugation, dominance and control among racial groupings. The fly-past of helicopters saluting the inauguration of democratically elected governments of the affected SADC States could not have simultaneously drowned that decrepit culture away with their noises.

The BBC[15] archive has a chilling record of self-reports that show the potential indelibility of the psychological and social scars created by apartheid culture in the SADC. The following two are indicative:

> 1. I was the first black girl at an all white school in Zimbabwe in 1979. I was seven years old and very afraid. One of my little classmates chose to spit in my face for being a kaffir. That affected me terribly and sent me on my nationalistic journey.
>
> 'Africa for Africans', I said to anyone who cared to listen.
>
> When, the following year on November 11 the whole school sang the Rhodesian national anthem, which incidentally I didn't know because as

a black child I had never learnt it, I realised that white people will never change and they had to leave our country.

Ian Smith was the devil who should have had more foresight and compromised with the black population in 1965. Today, Zimbabwe's history would be different. However, I am deeply touched by the stories of being countryless and all that.

It is simple, my white brethren. Change your birth certificates to Zimbabwean ones and get Zimbabwean passports, that is if you don't have them already.

Don't give up on home. Fight for it. Hold on to it because nothing lasts forever. It is our turn to be monsters in your eyes. That will change. You are family, a part of us and we will grow together. You will see.

Tambu, USA/Zimbabwean

2. Having read all the comments, the one that strikes deep in my heart is Murray Lammond's: 'As exiles from the land of our births we will never belong anywhere. I hope our children are spared the same wrenching sense of loss.'

I was 13 when Rhodesia was lost – too young to understand what had happened and what had been sacrificed for us.

Now at 37, I am suddenly struggling to come to terms that my birthland does not exist and that I have no identity.

How can one reconcile that Rhodesia was hung out to dry by the British? [They were] not prepared to accept UDI, but more than willing to throw her to the dogs 15 years later anyway.

I am Rhodesian.

James, UK

What these two individual flows of consciousness show is the strong existence still among members of SADC communities of a binary opposition to otherness which recommends the view that any possible reconciliation on the matter of the possible correction of the economic and social legacy of apartheid-rule is likely to be difficult to achieve. It is not surprising that the Zimbabwe economy has been sacrificed in the last decade or so over this same matter. Litigation of this matter in national courts of SADC States,[16] the Windhoek-based regional SADC Tribunal[17] and even at the Washington-based International Centre for the Settlement of Investment Disputes[18] (ICSID) has shown that this is probably a purely political matter that falls beyond the purview of judicial litigation.

This is certainly the view taken by the Zimbabwe government which by section 16 B of its Constitution has ousted both the application of the Bill of Rights provisions contained in Chapter III of the same Constitution and ousted also the competence of any court of law to entertain an application querying the actual appropriation of land by government for resettlement purposes.

Chidyausiku CJ stated in *Commercial Farmers Union and Others v The Minister of Lands and Rural Resettlement and Others (Zimbabwe)* (2010) that former owners and/or occupiers whose land has been acquired by the acquiring authority in terms of section 16 B (2)(a) of the Constitution of Zimbabwe could not challenge the legality of such acquisition in a court of law. This is because the jurisdiction of the courts has been ousted by section 16 B (3)(a) of the Constitution.[19] However, former owners and/or occupiers of compulsorily acquired land could require any such appropriations to be scrutinized for their procedural propriety. Regardless, the outcome would still be the same one because ultimately courts tend to regard matters of high public policy as unjusticiable.

The doctrine of separation of powers applies to exclude from judicial scrutiny matters of public policy. Judicial attempt to control such policy decisions is rare and when it occurs, it is always regarded as an intrusion into the proper decision making competence of the executive. In *R v Commissioner for Administration ex parte Dyer* (1994) Simon Brown LJ stated that: 'Matters of national policy are not open to challenge before the Courts other than on the basis of bad faith, improper motive or manifest absurdity. Matters of national economic policy are for political – not judicial-judgment'.[20]

This makes the SADC decision in the *Campbell* case a curious one as it referred directly to policy matters of national constitutional importance – the domain of executive and not judicial competence. Although the SADC Tribunal proceeded to give judgment in favour of over 75 aggrieved white Zimbabwean farmers whose land had been appropriated without compensation for the purpose of correcting apartheid-rule's legacy of unequal land use/allocation along racial lines, the government of Zimbabwe has described that judgment as an exercise in futility, and the SADC Tribunal as a daydreamer.[21]

In a decision of 26 November 2010 the Supreme Court of Zimbabwe made it clear that its own decisions were final and that, decisions of the SADC Tribunal were 'at best persuasive but certainly not binding'. This is because the provision establishing the SADC Tribunal had not been transformed into national law. Consequently it 'enjoyed no legal status in Zimbabwe'.[22]

Practice of successive apartheid-rule administrations on the one hand, and that of the majority-rule administrations on the other both regard land use/allocation as a constitutional law matter, that is an executive matter and not a judicial one. Constitutional laws of any nation are supreme laws that defer to no other laws except in accordance with the Constitution itself. They are basic norms upon which all other laws and administrative practices of the system derive their validity.

Nonetheless, the challenge of reconciling the binary divide between the expectations of beneficiaries of apartheid-rule's constitutional land laws on the one hand, and those of the black majority in the democratic dispensation on the other appears to have been matched so far only by SADC States' lackadaisical approach to the need to de-school agents from apartheid-rule's distorted psychology which had premised the significance of human worth on one's skin-colour.

Evidence is very thin on the ground that affected SADC governments have deliberately targeted the invisible legacy of apartheid-rule as a means of facilitating their own counter-apartheid-rule land reforms. Yet without a sufficient enough accomplishment of that task, they risk dismal failure not least because the physical manifestations of apartheid-rule depended on an entrenched culturalization that premised the significance of human dignity on skin colour. Whites creamed off all the economic and social privileges while blacks were reduced to servants, squatters and scroungers in their own lands. This recommends the view that from the outset, SADC reforms should have been premised on winning people away from the distortions of apartheid psychological training to the ideals of social justice and equality.

The failure of SADC majority-rule governments to ensure this could be attributed to wishful thinking at best, or sheer recklessness. But just as their frustrations with lack of progress in the transfer of land from whites to blacks via the willing seller willing buyer process and other pacific processes shows, they have got it wrong. They appear to have imagined that mindsets would change without help. This represents a serious underestimation of the distortions of the psychological training of apartheid and the effect that it had on their populations.

Neither has the UN perceived this to be a need that ought to have been factored into the reconstruction agenda in each of these States. It must be logical to expect that if something had been legally insisted upon for generations, and had had the benefit of cultural approval through the socialization, educational and ecclesiastical teachings of society, then to counter its effects in the new order would require the deliberate, targeted, funded and monitored de-schooling of its falsehoods and the inherent deprivations of its constitutional laws. In operational services they call this type of de-schooling debriefing of operatives. Apartheid-rule's operatives badly need debriefing in order for them to function normally in the democratic dispensation.

Substituting equality for inequality would sound like a rational choice to most people. However, the psychologically distorted operatives of apartheid-rule think not. By contesting land reform measures, they appear to be assuming the legitimacy of their own property rights. This is because:

> Most of the injustices perpetrated by successive apartheid governments between 1948 and 1990 were committed in the name of the law. Millions were deprived of their South African citizenship in order to provide the Bantustan states with citizens, millions were arrested and imprisoned for violating influx control laws which required Africans to produce identity documents ('passes') on demand by a police officer and prohibited their free movement; and millions were forcibly relocated in order to achieve territorial and residential segregation. Thousands were detained without trial under arbitrary security laws and imprisoned for opposing apartheid. Many of these were mercilessly interrogated in solitary confinement under laws that permitted such treatment. The entire population was classified along racial lines and racial 'purity' was maintained by laws which prohibited social mixing,

> sexual relations, and marriage between different groups. Those classified as 'nonwhite' were denied the franchise and given inferior education, health care, social welfare benefits, and housing.[23]

Pursuit of the ideals of the democratic dispensation, including the substitution of equality for inequality in social reconstruction will stall if it fails to recognize and account for the deep seated cultural resentment among adherents of apartheid-rule culturalization. De-schooling from apartheid-rule culture should be an integral part of the SADC tool-kit for correcting the economic and social legacy of apartheid-rule. It should be strongly funded by whoever has an interest in the success of SADC States. External and local funding bodies will do well to support its initiatives. It ought to take precedence as a natural extension of the political opposition to apartheid in the region, alongside economic and social reconstruction in the democratic dispensation. In fact, it is the indispensable matrix without which apartheid-rule's legacy of economic and social inequality will be difficult to correct in the SADC.

Apartheid ideology had been practiced with ruthless efficiency. In the end it had compelled those on either side of the divide to wage war either in its defence or against it. The configurations that have created the impasse in the SADC land reform initiatives can be traced back to the determination of ill equipped and often ill-trained freedom fighters to reclaim their lost dignity, and that of the white oppressors to keep it.

Tor[24] of the Norwegian Africa Institute (Nordiska Afrikainstitutet) writes that by 1959 the white minority governments of the SADC had become so convinced of the need to keep Southern Africa under white rule that they ' … not only rejected popular democratic demands, but intensified their oppression of the black populations'.[25] Consequently, they had introduced emergency legislation throughout the Federation of Rhodesia and Nyasaland, and made massive arrests and banned the leading nationalist organizations in Malawi (Nyasaland), Zambia (Northern Rhodesia) and Zimbabwe (Southern Rhodesia).[26]

The MPLA and UPA (FNLA) had begun their armed resistance against settler colonial administrators of Angola in February/March 1961, followed by FRELIMO in Mozambique in September 1964. ZANU had begun its armed resistance against Ian Smith's Rhodesia Front regime in April 1966, followed by SWAPO in Namibia in August of the same year. Frustrated by deliberate exclusion from universally recognized democratic rights, and oppressed in their own lands, and having exhausted the limited peaceful avenues at their disposal, the people of southern Africa eventually turned to violent insurrection for freedom.[27]

These struggles are habitually referred to as the 30 years war.[28] Millions of lives were lost. The memory of those lost in these struggles often serves as a point of renewal for the case to either defend the legacy of apartheid-rule or to seek to correct it. This also serves to promote the victim mentality on either side of the continuum.[29] But what is required of the opposing parties is their mutual recognition of their unfortunate inheritance from apartheid-rule, of mindsets that need reconstruction about the significance of the inherent dignity of individuals regardless of colour.

9.2.1 Primary reconstruction challenges in SADC States[30]

SADC States' transition from apartheid-rule's basic constitutional norm of racial exclusivity and racial inequality in all forms of social ordering, to the new basic norm of equal treatment for all in the democratic dispensation has become their biggest reconstruction challenge. Mendez has framed the challenge thus: How should States go about establishing the objectives of the new democratic dispensation, including justice, equal treatment and land redistribution 'without falling into tokenism and false morality that only thinly disguises the perpetuation of impunity'?[31]

Particularly on the SADC land issue, commentators appear to be encumbered by other considerations which compel them into selective rather than holistic approaches. Most tend to frame the parameters of their analyses rigidly and in isolation from other significant factors. For example, some position their discussions of land reform in terms of its possible impact on food security; or on the labour relations between black farm labourers and their white employers; or on poverty alleviation and then proceed to make generalized recommendations about land reform in its entirety.

Some focus only on the 'current context' of the SADC land issues, that is, the outcomes of colonial administration of land, and totally ignore the 'underlying context', that is, pre-colonial land rights of natives. Consequently, even their pleas to resort to the principle of the rule of law as the solution to land disputes become problematic because they seek to privilege constitutional land laws of one era over those of another, and often without any justification. In such instances, the law's previous violence on blacks, seen for example through the expropriation of their lands without compensation and forced removals and prohibitions to return is then perpetuated by the law when it ousts the role of 'underlying context' in the determination of land disputes between the dispossessed land hungry and beneficiaries of apartheid-rule. The SADC Tribunal in *Mike Campbell (Pvt) Ltd and Others v Republic of Zimbabwe* (2009)[32] is a case in point.

The Tribunal casually stated the following and proceeded without any justification:

> [T]he applicants are, in essence, challenging the compulsory acquisition of their agricultural lands … under the land reform programme undertaken by the Respondent. We note that the acquisition of land in Zimbabwe has had a long history. However, for the purposes of the present case, we need to confine ourselves only to acquisitions carried out under section 16B of the Constitution of Zimbabwe Amendment Act 17 of 2005.

The SADC Tribunal's condonation of colonial constitutional laws that had been applied to expropriate native land without compensation, with its rejection of a majority-rule government's own laws of similar quality appears to conflate and confuse matters of acquisition of territory – which is the province of international law, and the acquisition of property – which is chiefly the province of domestic law.[33]

In *Calder v Attorney-General of British Columbia*[34] Hall J rejected as 'wholly wrong … the proposition that after conquest or discovery the native peoples have no rights at all except those subsequently granted or recognized by their conqueror or discoverer'.

The seminal decision of the High Court of Australia in the *Mabo* case[35] extinguished fallacies about the uses of the international law doctrine of *terra nullius* starting with Vattel's eighteenth century approach which had declared the right of Europeans to bring unused lands into production anywhere they found them.[36] Such misuse of international law to arbitrarily empower and disempower one lot over another remains its biggest fault line. Until it can show that it has stemmed this particular problem international law will continue to discredit itself in the eyes of its subjects, users and observers.

The *Mabo* case has criticized the enlarging of the concept of *terra nullius* by international law as a means of trying to justify the acquisition of inhabited territory by occupation on behalf of the acquiring sovereign because it served to facilitate the development of dehumanizing administrative standards and procedures that contradicted the notion of equality of individuals before the law in colonies generally. Brennan J's judgment in the *Mabo* case is premised on a thorough and sound examination of the nexus between international law and common law in the enlargement of the doctrine of *terra nullius*. The decision urges a jurisprudential reconstruction of property laws to ensure social justice by abandoning discredited reasoning and practices. It advocates even, a total departure from corrupted and distorted psychologies of old legalisms that are manifestly unjust. Brennan J stated:

> If it were permissible in past centuries to keep the common law in step with international law, it is imperative in today's world that the common law should neither be nor be seen to be frozen in an age of racial discrimination.[37]
>
> The fiction by which the rights and interests of indigenous inhabitants in land were treated as non-existent was justified by a policy which has no place in the contemporary law of this country. The policy appears explicitly in the judgment of the Privy Council in *In re Southern Rhodesia* in rejecting an argument (66) ibid., at p 232 that the native people 'were the owners of the unalienated lands long before either the Company or the Crown became concerned with them and from time immemorial … and that the unalienated lands belonged to them still'. …
>
> Whatever the justification advanced in earlier days for refusing to recognize the rights and interests in land of the indigenous inhabitants of settled colonies, an unjust and discriminatory doctrine of that kind can no longer be accepted. The expectations of the international community accord in this respect with the contemporary values of the Australian people. The opening up of

> international remedies to individuals pursuant to Australia's accession to the Optional Protocol to the International Covenant on Civil and Political Rights ... brings to bear on the common law the powerful influence of the Covenant and the international standards it imports. The common law does not necessarily conform with international law, but international law is a legitimate and important influence on the development of the common law, especially when international law declares the existence of universal human rights. *A common law doctrine founded on unjust discrimination in the enjoyment of civil and political rights demands reconsideration. It is contrary both to international standards and to the fundamental values of our common law to entrench a discriminatory rule which, because of the supposed position on the scale of social organization of the indigenous inhabitants of a settled colony, denies them a right to occupy their traditional lands.* It was such a rule which evoked from Deane J. (69) *Gerhardy v. Brown* (1985) 159 CLR 70, at p 149 the criticism that–
>
> 'the common law of this land has still not reached the stage of retreat from injustice which the law of Illinois and Virginia had reached in 1823 when Marshall C.J., in *Johnson v. McIntosh* (70) (1823) 8 wheat, at p 574 (21 US, at p 253), accepted that, subject to the assertion of ultimate dominion (including the power to convey title by grant) by the State, the "original inhabitants" should be recognized as having "a legal as well as just claim" to retain the occupancy of their traditional lands'.[38]

This is an instance of the Court affirming the doctrine of consent: *quod omnes tagit* – that which touches all must be agreed to by all.

Unfortunately, other commentators presume land reform to be a project aimed at the mere reformation of the duality between subsistence rural existence and commercial farming existence. They then proceed to make general remarks about land reform policies. Yet others, unknown at all to the subject matter, will use any semblances of authority to attack anyone pointing to reconstruction of apartheid mindsets as a critical issue to land reform issues of the SADC. Of course, many have lost land, and mines, and kingly/queenly existences that could not be so easily restored anywhere else in the world except at the price of the indignities that apartheid-rule had ensured against the indigenous populations for the benefit of the settler Europeans.

Consequently and unsurprisingly, their theses insist on determinations that serve to justify unequal land use/allocation. This makes discussion of this matter extremely risky. For instance, Andy Ferreira, the former President of the Zimbabwe Tobacco Association has turned on the more than 120 white Zimbabwean farmers that have chosen recently to return to the country to farm on their former properties on the basis of leasehold deals agreed with the beneficiaries of Zimbabwe's recent land reforms, accusing them of betraying others and calling on international traders to 'shun tobacco grown on contested land as blood tobacco'.[39]

They ignore the fact brought home so plainly by Brennan J in the *Mabo* case. He acknowledged in para 63 of his judgment that:

1. To state the law as he had done involved the overruling of a long list of cases that had held the contrary.
2. However, to not do so, and maintain the authority of those cases would destroy the equality of all citizens before the law.
3. The common law of the land would perpetuate injustice if it were to continue to embrace the enlarged notion of *terra nullius* and to persist in characterizing the indigenous inhabitants as people too low in the scale of social organization to be acknowledged as possessing rights and interests in land.
4. Moreover, to reject the theory that the Crown had acquired absolute beneficial ownership of land is to bring the law into conformity with Australian history. The dispossession of the indigenous inhabitants was achieved by the recurrent exercise of a paramount power to exclude the indigenous inhabitants from their traditional lands as colonial settlement expanded and land was granted to the colonists.

Still, some insist that the international requirement to protect the individual from potential excesses of governmental authority under the liberal requirement of the principle of the rule of law[40] is the only way to settle the social and economic legacy of apartheid-rule in the SADC States. By which they mean abandonment of underlying context to safeguard current context as the SADC Tribunal had done in the *Campbell* case. Consequently, they insist that the law should protect apartheid-rule authored land titles and land should be transferred only on a willing seller willing buyer basis,[41] otherwise the legal interest of land holders will be compromised in the new democratic dispensation. In turn that would raise questions about the democratic credentials of the new order that supplanted apartheid-rule. They argue that failure to protect the legal interest of the white farmers in land would defeat the *raison d'être* of getting rid of apartheid-rule.

But this claim appears to disregard the challenge that opposite others habitually impute against the legitimacy of upholding the social and economic legacy of apartheid-rule by resort to the principle of the rule of law as justification in the new democratic dispensation. In their view, the upholding of the social and economic legacy of apartheid-rule in the new democratic dispensation would serve only to compromise the legitimate expectation of the majority, held throughout the hard, harsh, long years of sacrificial struggle against apartheid-rule that upon the attainment of freedom, equality in the distribution of social goods and disadvantages would naturally follow. It also raises the question whether the rule of law actually supports the protection of the social and economic legacy of apartheid-rule in the post-apartheid democratic dispensation.

The Report of the Secretary-General on the Rule of Law and Transitional Justice in Conflict and Post-Conflict Societies describes the rule of law as:

> A principle of governance in which all persons, institutions and entities, public and private, including the State itself, are accountable to laws that are publicly promulgated, equally enforced and independently adjudicated, and which are consistent with international human rights norms and standards.

> It requires, as well, measures to ensure adherence to the principles of supremacy of laws, equality before the law, accountability to the law, fairness in the application of the law, separation of powers, participation in decision making, legal certainty, avoidance of arbitrariness and procedural and legal transparency.[42]

The UN Human Rights Committee has helpfully clarified the application of this principle in relation to the requirement of non-discrimination – which is what the counter claims of title to property is being premised on in the cases that have so far come before national courts,[43] the SADC Tribunal,[44] and the Washington-based ICSID.[45] In its General Comment No 18,[46] it stated the following:

> The Committee also wishes to point out that the principle of equality sometimes requires States parties to take affirmative action in order to diminish or eliminate conditions which cause or help to perpetuate discrimination prohibited by the Covenant. For example, in a State where the general conditions of a certain part of the population prevent or impair their enjoyment of human rights, the State should take specific action to correct those conditions. Such action may involve granting for a time to the part of the population concerned certain preferential treatment in specific matters as compared with the rest of the population. However, as long as such action is needed to correct discrimination in fact, it is a case of legitimate differentiation under the Covenant.[47]

This linking up of the requirements of the principle of the rule of law with the requirement of non-discrimination by the UN Human Rights Committee shows that a balancing act in the determination of their effect is probably required on a case by case basis, having regard to the full context of the matter in order to ensure social justice.

Still some commentators advance utilitarian arguments around food security interests. They appeal to reason and not to emotional euphoria-based unrealistic sentiments of freedom which if followed through would directly lead to poverty that would punish nationals more than apartheid-rule could have done. Therefore, a wholesale reversal of land use would be illogical and catastrophic to the national interest. They argue that blacks lack the business skills, farming training and general knowledge of intensive large scale commercial farming required to maintain national food security. They insist that blacks could not be transformed overnight from subsistence farmers to commercial farmers.

However, they conveniently ignore the fact that apartheid-rule had denied the black majority the same opportunities that would have equipped them with all that they claim now disqualifies them from access to land. The liberals among these quasi-utilitarian thinkers advocate the directing of land-hungry blacks to skills training before they can be given access to the nation's prime land – *assimilado* arguments. But they seem to completely ignore two important facts.

One is that because apartheid had alienated blacks from land with the best agricultural potential and confined them to semi-desert lands with the least agricultural potential, those lands have now become barren and incapable of sustaining even the subsistence farming that natives have historically practiced. If anything, this has highlighted for the dispossessed, the unsustainability of their condition particularly after the end of apartheid-rule. Nonetheless these 'utilitarians' insist further that white commercial farms should not be converted to anything else less than what they represent, namely, food security engines that are critical to the survival of the SADC economies and States.

The second is that few vocations and professions train practitioners in the vacuum of a plain classroom behind a desk. Driving a car, piloting a plane, removing a tooth, etc are all learnt on the job, that is, behind the wheel of a car, behind the control column of the cockpit, on the dentistry table, etc respectively. Therefore, attempts to rationalize and maintain the contested social and economic outcomes of apartheid-rule in the new democratic dispensation through pleas to the principle of the rule of law serve also to perpetuate justifications often rehearsed during apartheid-rule to ensure the continuation of white supremacy.

Yet others attempt social justice arguments around constitutional reform as the cardinal premise upon which the salient economic and social legacies of apartheid-rule should be settled. Commentators habitually describe social justice as a people-oriented idea because to describe it, ' … we must look at what the people themselves think'.[48] Miller writes that social justice theory has always been, and must always be, a critical idea – one that challenges us to reform our institutions and practices in the name of greater fairness.[49]

Certainly this appears to be the view of the governments of the worst affected SADC States, namely, South Africa, Namibia and Zimbabwe. They appear to have inaugurated a new norm of customary international law on black economic empowerment (BEE) as their basic norm for managing and resolving apartheid-rule's social and economic legacy on their territories. This norm is supported by constitutional pieces of legislation, administrative procedures, and new government ministries and departments to oversee its practice.[50]

This array of positions and inflexions of its several combinations highlights the difficulty with the SADC land issues examined in this book. Each position represents a major element in the problem of unequal land use/allocation that is also the most salient visible legacy of apartheid-rule in the SADC. Briefly, these elements could be summed up as pleas for a new land relations policy that is premised on only one of the following: social justice; status-quo rule of law arguments; and food security concerns.

However, land reform that seeks a culture change that is capable of liberating agents from the invisible legacy of apartheid-rule does not appear to have been contemplated yet in the SADC. Nonetheless, it may be SADC States' only hope for successful land reform that does not derail their economic fortunes or prospects.

9.2.2 Towards a new, sustainable social reconstruction land relations policy?

This book advocates a new land relations policy (LRP) for the SADC which accounts for the primary elements in the SADC land issues, particularly the invisible legacy of apartheid-rule. This is justified by the fact that such a policy would compel the greatest legitimacy. Franck[51] has helpfully defined legitimacy as a system or rule's pull of its addressees towards voluntary compliance. While the numerical majority may insist on a strict social justice approach, they should recognize that failure to gain the support of the few that may still favour application of the principle of the rule of law approach that ignores the underlying context to the land issue may be catastrophic as these few may still have a key role to play in the management of potential turbulences that threaten reform programmes of this nature.

A credible and sustainable LRP for the affected SADC States should account for the expectation interest of agents on either side of the continuum, comprising the social justice protagonists on the one hand, and the current context only rule of law protagonists on the other. To achieve that, that policy should be capable first and foremost of liberating agents from the excesses apparent in their tabled initial positions and expectations in a manner that would extricate them from what Freire has helpfully described as protagonists' fear that limits the possibilities of freedom from oppression.[52]

Freire locates the problem in the fact that dehumanized beings are semi-authentic beings because it is not the function of being human either to be dehumanized by another or to dehumanize others. Consequently, agents experiencing this reality – whether as oppressors or as the oppressed, could be said in a sense to be in semi-authentic state of existence. Such a policy would be based on the premise that the attitudes of both the oppressor and the dispossessed oppressed in the SADC land issues had been learnt from their shared experience of apartheid-rule.

As an ideology, apartheid had been propagated and practiced with tremendous effect in the SADC. It had been taught in the family, the church, schools, employment relations forums, social relations, and everywhere. Shop attendants would not for instance let a black child try an outfit before buying it. They would use a measuring tape to determine whether the desired garment would fit or not. However, white children could try the actual garments for fitting before deciding on whether to buy or not. There were toilets for blacks and toilets for whites in public and work places. Several generations of people were raised on such principles and understanding of racial superiority and inferiority respectively.

The new democratic dispensation offers these psychologically distorted agents what Freire calls semi-authentic agents, the opportunity for liberation to authentic human existence. Just as their own nations had been re-born by the adoption of radically different new Constitutional arrangements at independence from apartheid-rule, these agents ought to be helped towards a radical reconstruction of their mindsets. From judges who had zealously developed and enforced common laws that championed apartheid-rule policies to shop-floor stewards who had refused blacks to try clothes prior to purchasing them while allowing their white counterparts to do exactly that, the paradigm shift requires de-schooling of old habits, old falsehoods peddled as truths, and so on. Formal and informal language patterns of the oppressor and those of the dispossessed oppressed mirror strongly engraved old habits and life-long attitudes whose resilience is playing out on the question of why it is right to banish apartheid-rule and yet seek to maintain its social and economic legacy.

Science has continually proved that man's biggest asset is his capacity to re-learn or re-format himself in accordance with his new reality in order to make himself authentic – adaptation. From those injured in the throes of combat to those psychologically scarred under the German Reich in Germany or the Ku Klux Klan supremacist ideology in America, to those bathed and drenched in apartheid-rule's supremacist doctrine in the SADC, the human being is always accessible to humanizing change. Rational choice theorists have found no reason to the contrary. Heath writes:

> If our rational choice explanation fails or is un-illuminating, then we shall assuredly have to turn to other explanations in terms of unconscious drives, habitual action or other forms of non-rational action. But I think we do well, until firm evidence to the contrary is available, to assume that our fellow men are as rational and intelligent agents as we usually suppose ourselves to be.[53]

Therefore, the de-schooling of agents from apartheid-rule habits and psychological distortions about the significance of human worth ought very much to be a part and parcel of the social reconstruction dynamic in the SADC. This is justified also by the fact that the psychological distortions of apartheid-rule had created semi-authentic beings that fit Freire's crisis of authenticity thesis:

> The central problem is this: How can the oppressed, as divided unauthentic beings, participate in developing the pedagogy of their liberation? Only as they discover themselves to be 'hosts' of the oppressor can they contribute to the midwifery of their liberating pedagogy. As long as they live in the duality in which to be is to be like and to be like is to be like the oppressor, this contribution is impossible. The pedagogy of the oppressed is an instrument for their critical discovery that both they and their oppressors are manifestations of dehumanisation.[54]

This raises the following question: by what standards and by what processes does one begin to dismantle apartheid-rule's legacy of unequal land distribution along racial lines without destroying food security capacity – one of the main fears of some agents; while ensuring also the protection of the expectation interest of both the dispossessed land-hungry majority and of the white minority that has most of the prime land of the SADC? Success or failure of SADC States' democratic dispensation programmes for social reconstruction will depend on the quality of the new LRP that they adopt. How does one ensure the expectation interest of diametrically opposed stakeholders who are nonetheless equally critical to the success of the envisaged social reconstruction land reform programmes?

This is a difficult question because many procedures and techniques which were eventually developed by both the General Assembly and the Security Council of the United Nations to promote and protect human rights had been hammered out on the anvil of universal moral opposition to South Africa's apartheid system of governance,[55] culminating in the creation of the elite norm of *jus cogens* on the prohibition against apartheid-rule as a crime against all of humanity. Steiner et al write that although South Africa had been the main focus, the situations in Southern Rhodesia – modern day Zimbabwe – and the southern African Portuguese colonies of Angola and Mozambique were also critical to UN attention in this respect.[56]

Therefore, there might be a prima facie case for a new LRP that is strongly inclined towards the social justice expectation interest because of the universal rejection of apartheid-rule. It would be counter-intuitive to enable the contested continuity of the social and economic legacy of apartheid-rule by shielding it through appeals to the principle of the rule of law. It would also undermine the significance of the law to any right thinking person.

Evidently, there is an ideological contradiction at the core of pro-status-quo arguments that are sometimes presented as food security and national development arguments[57] and at other times as *terra nullius*[58] arguments, and at others simply as rule of law arguments.[59] This contradiction misunderstands and underestimates the ultimate objective of why the social and economic legacy of apartheid-rule in the SADC should be corrected. It is this, freedom that offers a chance for authentic human existence for all agents of the community concerned is liberating and sustainable because it offers also the opportunity for self-actualization.

Humanistic psychology describes self-actualization as a person's fundamental tendency toward maximal realization of his/her potentials.[60] Maslow's theory of motivation suggests that individuals' lives mirror a hierarchy of needs that ascends from the basic biological needs to the more complex psychological motivations that become important only after the basic needs have been met. The needs at one level must be satisfied before one can begin to consider those at the next level:

> When food and safety are difficult to obtain, the satisfaction of those needs will dominate a person's actions and higher motives are of little significance. Only when basic needs can be satisfied easily will the individual have time and energy to devote to aesthetic and intellectual interests. Artistic and scientific endeavours do not flourish in societies in which people must struggle for food, shelter and safety. The highest motive, – self-actualization – can only be fulfilled after all other needs are fulfilled.[61]

Humanizing freedom liberates both the oppressor and the dispossessed oppressed from fear of one another that locks their life experiences to low to medium needs according to Maslow and therefore enables them a mere semi-authentic existence in which self-actualization could not be achieved. Fear of one another often imprisons agents in the incubator of semi-authentic existence where self-actualization is almost unattainable.

According to Freire, such liberation is a painful but necessary transformation from semi-authentic to authentic human existence:

> Liberation is thus a childbirth, and a painful one. The man or woman who emerges is a new person, viable only as the oppressor-oppressed contradiction is superseded by the humanization of all people. … the solution of this contradiction is born in the labour which brings into the world this new being: no longer oppressor nor longer oppressed, but human in the process of achieving freedom.[62]

Childbirth is often accompanied with enormous pain, screaming and shouting, sleeplessness and even prayer. Childbirth is never a tranquil affair. Waters break, uncertainty looms, flesh tears and blood gushes out. Reports of the birth are published. Dynamics in the SADC land issues are indicative of the liberating process of re-birth. Foreign relations policies between SADC States and Western States are dependent on it. Academic journals are filling up with attempts to analyze the SADC Land issues. National, sub-regional and international tribunals have been seized upon the matter and continue to proffer judgments on the matter. The SADC LRP is significant. It is a material issue to the SADC, the African Union (AU), the European Union (EU) and the world at large. Most importantly, it is significant for the nationals of affected SADC States themselves.

9.2.3 The social reconstruction challenge in perspective

South Africa's colonial history had begun on 6 April 1652, when the Dutch seafarer Jan van Riebeeck had landed on Table Bay with his three ships[63] and ended on Freedom Day, 27 April 1994, the day that the first democratic elections were held, resulting in Nelson Mandela's inauguration as South Africa's first democratically elected leader. Though the doctrine of white supremacy had promoted the dispossession, subjugation and enslavement of natives in both the Boer and the British colonies of South Africa, the Anglo-Boer War of October 1899 to May 1902 had a seminal influence on the development of Afrikaner nationalist politics which benefited from the British reconstruction regime's prioritization of the re-establishment of white control over the land and compelling of the Africans back to wage labour.[64]

A 1905 report of the South African Native Affairs Commission had laid out the constitutional strategy for ensuring white supremacy. The report had introduced new rigidities into South African thinking about race relations by formalizing the idea of segregation more forcefully. First, ' … it envisaged the territorial separation of black and white as a permanent, mandatory principle of land ownership'.[65] The first union of South Africa government[66] had begun to implement that strategy with the adoption of the 1913 Natives Land Act that defined the remnants of native ancestral lands after conquest for African occupation and made it illegal for natives to purchase or rent property outside their reserved areas.

Eventually, these reserves comprised roughly 13 per cent of South Africa's total land surface. Moreover, 'Administrative and legal dualism reinforced the division between white citizen and black non-citizen, a dispensation personified by the governor-general who, as "supreme chief" over the country's African majority, was empowered to rule them by administrative fiat and decree'.[67] The Natives (Urban Areas) Act, 1923 served to entrench urban segregation by limiting natives' mobility by means of pass laws. It had also regularized job discrimination by reserving skilled work for whites and denying African workers the right to organize.[68]

The pass laws had ensured that natives were compelled to become wage earners under conditions dictated by their white employers. They denied them any bargaining power.[69] The promulgation of white supremacist constitutional laws; the adoption of segregationist administrative practices; and other government measures ensured the establishment of lasting foundations of apartheid social ordering in South Africa. Especially after the 1948 election which had brought the National Party into power on the ticket of apartheid-rule, successive governments had ensured even more rigorous and more authoritarian approaches for ensuring white supremacy and native domination.

The consequence was the establishment of a social ordering paradigm so inhuman in terms of its physical, psychological and social disenfranchisement of the human soul of both the oppressor and the oppressed. The General Assembly of the UN responded to this situation with a series of resolutions that eventually compelled a reluctant Western States dominated Security Council to act too, culminating in its Resolution 418 (1977) which imposed a mandatory arms embargo under Chapter VII of the UN Charter.[70]

General Assembly Resolution 3068 (1973) established the International Convention on the Suppression and Punishment of the Crime of Apartheid,[71] characterizing apartheid-rule as a crime against humanity. The intensity and frequency of UN condemnation of apartheid-rule in southern Africa resulted in the peremptory norm[72] against apartheid-rule. These few sacred rules include the prohibition against slavery, genocide, aggression and racial discrimination.[73] Harris[74] traces the concept of *jus cogens* to the requirement of treaty law that denies States capacity to enter into treaties that are contrary to *jus cogens*, namely, conduct that is fundamentally repugnant to all of humanity. Even a persistent objector could not escape being bound by a new rule of customary international law[75] (CIL) that has the character of *jus cogens*.[76] This is because it is not the proper vocation of human beings to pursue dehumanization. Freire[77] writes that:

> But while both humanization and dehumanization are real alternatives, only the first is the people's vocation. This vocation is constantly negated, yet it is affirmed by that very negation. It is thwarted by injustice, exploitation, oppression, and the violence of the oppressors; it is affirmed by the yearning

> of the oppressed for freedom and justice, and by their struggle to recover their lost humanity.

In fact, humanization has always been humankind's inescapable concern because of its virtues of freedom and self-actualization. Writes Hegel, 'It is solely by risking life that freedom is obtained; … (and) the individual who has not staked his or her life may, no doubt, be recognized as a Person; but he or she has not attained the truth of this recognition as an independent self-consciousness'.[78] Southern Africans have always privileged altruistic human and social endeavours that ensure the recognition, promotion and protection of the inherent human dignity of all agents of society. This virtue is enshrined in the principle of *humwe.*

Humwe is arguably one of Africa's oldest, most practised and most enduring ideas. *Humwe* is *Shona* for 'in this together' and 'us all'. *Humwe* requires society to ensure the welfare of all its agents by insisting on the fundamentals of equity, social justice and human security. In all matters pertaining to social-ordering and in particular the distribution of life's advantages and disadvantages *humwe* requires that all agents focus on the whole and not the sum of its parts. It insists on a knowledge-based human rights orientated paradigm of social ordering – what South Africa's post-apartheid government has popularised as *ubuntu*, meaning 'to be human'. In other words you achieve your own dignity by seeking to ensure the inherent dignity of others.

However, the realities of dehumanization, including the economic and social legacy of apartheid-rule in the SADC require deliberate and purposeful correction in order to restore affected SADC States to a path of *humwe* or *ubuntu*. Such corrections are helpful when they serve to liberate both the oppressor and the oppressed from the tangle of apartheid's dehumanizing legacies. They are counterproductive and also dehumanizing when they merely replace one form of dehumanization with another.

According to Freire:

> Dehumanization, which marks out not only those whose humanity has been stolen, but also (though in a different way) those who have stolen it, … (It) is a *distortion* of the vocation of becoming more fully human. This distortion occurs within history; but it is not an historical vocation. Indeed to admit of dehumanization as a historical vocation would lead either to cynicism or total despair. The struggle for humanization, for the emancipation of labour, for the overcoming of alienation, for the affirmation of men and women as persons would be meaningless. This struggle is possible only because dehumanization, although a concrete historical fact, is not a given destiny but the result of an unjust order that engenders violence in the oppressors, which in turn dehumanizes the oppressed.
>
> Because it is a distortion of being more fully human, sooner or later being less human leads the oppressed to struggle against those who made them so. In order for this struggle to have meaning, the oppressed must not, in seeking to regain their humanity (which is a way to create it), become in

> turn oppressors of the oppressors, but rather restorers of the humanity of both.
>
> This then is the great humanistic and historical task of the oppressed: to liberate themselves and their oppressors as well. The oppressors who oppress, exploit and rape by virtue of their power, cannot find in this power the strength to liberate either the oppressed or themselves. Only power that springs from the weakness of the oppressed will be sufficiently strong to free both.[79]

The question that the land issue raises is one of dealing with the physical, psychological, economic and social dehumanizing and distortive legacy of apartheid-rule in the SADC, particularly in the worst affected States of South Africa, Namibia and Zimbabwe. German control of modern-day Namibia (South West Africa) had begun in 1884, when the Chancellor, Otto von Bismarck, annexed all of South West Africa. It ended on 21 March 1990 when Namibia finally gained independence from its neighbour – South Africa. Zimbabwe's colonial time-line runs from September 1890 when the British Pioneer Column first settled in Harare and ends on 18 April 1980 when it gained political independence from Britain. Successive foreign administrations in both Zimbabwe and Namibia had taken legislative and administrative measures similar to the South African model, for the same purpose and to similar ends, so that the unequal land distribution challenges in all three States are not dissimilar.[80]

Majority-rule governments of Namibia, South Africa and Zimbabwe appear to be under torment of the visible and invisible legacies of apartheid-rule. For several reasons, unequal land use/allocation (the physical legacy) on racial lines has become synonymous with the resilience of apartheid's outcomes decades after the official end of the practice. This is because of the corresponding significance of land in the agrarian economies of the SADC. It is also because of the severity of the expropriation of native land without compensation that had occurred during apartheid-rule. Unequal land use/allocation has become an eyesore in the SADC. Further, it has been argued[81] that the path to reform is often made arduous and unduly complicated by stakeholders' concurrent pursuit of the 'ultimate victim' status in the estimation of significant others, including foreign donors to the affected SADC State. This shows the complex challenges attendant upon the task of national reconstruction in post-apartheid SADC States.

The former oppressor and his former victim have varying expectations whose management and reconciliation under the new basic norm of equality for all threatens their newly found transient position of a new beginning.

9.3 The significance of land ownership in the SADC[82]

The value of land anywhere is not difficult to rate. According to Gray, land ownership is inevitably an expression of social status and an instrument of social engineering, ' … quite apart from the residential dimension, the importance of land as a form of property becomes almost incalculable when it is borne in mind that land has an enormous economic significance in terms of investment, business and agriculture'.[83]

In the predominantly agrarian economies of the SADC land had been the object of much colonial scientific research to discover its virtues right from beginning. Land had been immediately classified into zones according to its potential for agricultural production. Zone I comprised the most fertile soils in areas with the most favourable weather, while Zone VI onwards comprised the poorest soils with the least favourable agricultural production. Land had been rated for its agricultural potential.

Land ownership and use had been the focal point of earliest and continuing colonial constitutional laws, resulting in the creation of both commercial farmlands for whites and reserve trust lands for Africans according to their tribal customs. The latter were called Bantustans in South Africa and Tribal Trust Lands in Zimbabwe. Commercial farms were strategically established for crop production and animal husbandry in the zones with the best farming potential while Bantustans and Tribal Trust Lands were conveniently situated in residual lands in areas with the least farming potential. Land became the subject of calculated constitutional laws which created two classes, namely, the vanquished dispossessed and the victorious over takers.

Consequently, the utility of land determined who owned it with whites who comprised only 5 per cent of Rhodesia's population at independence in 1980 owning outright up to 95 per cent of the best land while native blacks who comprised over 90 per cent of the population struggled to eke a living in the dry and drought prone Tribal Trust Lands – a feat repeated across the colonies of the SADC. The expropriation of native land had occurred without compensation and without appeal.[84] It had been intended and therefore sanctioned by constitutional laws. It had converted natives from farmers to wage earners that depended on selling their labour to European enterprises in order to pay the new taxes imposed upon them by government. Such is the prime legacy of land distribution and use in post-apartheid-ruled SADC States.

Deborah James has correctly summarized the position of the dispossessed and that of the over takers as follows: ' … being "landed" encompasses a wide variety of actual positions (while) being "landless" implies an even wider divergence'.[85] Therefore, any effort to try to secure land for a formerly dispossessed group simultaneously poses a threat to those that previously had a monopoly on it.[86] That can result in an unhelpful binary opposition characterized first and foremost by counter-victimology arguments of stakeholders that are premised on a selective and skewed appraisal of the context.

Such arguments have a tendency to characterize the struggles of the dispossessed to regain their land as illegal and contrary to human rights norms by labelling them as 'land invasions' in South Africa; and 'squatting', 'land seizures' or 'land grabs' in Zimbabwe. This negative labelling of what are possibly legitimate struggles depending on whether one chooses a partial or holistic appraisal of the problem of unequal land use/allocation is counter productive because it does not in any way bring the stakeholders anywhere near to Freire's dynamic of a mutually 'otherness-enhancing' resolution strategy that is capable of liberating both the oppressor and the oppressed.[87]

Moyo writes that the labelling of war veterans' politically organized reclamations of farmland lost to colonial authorities at conquest is counter-intuitive, anti-human rights and unhelpful.[88] Liberals had supported the same war veterans during their struggle against colonial domination. The same liberals often premised their support of these guerrilla freedom fighters on the axis of self-determination and human rights. Indeed, apartheid itself had been characterized by international law as a crime against humanity. There is inconsistency in seeking to enlist human rights arguments in support of the emergent resistance of white farmers to land reform in the SADC now. It contradicts the African wisdom that: 'You do not kill off an old lion by feeding its cubs'.

9.3.1 Critical elements in the SADC land issues

Bystander attribution theory shows that *a* + *b* caught up in a milieu, are often blinded by the intensity of their situation that it often requires *c*, a bystander, to bring them both to the awareness of the manifestly apparent. Consequently, *a* + *b* may appear to *c* to be fumbling or even avoiding what to him is self-evident. This is true of the protagonists in the land issue.

Why for instance can commercial farmers not accept that unequal land use/allocation that is traceable to unjust constitutional apartheid-rule policies and laws is first, incompatible with the democratic dispensation's basic norm of equality for all, and second, no longer enforceable because domestic courts have now been given by the new majority-rule parliaments, new constitutional land laws that regard apartheid land titles as illegitimate?

Why for instance do commercial farmers attach human rights and rule of law arguments to their claims of justiciability of the land issue and not to indigenous claims of their unjustly disposed fellow black folk?

Unjustifiable as it may be, it could be explained as a manifestation of the extent to which the invisible legacy of apartheid-rule had distorted individuals' minds. Those distortions could be responsible for imbuing a false sense of victimhood among those agents that must now conform to the requirements of the new norm of equality. Climbing down from ascribed status to achieved status that requires everyone to begin on a path of earned rather than swindled advantages is likely to be painful though it is beneficial in that it liberates both the oppressor and the oppressed.

Atkinson et al write that both *a* + *b* commit the fundamental attribution error when they make a dispositional attribution about their own behaviour when they should instead be making a situational attribution.[89] White farmers that oppose land reform also tacitly appear to still insist on apartheid but lack only the platform to uphold it from. Thus, they hurry to this court and that court and the other because apartheid conditioning still informs them that the law must, and ought to protect their racial and class interest if it is real law. This is incompatible with the reality that equality has formally substituted inequality as the basic norm of social engineering in the SADC.

Similarly, SADC governments that presume that all agents of their societies have by some magical inspirational overcome the conditioning of apartheid-rule to accept equality as the new basic norm severely misunderstand the impact on individuals of the psychological distortions of apartheid-rule.

The fact is that blacks are as much victims of the psychological distortions of apartheid-rule as their white folk. Challenging his own Civil Rights Movement to understand its oppressors' own need for liberation from the psychological distortions of racial prejudice in America, Martin Luther King Jr[90] had asked them to stop and reflect on what it must mean to grow up being told everyday that blacks were inferior to whites; that God himself had ordained that order among men; and that blacks were uncultured, and whites civilized.

Psychological damage of individuals wrought by apartheid laws may be physically invisible. However, the bitter social and sometimes fatal skirmishes between both black people and white people in reaction to SADC governments' slow implementation of the requirements of equal treatment for all people regardless of skin-colour has made it very real and perhaps bigger and more dangerous than the physical manifestations of the legacy of apartheid-rule such as unequal land use/allocation.[91]

Helping white people and black people to overcome the psychological distortions of apartheid about the significance of human worth should be the starting point of all social reconstruction efforts in SADC States. This includes educating white judges and black judges that sit on national and sub-regional courts and tribunals to defer to the requirement of the doctrine of separation of powers which applies to exclude from judicial scrutiny matters of public policy to do with constitutional laws aimed at social reconstruction. In such cases, the function of the Court/Tribunal is to deal with the procedural propriety and not substantive mandate of the reform element, and then only, when it can be shown that the public authority had exercised his authority in bad faith, or with an improper motive or in a manifestly absurd way.

9.4 Concluding remarks

This book has examined the challenges attendant upon efforts to implement the new basic norm of equality that challenges apartheid-rule's legacy of unequal land use/distribution along racial lines. Successful implementation of this corrective measure would bring enormous benefits to the sub-region. First, it would authenticate the existence of the majority that had been excluded under apartheid-rule from participating in the development of their own economies by enabling them to participate and contribute to the development of their own lives, local communities and country's economy.

Second, it would put paid to the dispossessed black majority's burden of social injustice authored by expropriation of their lands by colonialists without any compensation. Third, and most importantly, it would liberate both the oppressor and the oppressed from apartheid-rule's distortion of the significance of human worth according to skin-colour.

Fourth, it would create space for both the oppressor and the oppressed to begin to function as authentic beings that are truly capable of attaining self-actualization – something that was totally unachievable for them both under apartheid-rule. This is because apartheid's social-ordering requirements had conditioned both white and black to:

i) Accept as normal and natural the economic and social inequalities in the allocation of goods and services in their communities according to race.
ii) Regard the rule of law as the application of laws to secure and ensure their positions of inferiority and superiority respectively and to entrench oppression and subjugation respectively.
iii) Regard human rights as a subject matter applicable for the benefit of the oppressor, but not the oppressed. While the oppressed non whites had opposed apartheid regimes even with their lives, the benefactors of apartheid had habitually returned those administrations into power at each election, something that only they could have stopped.

SADC history shows that apartheid administrations in Namibia, South Africa and Zimbabwe had fiercely pursued the culturalization of generations of both whites and non-whites into semi-authentic existence by teaching and enforcing through the law, the view that racial superiority of whites over non-whites was a divine principle to be served by all people. By the oppression and subjugation of non-whites (the oppressed) by their white counterparts (the oppressor), inequality was presented not only as natural, but also as Godly. In this light, both the oppressor and the oppressed were a creation of the apartheid legal order – victims of it even.

If unequal land use/distribution is the foremost physical manifestation of the legacy of apartheid-rule in the SADC, then the psychological mindset that insisted that the oppressor was justified and will always be justified by history, the law, and God himself was its invisible but most powerful legacy. It is the latter legacy of apartheid-rule that now stands in the way of SADC States' attempt to substitute equality as the basic norm of social-engineering for inequality along racial lines under apartheid-rule.

Apartheid had compelled whites to develop the mindset that they had a guardianship duty towards Southern Africa which they had been divinely appointed to subdue and monopolize. This justification of apartheid-rule had a strong following especially in the Dutch Reformed Church. Consequently, non-whites, the law, and everything else had to serve the interests of white supremacy. It is easy to see how whites ended up believing in apartheid, and keeping apartheid regimes in government at every election. They could see a convergence of political power, the application of the law, and their social circumstance confirming the doctrine of white supremacy. Eventually, they believed more and more in apartheid as demonstrated by their commitment to send their children and grandchildren to war to die in its defence against black majority-led liberation movements, and to keep apartheid governments in power. They became dependent on apartheid and had become conditioned to its psychology which had distorted the significance of human worth according to skin-colour.

The legal enforcement of apartheid had created semi-authentic beings whose choices of friends even, and about who could stay over at one's house for the night were regulated by the law. Apartheid's culturalization of individuals along distorted conceptions of the significance of human dignity on racial lines raises a very simple but profound question, namely: What actions have SADC governments deliberately undertaken to de-school and liberate their populations from apartheid-rule's distortions about the significance of human worth? This is significant because the visible salient economic and social legacy of apartheid-rule grew out of the invisible but cancerous educational legacy of apartheid-rule culturalization.

This invisible legacy of apartheid-rule, namely, the psychological distortion of the significance of human worth according to skin-colour has become the SADC's biggest challenge to the possible implementation of its preferred new basic norm of equality that seeks to correct the salient economic and social legacy of apartheid-rule, namely unequal land use/allocation. It appears that to stand a good chance of success SADC States must first take deliberate measures to sufficiently reconstruct the mindsets of the oppressor and of the oppressed into authentic beings. This is because generally speaking apartheid rule had compelled people into semi-authentic existence. Many remain trapped in that mindset. Some do not even wish now to come out of it. For SADC States to seek to address the salient physical manifestations of the economic and social legacy of apartheid-rule regardless of the burden of the invisible legacy of apartheid rule described above is at best wishful thinking and at worst reckless and negligent. It is as illogical as expecting a child to walk before they have even learnt to stand up straight. It leads only to the clashing of heads, social chaos and economic ruin as some States have recently learnt.

Unless agents are sufficiently liberated from the worst effects of apartheid's culturalization, particularly its psychology of determining the significance of human dignity according to skin-colour, whites will tend to resist and obstruct attempts to correct unequal land use/allocation initiatives that are required by the new basic norm of equality for all. Through their national courts, the Windhoek-based SADC Tribunal, the Washington-based ICSID and whatever next, they will seek to establish that they are the new victims of brutal SADC regimes. The decline of Zimbabwe's status from being the bread basket of Africa in the first ten to fifteen years of its political independence from Britain in 1980 to a basket case in the last ten years is demonstrative enough. The cost of neglecting the need to de-school and reconstruct agents on either side prior to implementing land reform policies is enormous but avoidable.

Both the violent land invasions and white farmers' resistance to the implementation of the equalizing new legislation through the Zimbabwe Courts, the SADC Courts and the Washington-based ICSID have helped no one. Both the Zimbabwe government and its white farmers and the land-hungry peasants could have done a better job than to reduce the country to a failed State. South Africa and Namibia, which are in exactly similar circumstances to Zimbabwe, are already tottering on the brink of a Zimbabwe-type social explosion. They have every reason to begin to consider a new land relations policy that prioritizes restoration of agents to authentic beings, liberated from apartheid-rule's psychology of distortion which had based human worth on skin-colour.

Only the genuinely sufficiently liberated oppressors and genuinely sufficiently liberated formerly oppressed persons can successfully participate in the exercise to correct apartheid-rule's salient legacy of land reform in the SADC. Discovery of that degree of sufficiency within any community is a matter of fact to be determined by the relevant authorities. The pedagogy of the oppressed is a potential instrument for ending agents' semi-authentic existence.

We realize our humanity only when our capacity to recognize, promote and protect the inherent dignity of others overtakes our previously learnt disregard of others' worth as lesser humans than ourselves because of their religion, or because of the colour of their skin, or because of their age. The possible reciprocation of that dynamic is what best demonstrates our capacity to engage in the moment of social rebirth which the land reform programmes of the SADC requires.

Based on the foregoing discussion, it is possible to recommend a new land relations policy premised on 'pedagogical counter-apartheid-rule psychological distortions of the significance of human dignity' – PECAPDISHD, for the SADC. The policy's point of departure is that apartheid-rule's psychological distortions of the significance of human worth along racial lines is the invisible but biggest stumbling block to SADC States' effort to correct the economic and social legacy of apartheid-rule. Substituting equality for inequality as the basic norm of social engineering in the majority-rule dispensation will not alone achieve the desired correction of the salient social and economic legacy of apartheid-rule, namely, unequal land use/allocation along racial lines.

PECAPDISHD is premised on rational choice's assumption that our fellow humans are as rational and intelligent agents as we usually suppose ourselves to be. Therefore, with the appropriate pedagogic interventions in the democratic dispensation, most people would turn away from apartheid-rule's deceitful distortions about the significance of human worth along racial lines and embrace the path of equity and social justice because of its overall promise of authentic human existence that also offers the possibility of self-actualization.

It is also premised on the thesis of Paulo Freire's pedagogy of the oppressed that, knowledge and humility flowing from the oppressed to the oppressor about the unsustainability of their shared existence/situation has enormous potential to liberate both the oppressor and the oppressed and lead them both on a course with greater promise of harmony. PECAPDISHD could follow the following procedures which could be varied of course according to relevant circumstances on the ground.

Step 1: Design and implement educational campaigns led by national Governments and involving the AU, SADC, United Nations Educational, Scientific and Cultural Organization (UNESCO), the International Labour Organization (ILO), and others interested in countering-apartheid psychology's distortions of human dignity in the SADC. National governments are responsible for co-ordinating the intervention within their individual countries and evaluating progress periodically, making adjustments as necessary. The campaigns should esteem local and international conceptions of the significance of human dignity and social justice. These could include international human rights virtues discussed in General Comment No 18 of the Human Rights Committee, especially paragraph 10, and southern Africa's own age-old social engineering principle of *humwe/ubuntu/ubwananyina*. *Humwe* literally means: 'We are in this together'. Therefore, it is in our common interest to co-operate in order to succeed. It is a principle of individual and social altruism for the benefit of the whole. Schools, colleges, universities and grassroots campaigns should be used/involved.

Step 2: Draft legislation inspired by outcomes of Step 1 above with the input of experts from a wide section of the professional bodies concerned. The legislation should ensure equal access to land without regard to sex, religion or any other distinction. Ensure also that lands made available for rural resettlement occur also in areas with the nation's most prime land and the best potential for agricultural production.

Step 3: Begin the transparent, non-partisan implementation of the land reform plans, ensuring women's access to land *qua* individuals.

Steps 1 and 2 above would serve also to prepare both the oppressor and the oppressed for a substantive cultural change by allowing them to rationalize their situation and change their disposition from one of opposition to one another to cooperation with one another. They would also serve to give ordinary people a sense of collective empowerment over their own affairs/situation as well as a sense of ownership of the intended outcomes. This would give the land reform process greater chances of success as those directly involved would be more likely to support it. It would also oust the sense of victimization that some white farmers have used to seize the courts in opposition to land reform.

The PECAPDISHD approach would significantly reduce or even eliminate the potential for anxiety, opposition, commotion, confusion and desperation in the land reform programmes being considered in some SADC States.

Arguments that attempt a rationalization of the status-quo to arrive at the recommendation that unequal land use/allocation should not be tempered with for food security and national prosperity reasons demonstrate the resilience of apartheid culturalization psychology and point to the extent of de-schooling required before equalizing measures can begin to enjoy the support required for land reform programmes to succeed in the SADC. This is because they reinforce apartheid culturalization's ambivalence to the semi-authentic existence of the land-hungry dispossessed non-white majority and still regard sacrificing of the majority interest for the minority as a humane way of conducting public affairs.

They disregard social justice and self-actualization arguments with impunity and human rights mean only the rights of the oppressor – an anti *humwe/ubuntu/ubwananyina* approach. They require of the law subservience to the status-quo. When the law fails to do that, it is not law anymore. They feed victimization and corruption pleas against majority-rule governments. They prolong change and maintain the binary opposition between the oppressor and the oppressed, perpetuating a state of semi-authentic existence for affected SADC States. Pro-status-quo rationalization arguments are unhelpful in the circumstances. They only point to the depth of apartheid-rule's psychology of distortion regarding the significance of human worth.

Attempts to correct unequal land allocation through the willing buyer willing seller approach have not delivered the expected exchanges. In fact, both the Mbeki and the Mugabe administrations have decried this approach, claiming that it gives whites control over where the landless blacks will end up, and when, and where they will never be able to set up. Moreover, whites do not always give up the best land.

Notes

1 Treaty of the Southern African Development Community (SADC). Done at Windhoek, Namibia on 17 August (1992) 5 RADIC (1993) 415.
2 UN Declaration on the granting of independence to colonial countries and peoples 1514 (XV) adopted at the 947th plenary meeting, 14 December 1960. See also Denis Judd (1996) *Empire: The British imperial experience, from 1765 to the present* (London: Fontana Press).
3 Allen F. Isaacman (ed) (1988) *The Life History of Raul Honwana: An Inside View of Mozambique from Colonialism to Independence (1905–1975)* (London: Lynne Rienner Publishers), pp 12–13.
4 Ibid, p 13.
5 J. Verkuyl (1992) 'The Dutch Reformed Church in South Africa and the ideology and practice of Apartheid', in E. S. Reddy (ed) *The Struggle for Liberation in South Africa and International Solidarity* (New Delhi: Sterling Publishers).
6 Susan Rennie Ritner, 'The Dutch Reformed Church and Apartheid' (1967) *Journal of Contemporary History*, 2: 17, 24.
7 See W. A. Landman (1968) *A Plea for Understanding* (Cape Town: Ned Geref Kerk Uitgewers); J. A. Loubser (1987) *The Apartheid Bible: A Critical Review of Racial Theology in South Africa* (Cape Town: Maskew Miller Longman).
8 See also Richard Elphick and Rodney Davenport (1997) *Christianity in South Africa: A political, social and cultural history* (Berkeley, CA: University of California Press); A. S. Geyser (1960) *Delayed Action* (Pretoria: NC Kerkboekhandel).
9 Verkuyl, above, n 5.
10 Verkuyl, above, n 5.
11 Verkuyl, above, n 5.
12 Alan Paton (1948) *Cry the Beloved Country* (London: Macmillan).
13 Athol Fugard (1963) *Blood Knot and other plays* (New York, NY: Theatre Communications Group Inc).
14 Donald Woods (1978) *Biko* (Ontario: Fitzhenry and Whiteside).
15 Available at <http://news.bbc.co.uk/onthisday/hi/witness/march/2/newsid_3497000/3497239.stm> (accessed 10 December 2010).
16 See also *Commercial Farmers Union v Minister of Lands, Agriculture and Resettlement and Others* SC/132/2000; *Ndebele-Ndzundza Community concerning the farm Kafferskraal*, No 181JS

LCC3/00, judgment of 23 December 2002; *Commercial Farmers Union v Comrade Border Gezi and Others*, Case No HC 3544/2000.
17 See also *Mike Campbell (Pvt) Ltd and Others v Republic of Zimbabwe* (2009) 48 ILM 534.
18 *Bernardus Henricus Funnekotter and Others v Republic of Zimbabwe* (2009) ICSID Case No ARB/05/6 judgment of 22 April 2009; *Piero Foresti, Laura de Carli & Others v The Republic of South Africa* (2010) ICSID Case No ARB (AF)/07/01 judgment of August 2010. See also <http://www.arbitration.fr/3.html> (accessed 10 December 2010).
19 *Commercial Farmers Union and Others v The Minister of Lands and Rural Resettlement and Others* (Zimbabwe), judgment No SC31/10, Const Application No 81/10, decision of 26 November 2010, p 27.
20 *R v Commissioner for Administration ex parte Dyer* [1994] 1 WLR 621.
21 See Ben Chigara (2009) 'Introductory note to SADC Tribunal – Mike Campbell (PVT) LTD and Others v Republic of Zimbabwe', *International Legal Materials*, 48: 530.
22 *Commercial Farmers Union and Others v The Minister of Lands and Rural Resettlement and Others* (Zimbabwe), judgment No SC31/10, Const Application No 81/10 judgment of 26 November 2010, p 4.
23 John Dugard (1887) 'Retrospective justice: International Law and the South African Model', in A. J. McAdams (ed) *Transitional Justice and the Rule of Law in new Democracies* (Notre Dame, IN: University of Notre Dame Press), p 270.
24 Sellstrom Tor (2002) *Sweden and National Liberation in Southern Africa*, Vol. II: Solidarity and Assistance 1970–94 (Stockholm: Elanders Gotab), p 24.
25 Ibid.
26 Ibid.
27 Ibid.
28 Ibid.
29 See also Ben Chigara (2003) 'The Inherent Dignity of Mankind and the Contest for Labels in the Land Issue', *Nordic Journal of International Law*, 72: 369.
30 See also Stephen Greenberg (2009) 'Crisis in Land Reform: The way out is not complicated', The South African Civil Society Information Service, available at <http://www.sacsis.org.za> (accessed 10 December 2010); R. Hall (ed) (2009) *Another Countryside? Policy Options for Land and Agrarian Reform in South Africa* (Cape Town: Programme for Land and Agrarian Studies (PLAAS) School of Government, University of the Western Cape 2009); Sam Moyo and Paris Yeros, 'Zimbabwe ten years on: Results and prospects', available at <http://www.pambazuka.org/en/category/features/54037> (accessed 10 December 2010); O.O. Olubode-Awosola and others (2008) 'Mathematical modelling of the South African land redistribution for development policy', *Journal of Policy Modeling*, 30: 841; Lungisile Ntsebeza and Ruth Hall (eds) (2007) *The Land Question in South Africa: The Challenge of Transformation and Redistribution* (Cape Town: HSRC Press); Ruth Hall (2004) 'A Political Economy of Land Reform in South Africa', *Review of African Political Economy*, 100: 213.
31 Juan E. Mendez (1997) 'In defense of Transitional Justice', in A. J. McAdams (ed) *Transitional Justice and the Rule of Law in New Democracies* (Notre Dame, IN: University of Notre Dame Press), p 1.
32 (2009) 48 ILM 534.
33 Per Brennan J in *Mabo and Others v Queensland (No 2)* [1992] HCA 23, para 45.
34 (124) 1973 SCR 416.
35 Above, n 33.
36 Above, n 33, para 33.
37 Above, n 33, para 41.
38 Above, n 33, para 42 (emphasis added).
39 'Recriminations as some white farmers return', *New Zimbabwe*, 4 December 2010, available at <http://www.newzimbabwe.com/news-3962-Recriminations%20as%20white%20farmers%20return/news.aspx> (accessed 10 December 2010).
40 See also Tom Bingham (2010) *The Rule of Law* (London: Allen Lane), pp 110, 171.

41 A cardinal requirement of the Lancaster House Agreement, London (1979) that ended settler apartheid-rule of Rhodesia, now Zimbabwe. Also trialled by the Mandela and Mbeki post-apartheid-rule governments. The main criticism of this approach is that white farmers hold back the nation's prime land and continue to dominate it, giving only some of their unfavourable lands. See also Lungisile Ntsebeza and Ruth Hall (eds) (2007) *The Land Question in South Africa: The Challenge of Transformation and Redistribution* (Cape Town: HSRC Press), pp 87–92.
42 S/2004/616.
43 *Commercial Farmers Union v Comrade Border Gezi and Others*, Case No HC 3544/2000.
44 See also the *Campbell* case, above, n 17.
45 The *Bernardus* case, above, n 18; the *Piero Foresti* case, above, n 18.
46 10 November 1989, available at <http://www.unhchr.ch/tbs/doc.nsf/0/3888b0541f8501c9c12563ed004b8d0e?Opendocument> (accessed 10 December 2010).
47 Ibid, para 10.
48 David Miller (1999) *Principles of Social Justice* (Cambridge, MA: Harvard University Press), p ix.
49 Ibid, p x.
50 For a detailed examination see Ben Chigara (2011, forthcoming). 'European/Southern African Development Community (SADC) States' Bilateral Investment Agreements (BITs) for the promotion and protection of foreign investments v. Post-apartheid SADC Economic and Social Reconstruction Policy', *Journal of International Trade Law and Policy*, 10(3).
51 Thomas Franck (1990) *The Power of Legitimacy Among Nations* (Oxford: Oxford University Press).
52 Paulo Freire (1996) *Pedagogy of the oppressed* (London: Penguin Books), pp 18, 28, n 3, 29–51.
53 Antony Heath (1975) *Rational Choice and Social Exchange: A critique of exchange theory* (London: CU), p viii.
54 Freire, above, n 52, p 30.
55 Henry Steiner and others (2008) *International Human Rights in Context: Law, Politics, Morals* (3rd edn, Oxford: Oxford University Press), p 836.
56 Ibid.
57 See especially Olubode-Awosola, above, n 30.
58 The idea that land that white farmers own was vacant and belonging to no one else when whites first occupied it. Consequently, they owe no one recompense or any form of consideration. Discussing the application of this principle under international law, see also B. Chigara (2008) 'Terra nullius', in Peter Cane and Joanne Conaghan (eds) *The New Oxford Companion to Law* (Oxford: Oxford University Press), pp 1160–61.
59 See also the *Campbell* case, above, n 17; the *Commercial Farmers Union* case, above, n 19.
60 Rita L. Atkinson and others (1990) *Introduction to Psychology* (10th edn, London: Harcourt Brace), p 525.
61 Ibid.
62 Freire, above, n 52, p 31.
63 Rodney Davenport and Christopher Saunders (2000) *South Africa: A Modern History* (London: Macmillan), p 21.
64 *South Africa Yearbook 2009/10* (Pretoria: Government Communication and Information System), p 30.
65 Davenport and Saunders, above, n 63, p 240.
66 The Union of South Africa achieved political independence from British rule in 1910. Chronicling the events leading up to freedom, see also Davenport and Saunders, above, n 63, pp 251–70.
67 *South Africa Yearbook 2008/09* (Pretoria: Government Communication and Information System), p 35.
68 Above, n 64, p 32.

69 Above, n 64, p 32.
70 See also Steiner and others, above, n 55, pp 836–37.
71 30 November 1953, available at <http://www.un.org/Depts/dhl/resguide/r28.htm> (accessed 10 December 2010).
72 Article 53 of the VCLT (1969) provides that any agreement concluded between States is null and void if it conflicts with norms *jus cogens*. 'A treaty is void if, at the time of its conclusion, it conflicts with a peremptory norm of general international law. For the purposes of the present Convention, a peremptory norm of general international law is a norm accepted and recognized by the international community of States as a whole as a norm from which no derogation is permitted and which can be modified only by a subsequent norm of general international law having the same character'.
73 See also *Nicaragua* (1986) *ICJ Reports* 100.
74 David Harris (2010) *Cases and Material on International Law* (7th edn, Sweet & Maxwell), pp 32–33.
75 Whereas customary international law recognises consent as a function of obligation *jus cogens* does not. (*Anglo Norwegian Fisheries* (1951) *ICJ Reports* 116; *Asylum* (1950) *ICJ Reports* 266). See also also Mario Prost and Paul Clark (2006) 'Unity, Diversity and the Fragmentation of International Law', *Chinese Journal of International Law*, 5: 341; Patrick Kelly (2000) 'The Twilight of customary international law', *Virginia Journal of International Law*, 40: 449; Ben Chigara (2000) *Legitimacy Deficit in Custom: A deconstructionist Critique* (Aldershot: Ashgate).
76 Harris, above, n 74.
77 Freire, above, n 52, pp 25–26.
78 George Wilhelm Hegel (1967) *The Phenomenology of Mind* (New York, NY: Harper and Row), p 233.
79 Freire, above, n 52, p 26.
80 See especially Ben Chigara (2004) *Land Reform Policy: The Challenge of Human Rights Law* (Aldershot: Ashgate), pp 1–31.
81 Chigara, above, n 29.
82 Chigara, above, n 80, pp 14–25.
83 See Kevin Gray (1987) *Elements of Land Law* (London: Butterworths), p 6.
84 See also Chigara, above, n 21.
85 Deborah James (2002) 'Human rights or property? State, society, and the landless in South Africa' (LSE, Research Online), available at <http://eprints.lse.ac.uk/archive/00001028> (accessed 10 December 2010).
86 Ibid.
87 Freire, above, n 52.
88 Moyo and Yeros, above, n 30.
89 Atkinson and others, above, n 60, p 696.
90 Martin Luther King Jr (1981) *Strength to love* (Philadelphia, PA: Collins Fount Paperbacks).
91 See also Ntsebeza and Hall, above, n 30, p 107.

Bibliography

Atkinson, Rita L. and others (1990) *Introduction to Psychology* (10th edn, London: Harcourt Brace), p 525.

Bingham, Tom (2010) *The Rule of Law* (London: Allen Lane), pp 110 and 171.

Chigara, Ben (2000) *Legitimacy Deficit in Custom: A deconstructionist Critique* (Aldershot: Ashgate).

Chigara, Ben (2003) 'The Inherent Dignity of Mankind and the Contest for Labels in the Land Issue', *Nordic Journal of International Law*, 72: 369.

Chigara, Ben (2004) *Land Reform Policy: The Challenge of Human Rights Law* (Aldershot: Ashgate).

Chigara, Ben (2008) 'Terra nullius', in Peter Cane and Joanne Conaghan (eds), *The New Oxford Companion to Law* (Oxford: Oxford University Press), p 1160.

Chigara, Ben (2009) 'Introductory note to SADC Tribunal – Mike Campbell (PVT) LTD and Others v Republic of Zimbabwe', *International Legal Materials*, 48: 530.

Davenport, Rodney and Saunders, Christopher (2000) *South Africa: A Modern History* (London: Macmillan), p 21.

Dugard, John (1997) 'Retrospective justice: International Law and the South African Model', in A. J. McAdams (ed), *Transitional Justice and the Rule of Law in new Democracies* (Notre Dame, IN: University of Notre Dame Press).

Elphick, Richard and Davenport, Rodney (1997) *Christianity in South Africa: A political, social and cultural history* (Berkeley, CA: University of California Press).

Franck, Thomas (1990) *The Power of Legitimacy Among Nations* (Oxford: Oxford University Press).

Freire, Paulo (1996) *Pedagogy of the oppressed* (London: Penguin Books).

Fugard, Athol (1963) *Blood Knot and other plays* (New York, NY: Theatre Communications Group Inc).

Geyser, A. S. (1961) *Delayed Action* (Pretoria: Craft Press).

Gray, Kevin (1987) *Elements of Land Law* (London: Butterworths).

Greenberg, Stephen (2009) 'Crisis in Land Reform: The way out is not complicated' (The South African Civil Society Information Service), available at <http://www.sacsis.org.za> (accessed 10 December 2010).

Hall, Ruth (2004) 'A Political Economy of Land Reform in South Africa', *Review of African Political Economy*, 100: 213.

Hall, Ruth (ed) (2009) *Another Countryside? Policy Options for Land and Agrarian Reform in South Africa* (Cape Town: Programme for Land and Agrarian Studies (PLAAS) School of Government, University of the Western Cape).

Harris, David (2010) *Cases and Material on International Law* (7th edn, London: Sweet and Maxwell).

Heath, Antony (1975) *Rational Choice and Social Exchange: A critique of exchange theory* (London: CU).

Hegel, George Wilhelm (1967) *The Phenomenology of Mind* (New York, NY: Harper and Row).

Isaacman, Allen F. (ed) (1988) *The Life History of Raul Honwana: An Inside View of Mozambique from Colonialism to Independence (1905–1975)* (London: Lynne Rienner Publishers).

James, Deborah (2002) 'Human rights or property? State, society, and the landless in South Africa' (LSE, Research Online), available at <http://eprints.lse.ac.uk/archive/00001028> (accessed 10 December 2010).

Judd, Denis (1996) *Empire: The British imperial experience, from 1765 to the present* (London: Fontana Press).

Kelly, Patrick (2000) 'The Twilight of customary international law', *Virginia Journal of International Law* 40: 449.

Landman, W. A. (1968) *A Plea for Understanding* (Cape Town: Ned Geref Kerk Uitgewers).

Loubser, J. A. (1987) *The Apartheid Bible: A Critical Review of Racial Theology in South Africa* (Cape Town: Maskew-Miller Longman).

Loubser, J. A. (1996) 'Apartheid Ideology: A Contextual Theology gone wrong?', *Journal of Church and State*, 38: 321.

Luther King Jr., Martin (1981) *Strength to love* (Philadelphia, PA: Collins Fount Paperbacks).

Mendez, Juan E. (1997) 'In defense of Transitional Justice', in A. J. McAdams (ed) *Transitional Justice and the Rule of Law in new Democracies* (Notre Dame, IN: University of Notre Dame Press), p 1.

Miller, David (1999) *Principles of Social Justice* (Cambridge, MA: Harvard University Press).

Moyo, Sam and Yeros, Paris (2009) 'Zimbabwe ten years on: Results and prospects', available at <http://www.pambazuka.org/en/category/features/54037> (accessed 10 December 2010).

Ntsebeza, Lungisile and Hall, Ruth (eds) (2007) *The Land Question in South Africa: The Challenge of Transformation and Redistribution* (Cape Town: HSRC Press).

Olubode-Awosola, O. O. and others (2008) 'Mathematical modelling of the South African land redistribution for development policy', *Journal of Policy Modeling*, 30: 841.

Paton, Alan (1948) *Cry the Beloved Country* (London: Macmillan).

Prost, Mario and Clark, Paul (2006) 'Unity, Diversity and the Fragmentation of International Law', *Chinese Journal of International Law*, 5: 341.

Rennie Ritner, Susan (1967) 'The Dutch Reformed Church and Apartheid', *Journal of Contemporary History*, 2(17): 24.

Steiner, Henry and others (2008) *International Human Rights in Context: Law, Politics Morals* (3rd edn, Oxford: Oxford University Press).

Tor, Sellstrom (2002) *Sweden and National Liberation in Southern Africa*, Vol. II: Solidarity and Assistance 1970–94 (Stockholm: Elanders Gotab).

Verkuyl, J. (1992) 'The Dutch Reformed Church in South Africa and the ideology and practice of Apartheid', in E. S. Reddy (ed) *The Struggle for Liberation in South Africa and International Solidarity* (New Delhi: Sterling Publishers).

Verkuyl, J. (2010) 'Recriminations as some white farmers return', *New Zimbabwe*, 4 December, available at <http://www.newzimbabwe.com/news-3962-Recriminations%20as%20white%20farmers%20return/news.aspx> (accessed 10 December 2010).

Woods, Donald (1978) *Biko* (Ontario: Fitzhenry and Whiteside).

Index

www.ingramcontent.com/pod-product-compliance
Ingram Content Group UK Ltd.
Pitfield, Milton Keynes, MK11 3LW, UK
UKHW020010200926
475702UK00014B/1806
* 9 7 8 0 4 1 5 8 5 9 7 4 5 *